CODES OF MISCONDUCT

Regulating Prostitution in Late Colonial Bombay

A SHWINI T AMBE

UNIVERSITY OF MINNESOTA PRESS

MINNEAPOLIS • LONDON

Portions of chapter 1 were previously published as "Colluding Patriarchies: The Colonial Reform of Sexual Relations in India," *Feminist Studies* 26, no. 3 (Fall 2000): 587–600; reprinted with permission of the publisher, *Feminist Studies,* Inc. Chapter 3 previously appeared as "The Elusive Ingénue: A Transnational Feminist Analysis of European Prostitution in Colonial Bombay," *Gender and Society* 19, no. 2 (2005). Portions of chapter 4 were published as "Brothels as Families: Transnational Feminist Reflections on 1920s Bombay Kothas," *International Feminist Journal of Politics* 8, no. 2 (June 2006): 219–42.

Published by the University of Minnesota Press
111 Third Avenue South, Suite 290
Minneapolis, MN 55401-2520
http://www.upress.umn.edu

Library of Congress Cataloging-in-Publication Data

Tambe, Ashwini.
Codes of misconduct : regulating prostitution in late colonial Bombay / Ashwini Tambe.
p. cm.
Includes bibliographical references and index.
ISBN 978-0-8166-5137-5 (hc : alk. paper) — ISBN 978-0-8166-5138-2 (pb : alk. paper)
1. Prostitution—India—Bombay—History—19th century. 2. Prostitution—India—Bombay—History—20th century. I. Title.
HQ240.B6T36 2009
363.4'40954792—dc22
2008053779

Printed in the United States of America on acid-free paper

The University of Minnesota is an equal-opportunity educator and employer.

15 14 13 12 11 10 09   10 9 8 7 6 5 4 3 2 1

For my mother, Sujata Tambe,
whose memory I cherish in untold ways,
and
for my father, Sudheer Tambe,
from whose pleasures I learn so much.

CONTENTS

ABBREVIATIONS

ARBJ	Annual Report of the Bombay Jails
ARBJD	Administrative Report of the Bombay Jail Department
ARPCB	Annual Report of the Police in the City of Bombay
ARPTIB	Annual Report of the Police in the Town and Island of Bombay
ARSCB	Annual Report of the State of Crime in Bombay
ARWPTIB	Annual Report on the Working of Police in the Town and Island of Bombay
BPPA	Bombay Prevention of Prostitution Act
CDA	Contagious Diseases Acts
COI	Census of India
CWMG	Collected Works of Mahatma Gandhi
GD	General Department
HD	Home Department
RACDAB	Rules for the Administration of the CDA in Bombay
RCP	Report of the Committee on Prostitution
RHBBC	Report of the Health of British Troops in Bombay Command
RWCDA	Report of the Working of the Contagious Diseases Act

INTRODUCTION: PROSTITUTION AND
THE LAW IN BOMBAY

One July afternoon in 2004, while conducting an interview with a public health professional in Mumbai about the city's sex trade, I experienced an uncanny feeling of displacement.[1] I was speaking to Dr. I. H. Gilada, a principal voice in AIDS-control circles in India, at his clinic off Grant Road. As he outlined his proposals for regulating prostitution, I found his words echoing, almost verbatim, those of a doctor called K. S. Patel who had worked at a venereal diseases hospital in the same area in the early 1920s.[2] I had come across Dr. Patel's confident recommendations to the colonial government just a few days earlier in a file preserved at the Maharashtra State Archives. His call for compulsory health checks and residential segregation of prostitutes, and his resigned acceptance of men's putative sexual needs, now spoke to me through the voice of a living person. Dr. Gilada, too, was calling for demarcating a zone for licensed brothel workers where they would receive regular medical checks. He argued that the demand for commercial sex could not be wished away and that the only way to protect the wider citizenry from venereal disease was to closely monitor sex workers.

This sense of déjà vu is familiar to anyone looking closely at the history of the sex trade in Bombay. Just as police reports in the 1930s complained that massage parlors were a new front for brothels, so also in the early years of the twenty-first century residents repeatedly expressed fears that the city was witnessing an "invasion" of brothels passing as massage parlors.[3] Just as Eastern European women settled in Bombay's wealthier brothels at the turn of the twentieth century because of upheavals in the Russian ghetto, women from former Soviet republics such as Uzbekistan were, at the start of the twenty-first century, to be found working as call girls in Mumbai's upscale hotels.[4] Just as police focused on relocating those in the most publicly visible stratum of the sex trade in the 1880s, such as European brothel workers, so also the government in 2005 displayed an inordinate fascination with the spectacle of "bar girls," the subject of recent films and books.[5] And just as the British activist Josephine Butler and the Ladies National Association in the 1880s used a campaign on behalf of Indian prostitutes as a means to increase their own political currency within Britain, so too contemporary antitrafficking advocates in the United States use egregious stories from Indian brothels as an emotive device to enlist global support.[6]

Some of these continuities are accidental, but many suggest patterns in the way publics and state officials relate to the sex trade. Perhaps the most interesting continuities are to be found in the realm of lawmaking. Many prostitution-related activities that Indian law rules as offenses remain unchanged in description since the formulation of the 1860 Indian Penal Code.[7] And this is not for want of political attention to these measures—nearly identical versions of prostitution laws have been passed over and over, with an astonishing degree of regularity. In some cases, parallels between laws can be found within the span of a single decade. In June 2004, for example, the state governor of Maharashtra (of which Mumbai is the capital city) presented the case for licensing sex workers as a response to the spread of AIDS.[8] The proposal created a furor, and I encountered a variety of contrasting responses to it, but by the end of the year the proposal had receded from public view. Although it had appeared novel, it in fact echoed an almost identical attempt made a decade earlier: in 1994, the proposed Maharashtra Protection of Commercial Sex Workers Act had mandated compulsory registration and medical testing of sex workers. It, too, had commanded great public attention when announced. It, too, died quietly after months of discussion, in the Legislative Assembly. In retrospect, the real purpose of such announcements seemed to be to remind the public of the state's commitment to a "cleaner" red-light district, rather than to usher in changes in the sex trade. The target of these proposals, in other words, was not prostitution as much as public opinion.

The history of prostitution in Bombay is riddled with such measures. Across the nineteenth and early twentieth centuries, the colonial government formulated laws that were enormously repetitive: activities such as procuring women and girls for prostitution, pimping, and soliciting men for prostitution elicited nearly identical legal measures in multiple eras. Procuring or enticement into prostitution was ruled an offense in 1827, 1860, 1921, and 1923; and brothel keeping was targeted in 1860, 1902, 1923, and 1930 (see "Chronology of Laws Relevant to Prostitution in Bombay"). In the very decades that saw an intensification of legislation on prostitution, 1860–1930, Bombay's sex trade grew vast in scale and became part of a cross-national circuit. The remarkable similarity in the moral panic about prostitution in various eras, independent of the actual trajectory of the prostitution in the city, pushes us to speculate that lawmaking served a purpose distinct from its actual effects on the sex trade. Could it be, as Pamela Haag (1999) has observed in the U.S. context, that laws presented a palliative vision of societies freeing themselves of sexual commerce? In other words, could it be that laws achieved discursively what could not be accomplished in actuality? While the expansion of prostitution over the past century might suggest that prohibitionist laws were simply ineffectual, could it be that lawmaking was instead a productive process that voiced and shaped public anxieties? Even more intriguingly, could laws have actually sustained particular forms of prostitution?

At the heart of this book is a methodological argument based on such questions. I argue that the law rarely works in straightforwardly efficacious ways, and that the contexts of colonial lawmaking and law enforcement on prostitution deserve to be treated as having distinct imperatives and as serving important but separate constituencies.[9] Whereas the process of lawmaking responded to a variety of public panics, the governing practices of police constables and inspectors, army medical examiners, magistrates, and municipal officials enacted administrative logics of separate, more limited ambitions. In focusing on the discrepancy between the language of law and law enforcement practices, my work departs from a textual approach that focuses principally on analysis of legal documents and legislative debates. It also challenges linear readings of how laws create effects; in keeping with Foucauldian insights, I assume that prohibitions do not end practices so much as rearrange the relative power of interested actors. In following micropractices of regulation, I am heeding the call of historical sociologists of law such as Mariana Valverde (2003), who remind us that studying the state need not only mean studying exalted national or federal sites but also the more quotidian forms of administrative functioning.

Such a focus on micropractices also opens up a specific perspective on colonial history. While imperial laws and policies were often framed in ways that appeared consistent with social and political currents in metropoles, those who administered and effected policies in colonies were often less committed, and sometimes even opposed, to these currents. Following the manner in which laws were executed then allows us to understand better the heterogeneity and limits of empire. It allows us to see how laws could be appropriated in unexpected ways by local nationalist elites, and also how colonial government functionaries could undermine the coherence and impact of colonial discourses. This book, then, offers the case of laws on prostitution as an argument for understanding imperial processes as more multifarious, and less orderly, than colonial discourses themselves projected.

LAW, SEX WORK, AND THE STATE

Laws on prostitution seem to recur across generations because they draw the attention of a far wider range of people than just those engaged in buying or selling sexual services. The figure of the prostitute performs so many metonymic functions—standing, alternately, for the heartlessness of exchange relations, the triumph of utilitarianism, the ills of industrialization, moral degeneracy, pervasive male sexual violence, declining public health, female deviousness, or even sexual empowerment—that state intervention in prostitution appears to affect not only specific bodies but entire polities. Laws aimed at curbing sex trafficking and medically monitoring prostitutes have engaged those across a political spectrum ranging from religious missionaries, nationalist social reformers, and military officials to feminists and labor organizers. Vibrant movements to decriminalize and unionize sex workers have used the issue as a lens to explore the very nature of work and citizenship. There is no doubt that prostitution attracts an unusually interested political gaze.

At a time when public health officials declare in alarmist terms that licensing sex workers is the only way to stem the AIDS pandemic, when the might of major intergovernmental bodies such as the UN and EU is arrayed against the shadowy figure of the transnational trafficker, and when

feminists of an abolitionist bent have gained the power to change laws in
countries such as Sweden and the United States,[10] greater reflection is war-
ranted on the relationship between lawmaking, law enforcement, and the
scale of the sex industry. Many of those engaged in formulating laws that
either prohibit or regulate the sex trade assume that the law works in sovereign ways to achieve its intended results (Halley et al. 2006). This study
of Bombay undercuts such an assumption, adopting in its framework the
potential for disjuncture between the legal discourses about prostitution,
law enforcement practices, and forms of prostitution.

An apt starting point for theorizing prostitution's legal status is the long-
standing and vexed feminist engagement with this topic. Questions about
the legitimacy of prostitution as sex work, and how the state should treat
prostitutes and their clients, have bedeviled feminist theorists for several
decades.[11] Fault lines reflecting varying approaches to sex, the body, and selfhood have clearly emerged. In the radical feminist view, prostitution is an
emblem of female sexual servility and male coercion. As an institution, it
denotes a group of women set aside for attending exclusively to men's sexual needs (Barry 1995). In the socialist feminist view, prostitution is one
among several pink-collar occupations that economically needy women rely
on to survive. Prostitution can nonetheless represent a particularly intense
form of alienation because, as Alisson Jaggar (1985) notes, rephrasing Marx,
it takes away from women that which is most their own—their sexual selves.
Socialist feminists such as Pateman (1988) examine in depth the nature of
the contractual exchange in commercial sex, arguing that its most troubling
aspect is that it relies overwhelmingly on making available for exchange a
specifically servile feminine body. Liberal feminists do not examine in the
same depth the nature of sex work but defend the right of sex workers to
practice their profession without harassment.[12] In the poststructuralist view,
sex work is a heterogeneous field of meaning because sex, and its relationship to the self, is itself indeterminate and multivalent. Chapkis (1997) and
others argue that the denigration of sex work relies on viewing sexual activity as the expression of an authentic self. If sexual activity is delinked from
selfhood, however, and seen in performative terms, then sex work can potentially be understood as a source of agency—depending on the control that
the sex worker exerts over the transaction (Bell 1994). In sex radical argu-
ments, commercial sex can destabilize normative gender prescriptions such
as female passivity.[13] Sex workers can, through their ability to set the terms

of the exchange, invert male dominance, enhance sexual exploration, and, through a sense of their own erotic autonomy, subvert the heteronormative sexual order.

Compelling as each of these positions is, this book does not advance any specific one in isolation. In approaching the problem of prostitution's status before the law, I view as ethically sound the position that sex workers should not be targets of the many forms of violence to which they are routinely subjected. At the same time, I do not equate this view with an endorsement of a liberal or sex radical position. Indeed I find especially convincing the socialist feminist view that in feigning desire, as potentially occurs in transacted sex, sex workers enact a form of deception and self-denial that is consistent more generally, and problematically, with femininity. While it is possible that for nonheterosexual sex workers a feigning of desire for men does not constitute a denial of their own desire, it is nonetheless the case that providing sexual services in exchange for money is too freighted an example of the normative expectation of feminine sexual inauthenticity. I also view the sex radical celebration of sex work as curiously silent on the modern historical ascendance of a market-based common sense that accepts all forms of exchange without probing their embedded incommensurabilities. The exchange of sexual services for money instantiates gendered social and economic hierarchies in multiple ways—large numbers of those who sell sex are women, poor, and belong to subjugated racial/ethnic groups— and therefore any blanket celebration of such exchange seems to me premature and jarring. However, I distance my position from the radical feminist certitude that all prostitution is rape and therefore violence (Barry 1995; MacKinnon 1993), which I find denies the heterogeneity of the forms and contexts of prostitution.

These varied positions on sex work/prostitution have implications for the thorny question of how the state should treat women who practice commercial sex. In the radical feminist view, the state should not endorse the inegalitarian sexual relations that prostitution typifies—after all, the argument goes, the sex trade overwhelmingly caters to only men's sexual desires, and indeed reifies these desires. In the liberal and sex radical view, when the state criminalizes prostitution, it is abusing its power by targeting an already vulnerable population. After all, those who most suffer the brunt of the criminalization of prostitution are not clients but sex workers. In yet another version of the liberal position, any welfare-conscious state should protect its population from ill health and hence oversee the sex industry in order to keep epidemics of venereal diseases in check. After all, regardless of their status before the law, sex workers are citizens and bearers of basic human rights, such as the right to life.

While the aforementioned positions cast the state in apparently contrasting roles, this book advances the argument made by postcolonial feminist legal theorists (Kapur 2005; Sunder Rajan 2003) and critics of governance feminism (Halley et al. 2006; Brown 1995) that it is important to always be alert to the possibilities of state coercion in all of the state's roles, including its protective roles. In the context of prostitution, regulation and criminalization are not contrasting state approaches but, rather, different modalities of state coercion. In particular, the current public health preference for regulation (expressed by Dr. Gilada's influential Indian Health Organization and shared by the Indian National AIDS Control Organization described in the Conclusion) belies the history of state abuse of regulation. Whereas state recognition of sex workers as an identifiable group in need of public health intervention might seem an improvement over previous trends of either ignoring or criminalizing sex workers, the state—both the colonial and post-Independence developmentalist version—is not a benevolent entity. The state's position is marked by an instrumentalist approach toward sex workers; it is much more committed to preventing ill health among the client population than among sex workers. It has been, and still is, likely to use measures that compromise the dignity and well-being of sex workers in service of the majoritarian goal of reducing infection rates across a "national population"—a goal to which sex workers have no necessary obligation, given the elitist and historically limited construct of the nation. What is sharply needed is the reminder that the state is an interested entity, a rhetorical actor performing for audiences, both domestic and international; international funding agencies, for instance, are crucial arbiters of state policies in neoliberal times. And the state is an entity with historically accrued prerogative and bureaucratic power that is very easily abused by its law enforcers.

In keeping with such a perspective, this book focuses on state-backed violence against prostitutes. Prostitutes in Bombay have largely remained victims of state violence whether laws swung between phases of regulation, acceptance, or abolition of prostitution. Although the social stigma attached to prostitutes has a long history, state-backed violence against Indian prostitutes is tied to the increasing involvement of the police, public health officials, and military administrators in controlling prostitution in the nineteenth century. I track the rise of this state-backed violence through reviewing prison records, police files, and census records over a span of eighty years.[14] Focusing on state violence is important because in the now-familiar debates on how to view prostitution/sex work, the one point on which a range of feminists often agree is that the disproportionate criminalization of women in prostitution is a serious problem. The loud call for decriminalizing sex workers has been rightfully motivated by the impulse to erode their stigmatization, invest their identities with greater dignity and recognition before the law, and spur improved health services.[15] This study demonstrates how decriminalization is nonetheless a complicated task, since the criminalization of prostitutes occurred in conjunction with the institutionalization of brothels. The very goals that drove state regulation—preserving public health and public order—led to the criminalization of women who did not work in state-sanctioned forms of commercial sex. Ultimately, my story of lawmaking and law enforcement in nineteenth- and early-twentieth-century Bombay underlines the role played by state actors in nurturing specific forms of prostitution while simultaneously increasing coercion of prostitutes.

THE SETTING: A PORT CITY

Bombay's red-light district, Kamathipura, is considered the primary node in South Asian trafficking circuits and the epicenter of the AIDS pandemic in India. Its role in this context has received heavy press coverage in recent years—a BBC news story about HIV prevention in India termed Kamathipura a "hotspot for the transmission of the disease" and a South African newspaper described Kamathipura as "the fleshy centre of India's HIV timebomb."[16] Several recent documentary films feature Kamathipura in addressing AIDS and trafficking in India, making this setting something of a genre.[17] In numerical terms, Bombay could have anywhere up to twenty thousand sex workers, which is comparable to metropolises renowned for sex tourism, such as Amsterdam and Bangkok.[18] But while such figures have made the city's sex industry a familiar site to international public health activists in the past decade, its red-light district actually has a much longer and more storied past.

The history of Bombay's sex trade is closely tied to the city's rise as a port, as indeed is much of Bombay's history. The earliest mention of Bombay as a port comes from records of the Silhara dynasty (810–1260 CE), but its rise as such occurred under British colonial rule after 1668, when the island became a part of Catherine of Braganza's dowry to Charles II in a marriage transaction between Portugal and Britain. At the time it became the regional headquarters of the East India Company in 1687, British colonial records described it as a "marshy outpost" (Dobbin 1972, 1). It slowly grew in prominence as an entrepôt connecting traders from Britain, China, Persia, and East Africa during the phase of mercantile colonialism from the late seventeenth to the nineteenth centuries. Although immigrants from neighboring areas had to be initially coaxed to move there—weavers and ship builders were drawn in from the previous company headquarters of Surat through gifts of land and offers of housing (Sheppard 1932; Rodriguez 1994)—within a hundred years, on the strength of its newly built docks, Bombay grew into a bustling international mart. Praise for its dry dock and ship-building industry was lavish: British administrators hailed the dock as better than any in Europe for its size and declared Bombay-built teak ships to be "50 percent superior to vessels built in Europe" (Hastings 1986, 4). By the end of the eighteenth century, its docks served vessels from the Persian Gulf, coastal Africa, Malacca, and China (Sheppard 1932), and its bazaars witnessed a remarkable confluence of peoples and products.[19] The island city became an asylum for merchants from the less politically stable neighboring areas of Gujarat and Konkan; these merchants shaped Bombay's economy of cotton and opium exports and imports of metals, silk, sugar, and cotton piece goods (Dobbin 1972; Dossal 1989).

With Bombay's rise to prominence as a commercial seaport, the city also became a key destination in a transnational sex trade circuit. After the opening of the Suez Canal in particular in 1869, women from as far away as Poland came to work in its brothels. The city had a significant client base of European sailors as well as resident soldiers (it was the headquarters of troops in Western India) and British administrators (it was the seat of provincial government). By the turn of the twentieth century, Bombay hosted the largest number of European prostitutes of all Indian cities.[20] In the 1920s, the scale of prostitution in the city brought on panicked comparisons with the United States and Europe, such as Bombay state legislator S. A. Sardesai's declaration, "In the city of Bombay alone, we have got 900

brothels. Have you heard [of] anywhere in the world [with] so many brothels? The capital of Germany . . . although it is a larger city than Bombay,
[has] only 40 houses . . . New York also [does not have] as many brothels
[as] Bombay" (HD 1926b, 4).

The growth of the sex trade also is linked with the city's emergence as
an industrial center. From the middle of the nineteenth century onward,
Bombay became a national industrial powerhouse with an expanding number of textile mills. Its population rose by over 65 percent between 1901 and
1921 as migrant workers flocked to the city to work in its mills (Edwardes
1910; Hazareesingh 2001). Many of these mills, and the apartment buildings housing mill workers, were built in central parts of the island, such as
Nagpada and Kumbharwada. Kamathipura, the heart of the city's sex trade,
was contiguous with (and one might say a part of) these very areas where
mill workers came to live (Kosambi and Brush 1988) (see Figure 1). Its brothels thus serviced the city's growing ranks of male migrant workers, many
of whom moved on a seasonal basis between the city and neighboring rural
areas (Chandavarkar 1998).

The scale of prostitution in Bombay, and the city's increasing national
prominence in the late nineteenth century, meant that the laws passed on
prostitution in this setting also set trends that influenced other parts of the
subcontinent. For instance, the city passed one of the earliest antisoliciting
measures in 1902 and was the first to ban brothels in the 1930s, leading
other cities to follow. In the period of international action against antitrafficking, Bombay was the seat of the national enforcement authority.[21] Bombay was also the setting for the rise of an influential pan-Indian nationalist
middle class, who directed national-level legislation on subjects related to
prostitution. Hence an analysis of Bombay's sex trade tells us a story both
about the rise of the city as well as the changing legal currents at a national
level.

PROSTITUTION AND THE "NARRATIVE OF DECLINE"

The "prostitute" first appeared as a criminal figure in laws in the colonial
period. In descriptions of prostitution in ancient and medieval India, prostitutes appear to have enjoyed a good standing before the state and even
state support (Joardar 1984; Mukherji 1931/1986; Sinha and Basu 1933). It
is only in the mid-nineteenth century that prostitutes became the target

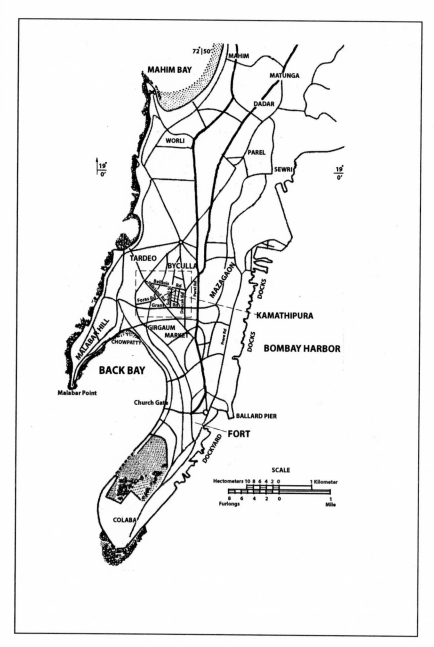

FIGURE I. Map of Bombay, highlighting Kamathipura. Adapted from *National Atlas of India,* 1960, Bombay plate 144.

of punitive laws under British colonial administrators, and the term "common prostitute" was inaugurated in Indian legal texts. Of course, comparing prostitution in ancient, medieval, and colonial periods is fraught with the danger of presentist interpretation, since several activities ranging from musical and dance performance to sexually serving soldiers have been translated from ancient and medieval texts as "prostitution," "harlotry," and "courtesanship" by latter-day historians. Nonetheless, across eras, the different types of activities classified as prostitution share two features: they were all forms of nonmarital sexual interaction, and the law did not penalize them.

Meyer's (1953) account of sexual life in ancient India notes that "harlots" were an important part of life in the city.[22] Vatsyayana's fifth-century BCE epic *Kama Sutra* classifies eight kinds of "courtesans," ranging from runaway wives to dancers.[23] Kautilya's *Arthashastra*, written circa 200 CE, provides examples of women who accompanied troops during war to provide entertainment and sexual service (Kautilya 1967, 63–65). Courtesans enjoyed an elevated social position particularly in the Gupta period (320–510 CE), the Turko-Afghan rule (1206–1526 CE), and the Mughal regime (1526–1707 CE) (Mukherji 1931/1986; Joardar 1984). In some cases, courtesans enjoyed options unavailable to married women, such as reading, writing, dancing, sculpture, and painting (Mukherji 1931/1986). Courtesans were also wealthy enough to become sources of tax revenue to the state under the Vijayanagara empire and under the Mughal emperor Shah Jahan (Manucci 1966).

In the eighteenth century, the Peshwa state in Maharashtra played a substantial role in training and supporting the artistic capabilities of dancing girls (Kadam 1998). As Wagle (1998, 20) notes, "prostitutes" were able to take complaints to courts when battered by customers, and "for a man to beat a prostitute constituted an offense." It is only in the mid-nineteenth century that prostitutes became the *target* of punitive laws that prohibited soliciting. Many scholars observe that women in the performing arts, such as courtesans and temple dancers, suffered an erosion of status in this period. The exclusivity of courtesans, for instance, declined in the latter part of the nineteenth century as their sources of patronage dwindled with the losses suffered by royalty and court culture in the colonial era. Dang (1993) and Oldenburg (1990) have mapped a steady degradation of courtesans, while Jordan (1993), Parker (1998), and Srinivasan (1988) have made similar observations with respect to temple dancing; Rege (1996) traces the devaluation of erotic folk songs such as *lavani*.

The common "narrative of decline" (John and Nair 1998, 12) and implicit romanticization of the past that inform such scholarship, however, bear some critiquing. In mourning the transformation of these varied activities into brothel work, many of these studies reproduce the construction of modern brothel workers as abject figures. In this sense, such scholarship does not interrupt the general stigmatization of brothel work. My book proposes a more nuanced view of brothel work, pointing to the opportunities it afforded some women, as well as the violence that pervaded it. Rather than mourning the loss of the cultural status of prostitutes, the book focuses on the constraints shaping brothel work, the dominant mode of organizing sexual commerce in industrial Bombay.

Feminist historians Nair (1996), Srinivasan (1988), and Whitehead (1995) have analyzed the criminalization of prostitutes in the colonial period as a dimension of Victorian sexual restrictiveness. Although this characterization has its merits, particularly because laws penalizing prostitutes were introduced in the late nineteenth century, it is also important to not read all changes in prostitution laws as a straightforward consequence of imported sexual mores. Instead, I argue that the British colonial state followed imperatives distinct from the British metropolitan state in the Victorian era, particularly when upholding prostitution in India. Colonial administrators resolutely characterized prostitution as a long-standing and invariable Indian custom, even though the forms and scale of the sex trade underwent a deep transformation in the colonial period. There was a political logic to administrators' position: the preservation of British prestige mandated clear racial and civilizational boundaries between Indian and English people, and Indian prostitution presented a powerful symbol of Indian moral degradation. At the same time, Indian prostitutes in military camps and ports provided sexual recreation for British soldiers and sailors, thus fulfilling practical ends, apart from their ideological uses. While abolitionist and anti-trafficking fervor consumed many legislators in Britain, British colonial administrators in India resisted its tenets, citing respect for local traditions. Contrary to its presumed civilizing mission, then, the colonial government institutionalized the very practices that it was called on to decry by Victorian ideologies. And rather than expressing a Victorian sexual restrictiveness, colonial prostitution laws expressed the pornographic imagination of the state, as chapters 3 and 4 will explain.

In devaluing the importance of Victorian restrictiveness as a framework, I am also probing the usefulness of Foucault's (1978/1990) conceptualization of nineteenth-century European sexuality. Many prominent scholars of South Asia (Guha 1997; Nair 1996; John and Nair 1998) have used Foucault's "apparatus of sexuality" as a model to understand colonial sexuality. Foucault's thesis that restrictions on sexual relations were productive forces and that they created new categories of sexuality surveyed by law is certainly apt. Yet I find that the Indian colonial context does not allow an easy transferral of Foucault's model, because bourgeois Indian mores were inflected by caste politics, and because the colonial state was far more coercive than the bourgeois European liberal state that Foucault studied. I thus explore the limits of Foucault's apparatus of sexuality, while drawing on his insights on how sexual prohibitions expand the scope of the state's gaze.

Apart from scholarship on the Victorian influence on performance arts, there are also several historical-sociological studies of economic compulsions that drove women to sell sexual services. Ratnabali Chatterjee (1993) focuses on the population of migrant women in cities, displaced by the labor surplus in agrarian areas. Imports from Britain drastically affected rural artisan activities, and widows who could previously make a living by spinning yarn were forced to leave villages; they arrived in cities to work as cooks, maids, or, eventually, prostitutes. Low earnings, as noted by Samita Sen (1999), led female workers in jute mills to work as part-time prostitutes. Pauline Rule's (1987) account of urban prostitution in nineteenth-century Calcutta emphasizes the role of demographic imbalances: as Calcutta became a primarily male city with a floating population of male sailors and migrant workers, prostitution increased. The sociological factors that these authors attribute to the growth of the sex trade—rural displacement and urban migration, demographic imbalances in cities, and female impoverishment—were certainly also of relevance to Bombay's history. The demographic imbalance in Bombay was quite dramatic: the proportion of females to males counted in Bombay censuses from 1870 to 1910 remained around 600 females to every 1000 males.[24] Such an imbalance can easily provide a naturalistic explanation for the male demand for prostitution. Nonetheless, such explanations are incomplete without a consideration of how institutional forces, such as laws and enforcement practices, fostered brothels and enabled regular male access to prostitution. In other words, sociological and demographic explanations alone cannot answer questions such as why and how an identifiable group of women termed prostitutes got marked by the law and segregated to identifiable neighborhoods (Walkowitz 1992).

Some of the best writing on institutional forces affecting prostitution in colonial India focuses on the Contagious Diseases Acts of the 1860s–1880s. Ballhatchet's (1980) engaging account of the conflict between colonial military administrators and British reformists is path-breaking in this regard. Banerjee's (2000) "history from below" of prostitutes in Calcutta also covers the consequences of the Contagious Diseases Acts, recovering the voices of prostitutes by analyzing songs, letters, and plays of the period. However, neither book extends beyond the Contagious Diseases Acts era, and Banerjee focuses exclusively on Bengal. D'Cunha's (1991) study of Indian laws on prostitution also focuses only on the Contagious Diseases Acts when discussing the colonial period. The Contagious Diseases Acts of the 1870s and 1880s do provide ample archival resources for study; in fact my analysis begins with that era in Bombay. However, the Contagious Diseases Acts cannot be seen as fully representative of a colonial approach to prostitution, because they were one specific historical moment in a longer process. These laws alone cannot explain the persistent criminalization of the prostitute in India. A grave need exists for studies that continue beyond this era and account for changes that took place through the subsequent sixty years of colonial rule. A grave need exists also for studies of contexts outside Bengal, since this region has assumed a prototypical stature in South Asian studies. A recent work that addresses these gaps is Levine's (2003) ambitious comparative study of how venereal disease was policed in four colonies of the British Empire. Spanning the period between 1860 and 1918, Levine explores multiple facets of the complex relationship between military medicine, racial categories, and prostitution. My book adopts a similar conceptual approach, exploring in greater depth the relationship between lawmaking and enforcement in a single site and over a span that includes important post–World War I nationalist developments.

Any study of the history of prostitution raises methodological questions about the forms and limits of historical sources, given the often hidden nature of this trade. Hershatter's (1998) remarkable study of twentieth-century Shanghai, informed by the insights of poststructuralist theory and subaltern studies, has been pioneering in its engagement with the rhetoricity of sources on prostitution—of how sources construct information for imagined audiences. In the case of Bombay, I find that certain kinds of official sources, such as police files, are remarkably forthcoming about prostitution; their richness confounds the assumption that urban prostitutes—a typically subaltern group—were marginalized into official invisibility. At the same time, the official treatment of prostitutes as a problem population, especially with regard to disease control and public order, means that while relevant official records extensively mention prostitutes, they keep the latter's voices muted. With the exception of court testimonies and petitions sent to the police, many sources do not contain even transcribed statements of brothel workers. In that now-familiar historiographical conundrum, the women's actions are profusely described but the women rarely represent themselves. Although Hershatter (1998) takes issue with Spivak's (1988) oft-cited claim about the inaudibility of subaltern subjects and emphasizes prostitutes' voices, I find formidable structural limits to prostitutes' self-representation within historical records.

Nonetheless, the prefigured limits of official archival sources drove me to engage more vigilantly with silences in texts and to underscore the rhetoricity of official sources. It also allowed me to assess the relationship of my subjects to official institutions, and prostitutes' identity construction before the law. Rather than conducting a probe into the "hidden world" of brothels—an enterprise with a long history of voyeuristic proponents—this book analyzes official sources for what they reveal about relationships between actors in the sex trade and the state.

I outline the phases of official approaches to prostitution thus: (a) the *regulationist* phase of the Contagious Diseases Acts, from around 1860 until 1890; (b) the *antitrafficking* phase, emerging at the turn of the twentieth century and lasting into the 1920s; and (c) the *abolitionist* phase, combining antitrafficking and nationalist discourses, from around 1917 to 1947. This book's chapters follow this broad historical sequence but are each organized around the specific colonial imperatives that informed legislation.

Chapter 2, for instance, focuses on the medical imperative of disease control undergirding the Contagious Diseases Acts. I argue that these laws should largely be read as a failure: while the laws were conceived as part of an ambitious imperial agenda, their enforcement in Bombay was selective and sporadic. The laws caused a rift between the police and the medical establishment and elicited opposition within Bombay's growing public sphere. I detail the strategies used by targeted women to escape medical checks and confinement.

Although the Contagious Diseases Acts had a largely ineffectual history in Bombay, police took advantage of them to closely monitor one group: European brothel workers. In chapter 3, I explore the police management of racial boundaries in Bombay's sex trade. I describe the conditions under which continental European women settled in brothels in Bombay and I detail the spatial allocation of European prostitutes to a specific neighborhood, Kamathipura. As the international discourse on prostitution shifted from disease control to antitrafficking, I show how Bombay police enforced League of Nations antitrafficking conventions in selective ways so as to leave the contours of European prostitution intact. In so doing, I illustrate the selective mandate of colonial governmentality.

In chapter 4, continuing a discussion of the marked racial stratification in Kamathipura, I provide a contrasting sketch of the milieu of Indian brothels, featuring how violence, at the hands of supervisors and the police, shaped the lives of Indian prostitutes. I use a 1917 court case about the murder of an Indian brothel worker, Akootai, as an occasion to think about the historiographic possibilities of recovering subaltern contexts.[25] Chapter 5 connects the aforementioned 1917 murder trial with wider political, social, and demographic currents and analyzes the rise of abolitionist laws in the 1920s and 1930s. I explain how nationalists and women's organizations participated in constructing Indian prostitutes as abject figures in need of rescue, and I offer a general feminist critique of both nationalist and British administrative positions as well as a specific critique of Gandhi's views on prostitution. I close by reflecting on how the various legal currents examined in this book have increased the violence toward prostitutes. Taken together, my account of prostitution laws across the span of the late nineteenth and early twentieth centuries illuminates the limits of state-led reform. The Conclusion considers the implications of my study for contemporary efforts to regulate the sex industry.

The Colonial State, Law, and Sexuality

In the nineteenth century, women in India increasingly became direct objects of colonial law. Measures such as banning widow immolation in 1829, allowing widow remarriage in 1856, prohibiting female infanticide in 1870, and raising the age of consent for consummation of marriage to twelve in 1892 constitute a commonly cited narrative of incremental legal reform (Tambe 2000). Interestingly, these reformed practices were often related to widely circulating conceptions about female sexuality: early marriage, for instance, was increasingly seen to fuel sexual precocity among girls, and remarriage for widows was believed to channel their potentially untrammeled sexuality in appropriate directions. A number of feminists studying the era have suggested that laws configured a new sexual order in the late colonial period (Chakravarti 1998; Nair 1996a; Sarkar 2000). The criminalization of prostitutes may be seen as one dimension of this sexual order. This chapter situates laws on prostitution within the context of such wider changes that occurred under colonial rule.

The notion of a colonial sexual order raises a number of questions: What was distinctly colonial about the control of sexual practices in nineteenth- and early-twentieth-century India? What was the role of the colonial state in the control of sexuality? And, in broader terms, how is the relationship between the state and the control of sexuality to be conceptualized? These questions have been addressed, to differing degrees, by feminist historians, subaltern studies historians, Cambridge School historians, legal historians, and Foucauldian theorists of sexuality. Rather than asserting a false unity to each group by reviewing them as distinct bodies of theory, this chapter explores relevant scholarship on the relation between the colonial state, law, and gender and sexuality.

Several historians have provided periodizations of the British colonial era in order to distinguish important shifts in the relationship between the colonial state, economy, and society. The most commonly cited turning point is the Revolt of 1857, which was followed by the dismantling of the East India Company and the start of direct Crown Rule, in 1858. Most historians agree that the revolt gave rise to increasing paranoia among British rulers and concern about consolidating its power.[1] On this basis, they define a transition from early colonialism to a period of high colonialism that generally stretches until the First World War. The period between the end of the First World War and political independence in 1947 was characterized by greater representative democracy and increasingly vocal identitarian movements built along the lines of religion, caste, and gender. Washbrook (1981) influentially explains this periodization in terms of the state's changing socio-economic imperatives: the state under the East India Company was essentially a mercantilist entity for which the appearance of continuity with previous regimes was necessary; it was followed by a high colonial period when a system of rule of law was attempted; the last stage, late colonialism between the two world wars, was marked by British attempts to broker power between social groups amid an incipient Indian nation-state.

Other attempts at periodization have been rooted in political philosophies informing British rule in India: Stokes (1959) and Hutchins (1967) mark shifts from a pragmatic respect for Indian rules and customs, shown by late-eighteenth-century administrators, to Utilitarian ideas introducing widespread social reform after the 1820s. The nineteenth century, then, became a prime witness to a British imperial will that sought to transform the world in its own image. Most authors agree that the second half of the nineteenth century, at which point this book begins, was notable for the rising importance of law and a penal structure. The phases of laws on prostitution—regulation in the late nineteenth century, antitrafficking in the early twentieth century, and abolitionism in the 1920s and 1930s—map broadly onto the phases of high and late colonialism. The phases of regulation and antitrafficking correspond to a time when Britons viewed their country's role as a dominant imperial power in increasingly racialized terms, drawing distinctions between competing imperial powers during the period of high colonialism. The currents of abolitionism, spurred by Indian nationalist reformers, reflect a period of greater colonial concessions to social movements and nationalist demands after the First World War.

THE COLONIAL STATE IN INDIA

The colonial state may be seen as a particular variant of state forms: one that instituted and mediated the power of an imperial center upon colonized economies. At the same time, it responded to imperatives distinct from both imperial and noncolonial state formations. In India, the British colonial state's legal and administrative apparatus conditioned a specifically colonial mode of production that changed the character of land, labor, and property relations and increased power at urban nodes of trade.[2] From the mid-eighteenth century onward, the state fundamentally restructured land relations through instituting private property rights in land, thus facilitating its own revenue raising. Settlement laws made all land that was not privately owned the property of the British Crown, thus reducing the amount available for small peasant cultivation and increasing displacement from rural to urban areas. As an urban-centric railway network was developed, agricultural production shifted in favor of cash crops, promoting a cash nexus in the economy. Indigenous industry was quelled in order to promote imports from Britain. The colonial state in India thus actively fashioned an economy whose logic was geared to the metropolitan center.

A key instrument of control instituted in the colonial period was a structure of state-sponsored legislation. Conventional historians present colonial rule as having introduced a rational and stable structure of lawmaking commonly referred to as a "rule of law" (Lingat 1998), although as I discuss later, feminists have contested the extent to which this structure was entirely new, and legal theorists have questioned its legitimacy given the absence of full citizenship for its subjects. Nevertheless, the legal paramountcy of the colonial state was backed by considerable physical force. The colonial state set up an order where it alone had legitimate recourse to violence: for instance, during Cornwallis's tenure as governor-general at the end of the eighteenth century, landholders were denied the right to police their own districts (Stokes 1959). The centralization of the armed forces and the use of the army to assist in matters of civilian order constituted the state's coercive base. The army even assisted in tax collection for a period (Washbrook 1981).

Changes in the fortunes of political parties in England had mixed effects on colonial policies. Hutchins (1967) convincingly argues that as the power of the Liberal Party grew in Britain, India became a refuge for Conservative policymakers. The era of the Contagious Diseases Acts is a good example: when the Liberal Party was in power (1868–74, 1880–86, 1892–94), conservative administrators in India fought to preserve the policy of regulated prostitution. At the same time, the widespread social reform introduced in Britain by the Liberal Party in the first decade of the twentieth century also spurred Indian legislators to pursue reform of colonial policies on prostitution. However, on the whole, the ethos of the colonial state remained resistant, in that it was consistently more coercive than the metropolitan state. The colonial penal system serves as an illustration: although prisons were introduced on a wide scale in the late eighteenth century in line with developments in Europe, they coexisted with more brutal forms of punishment such as capital punishment, public executions, and whippings (Arnold 1997).

The colonial state's heavy reliance on coercion has led Subaltern Studies scholars to characterize it as a dominant, and not hegemonic, structure.[3] They stress that the so-called rule of law that the colonial state instituted was established without the consent of the ruled, rendering it a different entity from the bourgeois liberal state in England (Guha 1997). While Subaltern Studies authors are right in pointing out that the colonial state had no legitimacy—with legitimacy understood specifically as fulfillment of the representative function of the state—practices of collaboration between intermediary classes and colonial administrators that strengthened British rule did exist. Such collaboration has been the subject of Cambridge School histories.[4] Bose and Jalal (1998), for instance, point out that British administrators received important support from princes and some rural elites in setting up the colonial state. The colonial state was able to extract higher levels of surplus than any previous state because of the help of its elite collaborators (Washbrook 1981). Early colonial laws on property and taxation favored existing hierarchies of caste and in many cases reinforced them by using differential tax assessments for each caste and redefining property rights along caste lines (Washbrook 1981). Such laws earned the colonial state the cooperation of upper castes, in many respects.

THE CONTEXTS OF LAWMAKING

Although new laws were introduced in the colonial period, they were never written upon a tabula rasa. Initial British attempts at lawmaking in India were marked by investigations into religious scriptures, in an attempt to maintain an illusion of continuity with the past. In appearing to uphold tradition, the colonial state secured elite cooperation and reinforced its own authority. Early British administrators, notably Warren Hastings and William Jones, commissioned Hindu priests *(pandits)* and Muslim clerics *(maulvis)* to draw up official interpretations of religious codes for dispensation of justice by a court system. The colonial quest for homogeneity in Hindu scriptures was an essentially modern impulse, and its result was the creation of an entirely new body of discourse that could be called "official knowledge," as Mani (1989, 89) points out. In commissioning the work of *pandits* and *maulvis,* the colonial state was in effect validating elite conceptions of sexual practices. The new official discourse for Hindus, based on interpretations by priests, had the effect of elevating Brahminical customs to become the norm, a power that they had not wielded earlier (Baxi 1986, Rudolph and Rudolph 1967, Singha 1998). The state's concern for the scriptural validity of laws declined somewhat when a reformist current overtook nineteenth-century colonizers and exerted pressure to transform Indian customs. As Stokes (1959) and Hutchins (1967) elaborate, the reformist pressure may be traced to the Utilitarian ideas of Thomas Macaulay and James Mill, which shaped a variety of statutes, regulations, and colonial institution building from the 1820s onward.

The new structure of legality was formalized through the following major changes: in 1833, the Charter Act established a single legislature for all of India; in the second part of the nineteenth century, the Code of Civil Procedure (1859), the Indian Penal Code (1860), and the Code of Criminal Procedure (1861) were passed. In 1858, the state also formally disavowed legislating on women's status by consigning it to "personal law" under the jurisdiction of religious authorities, or what was termed "community." The conventional reading by colonial historians is that this legality supplanted, or at least contended with, forms of authority based in the religious community.[5]

Based on an understanding of law as an expression of elite power, much Subaltern Studies scholarship makes the distinction between custom and law, at times romanticizing custom as the site of uncolonized practices and law as the "state's emissary" (Guha 1997, 40). There are, however, some pitfalls to placing custom and law in constant opposition. For one, this opposition assigns an unchanging quality to both custom and law (Anderson and Guha 1998). The sociologist of law Upendra Baxi (1992) also notes that to see law as a species completely different from custom is to perpetuate a quintessentially colonial characterization. He situates the prescriptions, prohibitions, and punishments enforced by custom as part of a grammar and practice of power, and thus also law.[6]

There is also a disagreement in legal history over the actual extent to which the colonial period introduced a "rule of law." Baxi sees the quest for certainty and order through law in the colonial period as more of an aspiration than an actual achievement. A look at case law, he insists, will reveal the ambivalence in the juridical decisions taken.[7] Bernard Cohn has also focused on a clash between indigenous and colonial legal processes, to which he attributes a failure of the British legal system in India.[8] Both of these scholars argue that a multitude of nonstate legal systems coexisted with colonial law, and that there were enormous continuities between colonial law and these systems.

Another basis on which the notion of the "rule of law" in colonial India may be questioned is a distinctive feature in the relationship between law and the colonial state: the judiciary did not, in practice, have an independent role of placing a check on the executive arm but rather was tied to the political structure of the government. The executive, composed primarily of British administrators, changed laws as it pleased, and judicial appointments were made from among civil servants. The enormous control wielded by the executive branch of the colonial state undercuts the claim of an impartial, stable "rule of law."

A characterization of colonial law on which historians converge, however, is that the law achieved the expression of imperial interests in timeless, universal terms. Disputes concerning law were expressed in terms of general statements of principle rather than particular statements of private interest. This made the law an especially powerful form of discourse and an important instrument of domination. Guha (1997) finds that the power of colonial law lay in the abstractions it generated: it took real historical figures and events and placed them outside history, by translating them into a discourse expressing the will of an omnipresent state. Guha terms this discourse a kind of appropriation, as it erased the perspectives that situated historical experience within the life of a community. On a social scale, the attempt at "rule of law" reflected a general urge to order, to imprint an ethos of abstract principles, and a new, less familiar, language of authority. Purportedly universal standards were the platform on which laws specifically conducive to colonial domination were passed.

FEMINIST INITIATIVES: CRITIQUING LEGAL DICHOTOMIES

Much feminist attention has been focused on the slew of laws passed in the nineteenth and early twentieth centuries that reformed women's status. Scholars such as Chakravarti (1998) question colonial historians' assumption that the state served a new ordering and rationalizing function. Chakravarti instead asserts that even in precolonial times, a rational structure of caste law existed, held together by the state. Countering historians who characterize the precolonial period as one with a multiplicity of caste laws with no fixed Hindu law, she argues that "discrete caste laws functioned within an overarching conceptualization" (1998, 186). As far as women's sexual practices were concerned, powerful and ordered forms of governance predated the colonial period. For instance, in the case of Maharashtra, the Peshwa state assumed responsibility for penalizing women for adultery. The state played a supportive role to the husband, aiding the community's control over female sexuality.

What was new in the colonial period, according to Chakravarti, was the emergence of a choice of laws used to govern women. Women became subject to a dual authority structure: their everyday lives continued to be subject to the social power of the community, while property-related disputes made them subjects of the state. An interlocking structure came into place, with both upholding male-dominant family forms. Nair's (1996a) analysis of law in the colonial period also supports the claim that a dual structure came into place.

From a broad feminist perspective, the two changes in the legal structure with greatest implications for gender relations were, (a) the creation of a "personal law" relating to marriage and family matters, and (b) the introduction of property rights as a factor in dispute settlement.

PERSONAL LAW

In the 1830s, a Law Commission began to draw up a body of substantive law, which led to the Indian Penal Code, passed in 1860. The Second Law Commission, which drew up the Code of Criminal Procedure in 1861, did not agree to codify Hindu and Muslim law, as it came on the heels of an 1858 injunction by Queen Victoria against interfering with religious beliefs.[9] It marked off a separate field of "personal law"—religion-based laws governing marriage, separation, inheritance, maintenance, and adoption. It declared that laws on marriage and inheritance were synonymous with religious laws, while isolating other kinds of laws as outside the ambit of religion. As Agnes (1999) notes, this version of the separation between the public and the private effectively granted religious authorities the power of control over women's economic and sexual mobility.

The colonial state solidified male dominance by granting male legislators the power to speak on behalf of women of their communities. Effectively, this move located women much more deeply within community structures; their identities were reified along religious and caste lines. Indian male legislators (whose numbers in the Central Legislative Assembly increased in the 1920s) wielded a dubious authority when speaking in the name of "their" women. As feminist scholars have roundly established, the needs and voices of actual women were often of secondary interest to legislators; it was the latter's own political positions, dramatized by the publicity stirred in political debates, that were of greater importance (Mani 1989; Nair 1996a; Sarkar 2001; Sinha 2006; Sunder Rajan 2003). Women's access to legislative forums was, at best, strained: they were elected in the 1920s to provincial councils but not to the Central Legislative Assembly.

PRIVATE PROPERTY RIGHTS

These rights played a decisive role in eroding an older social order. Kosambi (1996) notes that the colonial state's legal system became ever more powerful precisely because property was awarded in dispute settlements. More and more people chose English courts in urban centers over caste *panchayats*, as the stakes in disputes were raised. Kumar's (1998) analysis of adultery cases in early-twentieth-century Bombay also demonstrates that grievances were taken to court when they hinged on issues of property or money. Thus, the attitudes and predispositions of English judges set precedents on questions otherwise subject to community standards.

Having noted the importance of British-ruled courts in shaping Indian community practices, feminists are less likely than conventional historians to see state-and caste-based forms of authority as mutually exclusive domains. For instance, although Chakravarti (1998) distinguishes between state jurisdiction and caste-based forms of law, she argues that there were several cases of overlap between them, for which a body of case law was built up. Cases not resolved conclusively by caste councils *(panchayats)* were adjudicated by courts. English courts did inquire into *panchayat* decisions and even reverse them, especially when cases related to "public morality"—in which women were inevitably involved. Chakravarti cites, in this respect, cases involving second marriages by women. Among the Teli and Aheer castes, women were permitted to marry a second husband if the first husband contracted leprosy or took a second wife himself. The colonial state, however, charged such women with bigamy, citing a fear that "adultery would be legalized" (Chakravarti 1998, 136–37).

Feminist historians also offer a distinct analysis of the scope of the colonial state. Whereas Subaltern Studies Collective and Cambridge School historians view the colonial state as either reluctant or unable to affect the sphere of intimate relations, feminist historians demonstrate the colonial state's significant influence in this realm. They point to examples such as the enforcement of laws against female infanticide: the colonial state passed an act in 1870 declaring female infanticide a form of murder and called for monitoring family records of about half a million people in order to gauge sex ratios and identify infanticidal clans. Once the state declared clans to be infanticidal, police officers had to inquire into individual suspected cases in those clans. The colonial state carried out a surveillance exercise of such great magnitude successfully, showing that it could not only enforce laws involving the personal domain but could do so effectively (Panigrahi 1972).

In light of the proven capacity of the colonial state to propose and carry out ambitious social reform, feminists argue that the colonial state in fact held back from many reforms; far from being benign proreform spectators, colonial administrators often took patently regressive positions. Feminists view the state's inauguration of "personal law" and its policy of noninterference in matters relating to the intimate domain as a politically expedient stance in the face of pressures from religious revivalists and traditionalists. Nair's (1996b) analysis of Mysore demonstrates the conservative position of the colonial state through a contrast. As a princely state, Mysore was disconnected from formal colonial rule but was subject to similar reformist pressures as other parts of India. On the whole, it took more progressive positions on issues of social reform than the provinces under direct colonial rule. For instance, in 1893, an Infant Marriage Regulation was passed that prohibited all marriages to girls below eight years of age and all marriages by men above fifty years to girls below sixteen (Nair 1996b). In making such marriages themselves illegal, and not just their consummation, the Mysore government acted with less fear of political consequences than did the colonial government of India.[10] Such characterizations of the colonial state's political positions go against the current of conventional history, which narrates colonial reform as a steady linear process of women's advancement (Heimsath 1964; Natarajan 1959). According to this laudatory narrative, the colonial state encouraged female emancipation, with the progressive gender ideology of British rulers overcoming the orthodoxy of religious revivalists. Feminist scrutiny of the legislative debates, however, reveals collusion between British and Indian patriarchal forces as much as an apparent contestation between them (Tambe 2000).

If one were to view at a glance the key laws changing the family form across the late colonial period (Figure 2), one could see a reconstitution of

Marriage-related legislation	Non-marriage-related legislation
• Sati banned (1829) • Widow remarriage permitted (1856) • Intercaste marriage permitted (1872) • Age of consent to consummation of marriage raised (1891) • Age of marriage raised (1929) • Muslim Shari'at Application Act (1937) • Women's Right to Property Act (1937) • Indian Succession Acts (1865, 1925, 1929)	• Homosexuality criminalized (Indian Penal Code, 1860) • Devadasis restricted (Indian Penal Code, 1860, Devadasi Act, 1934) • Prostitution controlled (Contagious Diseases Acts, 1868–1888; and a series of abolitionist laws, 1902–1948) • Infanticide banned (1870) • Age of consent for nonmarital sexual relations raised (1925) • Women's labor restricted/protected (Factory Acts 1891, 1911, 1922, 1934) • Maternity Benefits (1929)

FIGURE 2. Laws affecting the form of the family, 1800–1947.

the sexual order. As Nair (1996a) observes, colonial laws "buil[t] walls between the sexuality of women in the familial and extra-familial domains"
(150). Taken together, these laws standardized the family form and devalued
women who fell outside this form. First, marriage was regularized through
laws that defined its ideal age, its forms and lines of descent. The most
prominent examples were laws permitting widow remarriage, banning sati,
and permitting intercaste marriage. Second, the notion of the male breadwinner became entrenched through laws limiting women's employability,
such as the Factory Acts. Third, the sexuality of infants and children became
a scientific concern and cause for raising the age of marriage. Finally, forms
of sexuality that were not rooted in formal alliances—homosexuality, prostitution, and concubinage—were increasingly prohibited. Nonmarried
women of various kinds, especially prostitutes, widows, and entertainers,
were denigrated.

THE COLONIAL STATE'S ECONOMIC AND IDEOLOGICAL IMPERATIVES

In order to understand the context of these laws better, it is worthwhile
examining the colonial state's general economic and ideological imperatives. Capitalist states have historically sought to regulate women's marriage, inheritance, and employment practices.[11] Through such measures,
they have assured the reproduction of the labor force and ensured the
security of private property. The colonial state in India had a long-term
interest in guaranteeing the reproduction of the labor force in preferred
economic sectors, such as tea and cotton, commodities that were in demand in Britain. Nair (1996a) and Kumar (1994) in their analyses of the
Factory Acts illustrate how labor legislation for women in industries and
plantations shifted with changing workforce requirements. For instance,
from 1850 to around 1900, when there existed a need for cheap and pliant
labor in plantations, and workers were recruited from afar, there was no
legislative concern over child and maternal welfare. As labor unrest grew
and birth rates declined, plantation owners began to target the perceived
"immorality" of single women workers and instituted pronatalist policies.
The notion of the male breadwinner was standardized through laws prohibiting the recruitment of married women, whose responsibilities were
now seen to rest in the household.

Apart from the reproduction of the labor force, the colonial state's interest was to ensure the security of property upon which its revenues were based. This imperative meant, at the level of family forms, encouraging stability in inheritance practices, which assured property transfer across generations. The many laws standardizing succession practices that were passed from the latter half of the nineteenth century reflect this imperative. The rising importance of the notion of property in land and the introduction of the cash nexus increased the stakes in inheritance practices. Family forms that did not conform to a dominant patrilineal type came under attack. Among the matrilineal Nayars of Kerala, for instance, colonial legal reform granted male members the right to bequeath property to their own wives and children. Nayar men's ability to acquire their own property through employment was also accelerated through their contact with the colonial administration. These developments eroded the matrilineal inheritance order. The female-headed households of *devadasis* (temple dancers) also grew weak as laws were passed curtailing their ability to adopt children and transmit property.[12]

Even as it standardized family forms, the British colonial state did not necessarily encourage family forms resembling the norm in Britain. For instance, it touted the advantages of the joint family in India, as this was an ideal family form for security against loans, with liabilities shared by all family members. As Washbrook (1981) observes, this family form served the interests of the ultimate creditor, the state. The colonial state supported widow remarriage even when the widow was marrying her brother-in-law (levirate marriage), in order to prevent fragmentation of land holdings. Widow remarriage in fact served the interests of the dead husband's family, because widows were expected to relinquish their claims to their husband's property upon remarriage (Carroll 1989; Chowdhury 1996). Thus, the colonial state in India promoted practices that were unacceptable in Britain.

The transformations wrought in property and land relations by the colonial state needed to be embedded within a sense of a social and moral order. Colonial administrators sought to maintain their moral and intellectual authority through a discourse of civilizational superiority. They justified colonial rule using a spatialized narrative of historical progress that fixed different parts of the world on a single hierarchical scale (McClintock 1995). One plank of this discourse was a hierarchizing of nations according to the status of their women. The colonial state presented itself as a representative of an advanced civilization that would introduce the upliftment of Indian women from centuries of suffering. The "lax morals" of Indian society became a staple of colonial discourse, and the tropical climate was said to conspire with the so-called innate corruptibility of Indians to produce widespread depravity. Early marriage, promiscuity among widows, and prostitution were seen as examples of these traits.[13] As the result, it was ideologically useful for the colonial state to not so much abolish these practices as keep their existence in public view, in order to buttress claims about racial distinctions between rulers and the ruled. In debates on early marriage, for instance, some British administrators played obstructionist roles, opposing reforms that would ban child marriage (Sinha 1997, 1999).

Apart from direct legislation, the colonial state also exerted an indirect influence by shaping the terrain upon which the discourse of Indian social reform arose. British administrators' claims about the inferiority of Indian civilization sparked a strong nationalist reaction, of which there were two variants: reformist and religious revivalist. Reformist efforts to improve the status of women were motivated by the goal of raising India's stature among the ranks of nations and ascending the colonial hierarchy of "civilized" nations. Religious revivalists, on the other hand, responded to the colonial hierarchy through an alternative narrative of the ancient glory of Vedic womanhood, desecrated through long periods of foreign rule (Chakravarti 1998, Roy 1995). Thus, although the reform process was a movement impelled by urban Indian intelligentsia, it was at least in part a response to the evangelical currents introduced by British rule. British administrators in turn reinforced this logic of provocation and response by seeking varied proofs of Indian "barbarity." Prostitution served as one such example.

PROSTITUTION AS AN EXEMPLAR

It is a commonplace of feminist theory that the cultural denigration of sexually promiscuous women assists in disciplining women in general.[14] Colonial prostitution laws played an important role in constructing such a dichotomous order. The colonial state introduced the term "common prostitute" to Indian legal discourse, thereby affirming the rise of a devalued, proletarian form of prostitution (Oldenburg 1990). By legally tolerating brothels, it also institutionalized the identity of the brothel worker. The colonial state's laws on seduction, enticement, and elopement also contributed to the dichotomous construction of respectable bourgeois womanhood and the prostitute. In allowing men to buy wives and criminalizing those who "stole" or "abducted" these wives, the law reinforced male property rights in women. Such laws set apart women who did not belong to men, such as prostitutes (Singha 1998).

The specific measures that the colonial state took to control prostitution were shaped by a racialized imaginary. As observed in several other contexts, the latter half of the nineteenth century gave rise to a specifically scientific racism among European colonizers, leading states to control interracial sexual unions and prevent miscegenation (Cooper and Stoler 1997, Stoler 1997). Such policies were a departure from the early stages of colonialism, when concubinage and even intermarriage with natives were permitted, as they saved colonizer men the time and financial responsibilities of European-style family life (Ghosh 2006). Studies of prostitution in military bases confirm that alarm over interracial mixing between soldiers and foreign women prompted regulated prostitution (Ballhatchet 1980, Enloe 1989, Moon 1997). For the colonial state in India, the most unwieldy segment of European males was the soldiers who, after the 1860s, served for short periods of seven years (Arnold 1993). Regulated sex between soldiers and prostitutes came to be seen as the most effective way in which the colonial administrators could prevent permanent unions developing with native women (see chapter 2). Chapter 3 demonstrates how the colonial state accommodated Eastern European women in Bombay brothels in order to reduce sexual contact between British men and Indian women.

Laws on prostitution also provide an excellent example of the colonial state's complicated economic imperatives. Prostitution in urban centers played a role in supporting the migrant labor system. Luise White (1990), in a study of colonial Nairobi, finds that prostitution benefited both the urban economy and the rural hinterlands: prostitutes subsidized their own rural families with their earnings and also reproduced urban wage labor through their services. Of the various types of prostitution, the brothel-based (malaya) form, particularly, included nonsexual services such as providing food, bathwater, and conversation. Being akin to nonlegal marriage in many ways, such relationships reproduced male labor power in the cities. The dual economic role of prostitutes served the colonial economic structure and was therefore not disturbed by the colonial state.[15] In the context of colonial India, Sen (1999) and others have argued that high male-to-female

population ratios in jute mill towns of Bengal sustained prostitution, although they do not echo White's corollary—that prostitution reproduced
male labor power. The link between urbanization and prostitution has not as
clearly been mapped in the case of Bombay, although Chandavarkar's (1994)
study of industrial growth in Bombay mentions in passing that prostitution
was prevalent in the 1920s, when the workforce consisted of a large number
of male migrants. Chapters 5 and 6 in this book look closely at this milieu.

Scholars typically see an ideological fit between Victorian and Brahminical standards in shaping the content of many laws on prostitution (Uberoi
1996; Whitehead 1995). For instance, a vociferous public movement against
the matrilineal family form of *devadasis* (temple dancers) was led by Brahmins and fed by Victorian notions of the dancers' "immodesty." The Victorian moral order in late-nineteenth-century Britain was in fact marked
by several features consonant with Brahminical standards: exalting the
mind over the body, and therefore mental labor over manual labor; sexual
restraint among women; and a stress on cleanliness, in both physical and
moral terms. Victorian norms relied heavily on theories of hygiene for enforcing minimal contact between upper and lower classes, while Brahminical standards had a long history of social rarefaction using the metaphor of
purity—from untouchability to the strict monitoring of bloodlines (Whitehead 1996). With regard to prostitution, therefore, a high degree of overlap
in the beliefs of bourgeois rulers and Brahmin elites was not surprising.

Yet it is also important to critically probe the assumption that prostitution laws in the colonial period were fueled principally by Victorian sexual
restrictiveness. Not only does the colonial state's history of tolerating prostitution belie this assumption but the very notion of Victorian sexual restrictiveness requires further questioning. Michel Foucault, whose writing has
recast the understanding of nineteenth-century European sexuality, importantly overturns many crucial assumptions about how Victorian sexual mores
functioned. In the following sections, I review Foucault's elaboration of the
modern apparatus of sexuality and then consider its relevance to the Indian
colonial context.

FOUCAULT'S "APPARATUS" OF SEXUALITY

Michel Foucault's varied writings have, in the past three decades, transformed scholarly understandings of European modernity. Of particular

relevance to this book is his conceptualization of how human beings were constituted as subjects, particularly following the overturning of juridical monarchies by bourgeois revolutions. He holds that as the aim of government shifted from preserving power of a sovereign to controlling a new entity, population, new tactics and techniques loosely classified as governmentality emerged, focused on individual subjects.[16] Dividing practices, evident in the rise of prisons, asylums, and clinics, condemned pathologized individuals to confined social and physical spaces. Sciences of classification became more and more elaborate and structured into disciplines. Techniques of domination based on increasingly penetrating knowledge systems turned humans into objects of study. At the same time, new ways of active self-formation produced new modes of subjectification. One example of these modes of subject formation was a rise in discourses about sex as a site of knowledge about the self.[17]

Foucault's *The History of Sexuality: An Introduction* (1990) traced the elaboration of sexuality in disciplines such as medicine, psychiatry, and anthropology in the nineteenth century. The repression of sexuality, assumed to be a hallmark of the Victorian age, was, according to Foucault, only one part of a larger dynamic of the intensification of attention to the body. Rather than being aimed at reducing sexuality, this repression was in fact a way of constituting a body that could be cared for, protected, cultivated, and most importantly, differentiated from others. Foucault viewed the attention to sexuality and selfhood as a feature of identity formation among bourgeois classes. Through its concern with knowledge about sex, the bourgeoisie endowed itself with a body possessing health, hygiene, descent, and race. The identification of sex with selfhood ultimately underlined class distinctions.

According to Foucault, the bourgeois preoccupation with sexuality was a transmutation of the aristocratic concern with bloodlines. Ancestry had been of greatest importance for the nobility but the bourgeoisie, having no such recourse to the past, viewed the health of its body and its progeny as crucial to its future. Older forms of prestige bestowed by alliances were displaced by more individualized mechanisms of self-improvement. Therefore, from the eighteenth century onward, a shift occurred away from a system of alliances based on marriage, development of kinship ties, and transmission of names. Because correct sex was the means by which longevity of the bourgeoisie could be secured, the act of sex came to have biological responsibility for the entire species. The science of the body ascended in importance, and along with it strategies and discourses concerned with sexuality, which Foucault together terms an apparatus of sexuality.[18]

The apparatus of sexuality was characterized by four key strategies, Foucault argued: (a) the "hysterization" of women's bodies, whereby the feminine body was seen as thoroughly saturated with sexuality and as vital to securing reproduction of the social body; (b) the "pedagogization" of children's sex, whereby children were seen to have a dangerous potential for sexual activity that needed to be checked by education; (c) the socialization of procreative behavior, wherein economic incitements and restrictions promoting procreative behavior of couples were introduced; (d) the "psychiatrization" of perverse pleasure, whereby sexual anomalies were clinically analyzed (Foucault 1990, 104–5). Scientific regimes of classification played a vital role in this new apparatus of sexuality: techniques for the state management of births, marriages, life expectancy, and fertility of the population came into being at this time, as did a "medicine of perversions" and program of eugenics (118).

In the new medicalized discourse on sex, previous categories of debauchery and excess came to be cast as perversions and pathologies. Prostitution can be viewed as one such reconfigured category (although Foucault mentions it only in passing). Whereas prostitution was previously cast as immoral behavior, it took on new dimensions as a pathological activity under modern regimes. It became a "crime" against the species on two counts: it involved heterosexual sex not aimed at correct procreation, and it was associated with venereal disease. Venereal disease assumed a particularly terrifying aspect as an affliction that crippled generations, and the prostitute became a symbol of its spread. A moral failing became recast as physical disease, echoing a shift found in understandings of alcoholism (Valverde 1998). The prostitute may also be classified alongside the many discursive figures that emerged from various European nineteenth-century preoccupations: "the hysterical woman, the masturbating child, the Malthusian couple, and the perverse adult" (Foucault 1990, 105). Like these figures, the prostitute became an object of knowledge in the nineteenth century in many imperial settings, crystallizing concerns about venereal disease, racial miscegenation, and urbanization. Unlike these figures, prostitutes were not only the focus of regimes of scientific expertise and pedagogy but also heavily controlled through mechanisms of law and punishment. The prostitute thus was a target of juridical, apart from governmental, power. Not only was she pathologized; she was also criminalized. If one is to use Foucault to gain insight into the process of the criminalization of the prostitute, it is important to engage with his theory of power, which calls for a fairly unconventional reading of law and punishment.

FOUCAULT ON LAW, POWER, AND PLEASURE

One of Foucault's innovations has been to understand sexuality in terms of public discourses that govern practices, rather than through mechanisms of repression such as taboo and law. This particular emphasis is a challenge to the standard account of the relation between sex and power, which holds sex as a prior energy that is then acted upon and restricted by power.[19] According to Foucault, such a reading, which makes sex equivalent to freedom, is symptomatic of a wider yearning to see pleasure as beyond power. The reach of power, however, extends to even the most intimate domains such as sex in ways that are not obvious; power in fact relies on *not* being obvious in these domains. It is a key feature of Foucault's political theory that power is understood not as external to freedom, acting upon it and repressing it, but, instead, constitutive of it. Our tendency to see power only as a limit placed on freedom may be based, he writes, on the kinds of institutions that prevailed after the Middle Ages: "juridical monarchies" that rested on law and transcended all heterogeneous claims to power (1990, 86–87). In place of this tendency, he offers a less centralized conceptualization of modern power—as an omnipresent complex of force relations. Within this framework, he intriguingly proposes, power is tolerable only on the condition that it mask a portion of itself. Therefore, the measure of freedom on which resistance is based is that which is left intact by power.[20] Thus, when sex is seen as an energy prior to power, we mistake the effects of power for the objective of power.[21] According to Foucault, standard analyses of the relationship of power to sex are marked by such a juridical hangover.

A major caution Foucault offers concerns prohibitions in general: he argues that although, on the surface, prohibitions appear like barriers to an activity, beneath the surface, they extend the lines of penetration by power. In other words, prohibited practices serve not so much as the enemy of power as a support to power's advancement. He relates as an example the campaign to control infantile sexuality, a task that was bound to fail but into which went an inordinate effort of corrective discourses and devices of surveillance by parents and teachers. By constituting child sexuality as a secret, this medico-sexual regime "forced it into hiding" so as to enable its "discovery" (1990, 41–42). Limits that were similarly created on other kinds of non-normative sexualities gave them a defined reality and thereby constituted them as vulnerable to power.

Foucault writes that such constitutive mechanisms of repression have a double impetus, of pleasure and power. There is pleasure in exercising a power that questions, monitors, watches, and searches out, and there is also a converse pleasure in fleeing from or evading this power. He thus conceives of a landscape of spirals of intertwined pleasure and power; in his scheme, the two mutually incite one another. As mentioned in my introduction, an irony in the history of state control of prostitution is that neither prohibiting nor regulating prostitution has had an adverse effect on its growth. Foucault's conceptualization of the relationship between pleasure and power in mechanisms of repression is a valuable contribution to understanding such a paradox. Laws on prostitution thus may be seen as repressing prostitutes while keeping intact a measure of freedom, thus *inciting* their own violation.

Foucault's theory of power presents a landscape not imprinted with absolute barriers of law but marked by points of saturation of power, pleasure, and knowledge. In this view, the laws on prostitution constituted a specific type of heterosexual commodified female sexuality on which medical, administrative, and penal attention could be focused. The prostitute was a figure who at once attracted the focus of institutions such as the medical establishment (which sought to understand venereal disease); the military (which sought to regulate the activities of soldiers and sailors); social groups such as the Indian bourgeois reformers (who formulated the ideal archetype of wife-mother); and British ruling elites (who were anxious about racial miscegenation). The series of legislations on prostitution need not be seen as absolute law but rather as an expression of the substantial discursive saturation around this figure.[22]

In seeing laws on prostitution as discourse, I do not strictly adhere to Foucault's (1990) usage of the term "law." Foucault makes the term function largely as a metaphor for sovereign restrictive power.[23] However, legal pronouncements may be seen as part of a field of contingent discourses.

Debates over laws, and even laws themselves, may be seen as a means by which circuits of communication were established between different establishments and social groups. In other words, the substance of the law was less an issue than the circuits it established; this insight is relevant when examining the pattern of increasing repressive legislation on prostitution mentioned in chapter 1. The political contests between Indian elites, reformers, and colonial administrators, discussed in previous sections, found an avenue in disputes over prostitution. The next section takes up the question of the direct relevance of Foucault's work for the history of colonial laws.

FOUCAULT AND COLONIAL HISTORY

Foucault's conceptualization of an apparatus of sexuality has been enormously influential because it offers a mode of analysis open to historical contingency. Yet the historicity implicit in Foucault's argument has been underemphasized in scholarship on colonial contexts. Two approaches define the scholarship on Foucault, sexuality, and colonialism: accounts that use Foucault's history as a theoretical model with which to compare changes elsewhere, and accounts that treat his work strictly as history and stress actual connections between the bourgeoisie in Europe and in colonial settings. The first type, which treats Foucault's work as theory, may be seen in writing on sexuality in India by Nair (1996a, 1996b) and Guha (1997); the second type, seeing Foucault's work as history, is more rare and describes to some degree the work on Southeast Asia by Stoler (1995, 1997).

Much of the writing on sexuality in colonial India assumes that Foucault's account of shifts from systems of alliance to an apparatus of sexuality describes a teleology applicable to other parts of the world. For instance, when Guha (1997) refers to Foucault in analyzing the control of sexuality in nineteenth-century India, he claims that unlike Europe, where the deployment of an independent apparatus of sexuality had taken place, sexuality in India was still subsumed in systems governing alliance. He maps sexuality in India along Foucault's schema, characterizing it as a system of alliances, even quoting Foucault's description directly: "a system of rules defining the permitted and forbidden, the licit and the illicit" (46). In a similar vein, Nair (1996a, 1996b) claims that the shift from the system of alliances that Foucault details in the case of Europe did not occur in the case of colonial India. She links the decisive changes in Europe to the rise of individualism, which the colonial economy did not engender, subordinated as it was to the metropolitan economy. In India there was a far less decisive break with the hierarchies of the traditional family. She argues, therefore, that women's sexuality remained firmly linked to caste and kin alliances (Nair 1996b).

Both Guha and Nair find Foucault's chronology to be theoretically valid: Guha finds that the changes Foucault describes were due to occur but had not yet done so, while Nair holds that the colonial period did not produce strong enough breaks with the past to introduce bourgeois liberal individualism. However, such a teleological understanding of Foucault's view of sexuality and power does not align with the specificities of colonial modernity. The colonial state, unlike the bourgeois liberal state, strengthened rather than weakened systems of alliance. The colonial state introduced a distinct order that reinforced property preservation and inheritance systems. It encouraged the standardization of marriage forms toward a patrilineal norm and reinforced the joint family as a means to preserve property holdings. Even by the teleological standards of liberalism, regression, rather than progression, occurred under colonial rule.

More to the point, though, Foucault (1990) was not writing a general theory of sexuality, even if his book does elaborate a theory of power. Foucault's primary aim in *The History of Sexuality* was to depict specific changes in his part of the world.[24] His formulation of the apparatus of sexuality is based on a cultural mosaic specific to European history, such as the confessional strain in Christianity that in turn served as a model of incitement to discourse on sex. Such features make any attempt to use Foucault for a comparative venture tenuous. Further difficulties arise when one tries to relate the types of power Foucault describes to power in the colonial setting. The colonial state, as described earlier, was distinct from the metropolitan state in legitimacy, use of force, and concentration of power. The colonial state was steeped in an illiberal ethos distinct from liberal metropolitan states. The democratic devolution of power to individuating networks of institutions and discourses was therefore not a necessity, although specific "modern" discourses and practices, such as systems of classification in the social sciences, medicine, and techniques of penal reform played an important role in the colonizing process (Arnold 1993, 1997). Also, with respect to sexual relations, as discussed earlier, the imperatives of caste played a key role in shaping norms. Although Guha (1997) and Nair (1996a) are correct in finding some similarities between the imperatives of European aristocratic and upper-caste norms, it is also important to note some distinctions: caste membership played a determining role across all ranks of Hindu society, and not just for an aristocratic minority; exclusionary practices were thus to be found across the range of social stratifications, and not just among the uppermost ranks.

The question needs to be then posed as follows: given that the colonial state was not identical with the metropolitan state but did incorporate some of its features, primarily its bourgeois character, were similar discourses of sexuality and techniques of control reproduced through the agency of colonial ruling classes? Such a question implies that changes have to be analyzed not as a structural necessity but rather as a consequence of contingent induction of mores by local privileged classes in contact with colonizing bourgeois (and not aristocratic) elites.[25]

The actual relations between metropolitan and colonial elites have been examined by Ann Stoler (1995, 1997). Stoler critiques Foucault by arguing that the history of sexuality in Europe needs to be charted with reference to its imperial ventures, echoing a similar earlier call by Spivak (1988). Unlike Guha (1997) or Nair (1996a), who adopts a teleological approach, she stresses the *simultaneity* of developments in colonies with the formation of European bourgeois identity. She finds that the colonial experience clarified metropolitan bourgeois notions of a specifically white identity. Through an analysis of varied microsites where sexualized relationships developed between colonizers and colonized, such as pedagogy, parenting, and tropical hygiene in the Dutch colonies, she is able to show that a racial grammar underwrote bourgeois culture in more ways than Foucault explored (1995).

Stoler's (1995) approach nonetheless necessitates a primary focus on colonizing elites and those who served them directly. The changes wrought for others who were colonized become less important in this framing. The greatest emphasis lies on bringing colonies into the ambit of imperial sexual history and considering the implications of colonial formations for metropolitan centers. Given this emphasis, as well as the drawbacks of the theoretical approach mentioned earlier, it appears that there is a small but important way in which Foucault's formulation remains to be extended to the context of colonial India: in identifying features of Indian bourgeois sexual norms that were a consequence of colonial contact, as well as in histories of those who were not immediately privy to interracial encounters.

A FOUCAULDIAN FEMINIST HISTORY?

Foucault himself did not, of course, write with feminist aims. As some feminists such as Hartsock (1990) have noted, Foucault does not have an explicit theory of the subordination of women. Nonetheless, with respect to this book, Foucault helps conceptualize some of the substantive changes that took place in Indian bourgeois sexual mores, such as more individualized constructs of sexuality and the self, the standardization of marriage, and the influence of medical discourses.

As noted earlier in this chapter, the colonial period saw increasing legislation on marriage, denoting its acceptable forms and minimum age. Although related to the system of alliance, these legislations could also be understood to reflect the bourgeois preoccupation with sexual practices. A characteristically bourgeois intensification of the body as an object of knowledge occurred in the debates that preceded and succeeded legislations on marriage in India. As Chakravarti (1998) points out, the Age of Consent controversy in the late nineteenth century brought unprecedented attention to the female body. It was indeed the most publicly conducted discussion on female sexuality that literate Indians had witnessed in their recent historical memory.

The knowledge system of medicine was also brought into play in nineteenth-century discourses, particularly in deciding the age of puberty for Indian women and its consequences on their maturity. Great emphasis on hygiene and health using scientific discourses was also prevalent in the early twentieth century, as Whitehead (1996) details.[26] She emphasizes the scientific maternalism that informed the discourse of women's groups, reformists, nationalists, and colonial administrators. Sanitary correctness became inextricable from the nurturing role played by mothers. This new archetype of motherhood influenced the Age of Consent controversy as well, as child brides and consequently young mothers were seen as incapable of fulfilling this role.

The construct of the ideal wife also shifted in the period toward a more individualistic standard. Chakravarti (1998) notes that the ideal of a companionate wife—one who was educated in issues of the day and in creating the home as a place of comfort for her husband—grew particularly strong among nineteenth-century reformers. Creating dyadic units in a culture of joint families was clearly a venture fraught with conflict, but the education of wives by husbands was a major vehicle through which such a unit was consolidated. This break from the traditional notion of the wife as a ritual partner of the husband changed the coordinates of self-formation among middle-class women. The newly defined figure of the cultured wife had greater potential for personal growth, and many middle-class women enthusiastically took to it. The most important dimensions of this new respectable middle-class woman according to Chatterjee's (1989) famous formulation, were spirituality, purity, and an accompanying sexual modesty. Although Chatterjee claims that the exalting of Indian women's spirituality was a means of elaborating Indian women's difference from the perceived worldliness of British women, it may be argued that this was also an expression of the stronger association between selfhood and sex, characteristic of Victorian bourgeois norms. That it was middle-class women's—and not all women's—sexual conduct that represented national character points to the peculiarly bourgeois quality of this formation. Middle-class womanhood in India was marked by the weight of responsibility to procreate and educate correctly, just as in Europe.

Within such a climate, it may be conjectured that prostitution became more denigrated, since it was precisely the link between sexuality and selfhood that was loosened by the nonintimate sex conducted by the prostitute and her client. Not only was sex delinked from appropriate procreation but the prostitute lacked access to the channels of appropriate education. Her possible knowledge of performance arts, such as dance and song, no longer carried the same cachet for racial and national advancement as did education. It was possible to focus opprobrium on the prostitute because she was neither an ideal woman in nationalist rhetoric nor one for colonial policy.

Several scholars have analyzed the opprobrium focused on the prostitute in the Indian colonial context, but most have conceptualized prostitutes' sexuality as a thing, an object of control (Srinivasan 1988; Oldenburg 1990; Rege 1996). The women they analyze are presumed to have a preformed sexuality that was then harnessed to specific ends or repressed by the state, community, religion, or patriarchy in general. Rege (1996) claims that there was a "drain" on the sexuality of *lavani* performers, which implies that their sexuality was a thing that could be taken away. Such analyses overly concretize sexuality. Foucault's history militates against such a reading of sexuality, emphasizing its polyvalent constitution through relations of power. The women were sexualized, in other words, by the very forms of power that appeared to extract their sexuality. Foucault's insight into the relationship between sex and power also urges us to refuse a nostalgic yearning for a time when sex was not subject to power, which, Foucault asserts, did not exist.

It would be misplaced, I have argued, to read colonial history in teleological terms with reference to Foucault's European history, not least because Foucault did not intend his description as a model. However, his elaboration of the dual-sided mechanism of prohibition, the mutual incitement of pleasure and power, and the constitutive power of discourse enables vital insights into the processes of laws on prostitutes and their criminalization. Although the nature of power in the colonial period was distinct from the milieu Foucault described—making for only a restricted use of his thought in this study—his understanding of the relationship between sex and power offers a useful caution: the co-implication of power and pleasure, and the expansive logic of prohibitions means that lawmaking and law enforcement on prostitution cannot be understood in linear, causal ways.

chapter 2

A Failed Experiment?
The Contagious Diseases Acts in Bombay

The Contagious Diseases Acts have been the object of several insightful historical studies during the past two and a half decades.[1] The astonishing ambition of these laws—of intricately monitoring sexual practices across swathes of the British Empire—make them a standard referent in colonial studies and feminist history. Indeed, the CDA as a topic appears to have been treated exhaustively: scholars have scrutinized the varied political forces that influenced the legislation, such as the colonial military and medical establishment, as well as its repeal, such as early British feminists, missionaries, and reformists.[2] Nonetheless, one aspect that has been relatively underemphasized is the gap between the language of the laws and law enforcement practices. Many studies of the CDA take the content of the laws as expressive of social experience and relate the laws as measures that accomplished the imperial control of sexuality and race.[3] It is tempting to read the laws in this manner because they provide a clear expression of imperial anxieties; nonetheless, such a reading risks mirroring the hubris of colonial imagination—of assuming that a set of standard laws could be effected evenly across continents. Even in the case of one country, India, alone, the Acts did not operate uniformly. Although scholars loosely pick examples from different Indian regions[4] or assume that one case, most often Bengal, speaks for all (Banerjee 1998; Chakraborty 1963; Rule 1987), the variation in the responses to these laws across regional contexts carries significant lessons.

The case of Bombay reveals a much less smooth-flowing story than the ones told so far. A closer look at CDA enforcement there reveals the limitations and contradictions of colonial power in its negotiation with local power structures. The Acts were dogged by problems in enforcement and political fissures in the administration and were assailed in the incipient nationalist public sphere. Although Burton (1994) and Ballhatchet (1980) attribute the repeal of the CDA to pressures within Britain, the local resistance to the laws and the nationalist responses that they enabled are factors that deserve greater attention. Rather than being an exemplar of colonial social control, then, the Acts serve to remind us of the importance of local contingencies affecting the reception of colonial laws, and the tenuous relationship between the rhetoric of lawmaking and its enforcement. This chapter demonstrates how the narrative of the CDA looks different if the laws are framed as a rhetorical success but an administrative failure.

ANTECEDENTS OF THE CONTAGIOUS DISEASES ACTS

The earliest reference to prostitution in Bombay laws emerged in the context of maintaining public order.[5] The first Police Rule, Ordinance, and Regulation of 1812, a set of rules that laid the basis for police administration of the city for nearly half a century, listed brothels as one of the several sources of disturbance to neighborhood peace.[6] Prostitution was presented as a trade that was instrumental to the commission of crimes; it was not, however, considered a crime on its own. Along with public bars, opium houses, and gambling houses, brothels were to be issued licenses that could be revoked if owners did not maintain order on their premises. Street brawls and drunkenness were actually noted as common problems in several historical accounts of early colonial Bombay, and they were attributed to the large number of liquor shops (Kapse 1987; Malabari 1910; Rodriguez 1994). In particular, it was the behavior of sailors that threatened the reputation of British ruling groups. In a census taken in 1814–15, the floating or migrant portion of the population of the island of Bombay was a hefty 60,000 out of 221,550 (Census of Island of Bombay 1864, i, ii). Imposing public order among this itinerant population, chiefly sailors, was a major concern of the police. In subsequent police regulations of 1827 and 1860, brothels or "houses of ill-fame" were specified in the same manner as in 1812, as a nuisance to public peace. Brothel keeping was not an offense, then, as long as it was orderly.

Enticing or "carrying away" women and girls *into* prostitution became a crime with the Police Regulation of 1827. However, what was criminalized was not so much the activity of prostitution as the deprivation of the husband or father of their wives or daughters.[7] Similar laws passed in the early part of the century in parts of North and East India treated husbands and fathers as the wounded party in cases where women and girls were "enticed away into prostitution."[8] The East India Company upheld the right of husbands to buy wives and parents to sell children, and it targeted the "enticing" of children and women into prostitution as an infringement on these property rights of husbands and parents (Singha 1998, 146–49, 156–58). The law thus largely enshrined male private property rights in women and children in such measures that apparently targeted prostitution.

Although prostitutes were not seen as criminals by law, the police nonetheless viewed them with suspicion. For instance, the secretary of the Government of India advised the Government of Bombay in 1838 that constables should be allowed to apprehend "every common prostitute . . . behaving in a notorious or indecent [manner]."[9] This 1838 note was the first recorded use of the term "common prostitute" in the Bombay context. It was echoed in the 1839 Police Act in England, which, Walkowitz (1980) argues, ushered in the prostitute as a criminal figure in that context. In Bombay, nonetheless, the prostitute did not figure as a criminal in the language of the law, except as a party to recruiting others into prostitution. The 1860 Indian Penal Code formally enshrined as crimes a range of acts that involved buying, selling, or kidnapping of children for the purposes of prostitution. Although the code had been under formulation for over twenty years since Thomas Macaulay first drew up a draft in 1837, it was only in 1860 that prostituting minors was added as an offense. According to Parker (1998), this measure was an outcome of the publicity received by an 1858 court case about the Cazee of Monghyr "leasing two female infants" to a brothel keeper (586–88). This case provoked outrage in Britain and intense political pressure to pass legislation on this issue. The Penal Code of 1860 subsequently introduced the key sections 372 and 373, aimed at protecting girls and women from being sold or bought into prostitution, which remain in place today.

Even as the law grew more refined in defining a host of activities associated with procuring women for prostitution, in military cantonments the state concomitantly *participated* in recruiting women for brothels. The story of regulated prostitution in military camps, or cantonments, is a familiar one to feminist eyes; in numerous contexts, military occupations have fostered the sexual instrumentalization of local women (Enloe 1989). The case of British India merits attention because of its scale. The British Army was stationed in over fifty cantonments across India, which made it one of the largest standing military presences in the colonial world (Arnold 1993). After the Revolt of 1857, a majority of the roughly 60,000 stationed soldiers were single, since their salaries were often insufficient to support children and spouses.[10] Soldiers were confined mostly to barracks, where the canteen and bazaar were their main avenues of entertainment. It is within these bazaar areas that regimental brothels were established. Regimental brothels were reserved for soldiers alone, managed by mistresses or *dhais* appointed by cantonment authorities to ensure that women were disease-free.[11] When one regiment left, the brothel was "taken over" by the regiment replacing it (Report of the Health of the Army 1909, 13). Apart from staving off soldiers' boredom, such brothels also bolstered the upper-class conviction that soldiers, drawn from the ranks of the poor, had uncontrollable sexual urges and were incapable of curbing their animal passions (Ballhatchet 1980). "Mercenary love," as prostitution was termed, was preferable to marriage with native women. It was also preferable to homosexual relations between soldiers, which were viewed as a sin, and to masturbation, which was believed to lead to physical and mental disorders.[12]

The only obstacle to this entrenched system of sexual recreation was the rising incidence of venereal disease. Because more British soldiers in India died from diseases than from combat, administrators were attuned to this problem. Between 1815 and 1855 alone, the death of soldiers from disease in India cost the British government ten million pounds (Arnold 1993, 64–65).[13] Venereal disease rates for British soldiers in India were also high compared to other parts of the empire (Levine 2003). Although it was European soldiers and sailors who introduced syphilis to India in the sixteenth and seventeenth centuries,[14] army officials in the nineteenth century viewed it as a scourge threatening the army from outside contact with low-caste Indian women. In keeping with precepts of colonial medicine that attributed disease to the Indian climate, sanitation, and mores, Indian women were seen as a part of a disease-bearing environment.[15] The first attempt to deal with venereal disease therefore came in the form of confining diseased prostitutes to buildings called "lock hospitals" for extended periods of time (Ballhatchet 1980). The reported incidence of venereal disease did not respond to this measure introduced in the 1820s and in fact grew higher toward the middle of the century (Ballhatchet 1980). As it became clear that the lock hospital system was not an effective solution, new rules emerged in the 1860s. The Cantonment Acts of 1864 instituted compulsory medical examinations for all practicing prostitutes in cantonments, apart from confining only those who were diseased. Medical authorities had to carry out regular checkups on prostitutes, and police had to enforce punitive measures if prostitutes refused.[16]

Interestingly, legislators foresaw no resistance to such measures: they assumed that poorer Indian women would not object to medical examination because they were free from any shame regarding their bodies. Legislators even held that a "special sensibility about corporeal examination," that quality idealized in Englishwomen, did "not exist in Indian women" (Parliamentary Papers 1888a, 234). Most importantly, officials held that prostitution was "a profession recognized in Hindu law books" and that "courtesans' regulation causes no offense to native sensibility" (Parliamentary Papers 1888a, 234). Because prostitutes appeared to play an organic role in Indian society, it was assumed that they would willingly cooperate with the colonial state.

With the Cantonment Act, all women in cantonments and surrounding areas came to be treated as if they were as completely under the control of medical officers of the army as soldiers. The increasing scope of the law reflected administrators' perceptions of the magnitude of the disease. In an important slippage, all Indian women, and not just registered prostitutes, were classified as potentially threatening sources of disease. The Contagious Diseases Acts, which were implemented soon after the Cantonment Acts, may be viewed as an outcome of the impulse to increasingly widen the span of regulated female subjects. So entrenched was the view of threats posed by Indian women that soldiers were confidently warned over decades that "the common women as well as the regular prostitutes [were] almost all more or less infected with disease" (Kitchener 1912, 58).

THE CDA IN BOMBAY:
SCIENTIA SEXUALIS IN A COLONIAL SETTING

In volume 1 of the *History of Sexuality*, Michel Foucault (1990) describes as *scientia sexualis* the medicalization of discourses concerning sexuality, and specifically the transformation of older forms of garnering knowledge through confession into techniques of scientific investigation and pathologization. The Contagious Diseases Acts can be viewed as *scientia sexualis* par excellence, enshrining into law medical techniques of garnering knowledge about bodies and sexual practices. In this section, I lay out the details of the Acts as passed in Bombay and then discuss their implications as a form of sexual surveillance.

A Contagious Diseases Act was first enacted in Bombay in 1870, following the passage of the Indian Contagious Diseases Act of 1868 in other parts of India and the British Empire such as Hong Kong.[17] It was suspended after a year and then reintroduced in 1880 and stayed in effect until 1888. The Act aimed to control venereal disease through enforcing medical checks on prostitutes, building on measures laid down in Cantonment Acts and applying them to cities. Within Bombay, which had a military garrison but which was more significant as a port, the CDA was a clear departure from earlier police codes dealing with prostitution as a social nuisance. The law expressed a will to control the entire population of women in prostitution, and not just those who were responsible for public disturbances. It specified where prostitution could be practiced, which prostitutes were acceptable, and how prostitutes could be monitored to ensure that they were disease-free. The law made it compulsory for women to be registered if they were going to practice prostitution anywhere.

The CDA envisioned an unprecedented degree of surveillance over prostitutes. Registered prostitutes had to present themselves every seven days for medical examination (RACDAB 1870, section VI). If a doctor detected venereal disease, the woman would be detained in a certified hospital until medical officers discharged her (RACDAB 1870, section VII). While in the hospital, she was not permitted to leave the premises and was required to follow a given schedule for waking, sleeping, and eating (RACDAB, section XII, regulation 5). All police officers and constables were authorized to ask prostitutes to show their registration tickets on demand (RACDAB 1870, section IV). Not possessing registration was grounds for imprisonment (up to one month) and/or a fine (up to Rs 100) (Indian Contagious Diseases Act of 1868, section 4). If a woman refused to show her registration, she could be punished with a fine up to Rs 50 and imprisonment up to fourteen days (Indian Contagious Diseases Act of 1868, section 7). Police inspectors, and not simply health officials, had to maintain registers of prostitutes. If the police commissioner so decided, prostitutes could be banned from residing in particular areas (RACDAB 1870, section IX). The police had to be notified of any change of address, and if a woman desired to have her name removed from the register, she had to apply in person to the police commissioner, followed by an application to the presidency magistrate. It was up to the commissioner to decide whether to exempt her (RACDAB 1870, section III). Copies of the law were translated into Marathi and Gujarati as well as English in order to communicate it across the population (RACDAB 1870, section IV, rule 26).

The CDA treated prostitute women in remarkably instrumental ways, subjecting them to humiliations rarely meted out to soldiers. There was a voyeuristic imperative written into the tasks for police and medical officers implementing the CDA. In the Bombay rules, police were not only required to note down in their registers the caste, residence, and age of each woman but also to describe her "complexion and general appearance, height, special marks of identification" (RACDAB 1870, appendix A). Not only did searching for and noting down such information involve an intensive surveillance; the information itself could serve ends unrelated to medicine, such as evaluating the relative attractiveness of various women for interested observers and supervisors. The procedures for the medical examination were also specified very intricately in the Bombay version of the Act. They dictated the manner in which the speculum had to be used: "The *speculum vagina* [had to be] used so as to fully expose the *os* and *cervix uteri* and every part of the vaginal canal" (RACDAB 1870, section IV, rule 32).

The highly technical language in the text of the law is noteworthy. At an obvious level, such language suggests that medical practitioners were involved in the framing of the Act, and that they were keen to prevent enforcers from finding loopholes, as occurred with the 1868 Act in Calcutta. At a more abstract level, such language indicates the thorough influence of a medicalized imaginary: medical techniques were seen as an acceptable means to uncover knowledge about sex. The insistence that doctors examine (and record) every part of the vagina expresses the familiar scientific principle of exhaustive searches for truths. The CDA were also not simply about diseases that affected the population as a whole; their disproportionate insistence on blaming women's (and not men's) bodies, and thereby studying women's bodies, allowed the production of knowledge about colonized women as sexual beings (Levine 2003).

The use of the law as an instrument to accomplish medicalizing women's sexuality is the distinctive colonial dimension of this form of *scientia sexualis*.[18] In Foucault's schema, laws, with their absolute injunctions relying on coercive power, belonged to the realm of sovereign or absolute power, the characteristic of juridical monarchies. The apparatus of sexuality that Foucault elaborated was based on more dispersed nodes of more liberal, governmental power. However, in the case of the CDA, the law—a technique of juridical power—facilitated the creation of the apparatus of sexuality. In other words, the colonial state, with its illiberal methods, set in motion forms of knowledge production that facilitated an "obsessive" search for sex, as Foucault (1990) termed it. Such a coincidence of techniques reflects the importance of not reading Foucault's schema in overly close teleological terms, and of treating the history of colonialism as a serious disruption of Foucault's classification of modern and premodern forms of power. The CDAs in colonies were not premodern versions of measures that emerged in Britain. The CDAs in colonies occurred simultaneously, broadly speaking, with those in England. Indeed, the application of CDAs in colonies such as Malta informed their application in Britain; knowledge garnered in the colonial settings facilitated governmentality in Britain.

Nonetheless, it is also important to reflect on the differences between the texts of the Bombay CDA and the English version of the CDA. The Bombay CDA's level of detail relating to the body was not a feature of the English version. It was also far more coercive than the English CDA. Whereas there were limits on the amount of time a woman could be detained by the police or by hospitals in England, Indian prostitutes could be forced to stay back for indefinite periods.[19] Indian prostitutes were to be compulsorily registered, whereas after 1883 in England the system became voluntary. The areas of residence for prostitutes were also specified. Attempts were made to separate prostitutes who serviced European men from those who served Indian clients (HD 1884). These differences are a reflection of not only the dominant (and nonhegemonic) character of the colonial state but the varying political climates in India and Britain. The rise of the Liberal Party and the growing abolitionist movement in Britain made measures conceived in Bombay politically impossible in Britain (Levine 1996; 2003). In England, the Act was never applied to London or other large cities; rather, it was restricted to port and garrison districts such as Portsmouth, Devonport, and Chatham (Moore, W.J. v/24/2289, 2–4). In India it was applied in cities as well as cantonment areas and became a measure enforced on civilians: because soldiers and sailors consorted with unregistered women, medical checks were carried out beyond the cantonment. The same problem in England did not result in measures aimed at the civilian population. The CDAs exemplified the colonial mode of seeing territories as laboratories and sites of observation where experiments could be carried out without provoking the resistance they might otherwise have met in the metropole (Cooper and Stoler 1997; Arnold 1993; Levine 1994, 2003).

Colonial medical officers saw Bombay as not only the site of a health problem but also an opportunity to study the means of controlling venereal disease among sailors. With its sizable population of sailors—amounting to 25,000 in 1885, for instance—the port city presented an urgent and compelling case. The chief medical officer of the Lock Hospital, Bryce Gordon, formulated an experiment to assess the health of the city's prostitutes by measuring the level of venereal disease on ships before and after leaving Bombay (RWCDA 1883, 7). The staff surgeon of a ship called HMS *Tourmaline* similarly compared the number of days spent in port with the level of infections on his ship (RWCDA 1883, 7).[20] In 1887, the medical officer indicated that he could pinpoint a single "source" of disease—the particular "contaminating" woman with whom sailors had consorted.[21] These experiments were each remarkably one-sided: the sexual promiscuity of sailors was held to be constant—only the "cleanliness" of prostitutes varied. Medical authorities perceived the "animal instincts" of soldiers and sailors to be a law of nature, which, if not "followed legitimately, (would) be followed illegitimately" (Government of Bombay 1886, 1). Contamination flowed only in one direction: from women to sailors or soldiers; prostitutes were "vehicles of disease" who "seized upon" soldiers and sailors (Government of Bombay 1886, 2). Because administrators viewed prostitutes as agents of disease, they thought that any methods the state used to control them were justifiable. Borrowing the doctrine of the father of regulation of prostitution, the French doctor Parent-Duchâtelet, they held that "individual liberty is a right to which prostitutes cannot pretend; they have abdicated their prerogative to it, and may be ruled by a different code of justice than that to which other members of society are subjected" (Government of Bombay 1886, 5).

While medical officers did not vary in their condemnation of prostitutes, they nonetheless differentiated between sailors and soldiers. They favored sailors, who, they believed, frequented licensed brothels, unlike the supposedly less discriminating soldiers. As the chief medical officer of the Bombay Lock Hospital described it: "The sailor coming on shore troubles himself but little about the clandestine prostitute. He is waited for at the bandar (port) by a procurer, commonly called a 'pilot,' who immediately takes him to the nearest brothel, and herein lies his safety, for all the public brothels are licensed and under the scrutiny of the executives of the Contagious Diseases Act" (RWCDA 1885, July 9). Soldiers, in contrast, were "in the habit of meeting [unregistered women] on the sea face or elsewhere" (RWCDA 1886, February). Any increases in incidence of disease were therefore attributed to the "trooping season" when soldiers were stationed in Bombay (RWCDA 1885, July 9).

The easy transposition of military goals onto the civilian medical sphere in India may be explained by the institutional structure of the British Raj. The medical authority ensuring health of the army was the Indian Medical Service. Although the foremost duty of this institution was serving military needs, it was also the chief arm of the incipient public health system and was employed in a wide range of civilian activities.[22] In fact, as Arnold (1993) points out, the distinction between its civilian and military role was not kept clear, and in 1910 roughly three-fifths of the Indian Medical Service's strength was deployed in nonmilitary duties. The experimental uses of the CDA demonstrate how the medical establishment combined its military and civilian mandates.[23]

The medical goal of experimental study carried an inherent potential for failure, however, given that a city could not be an ideal laboratory. The necessary seclusion of the people studied was patently impossible in Bombay. This was a city whose 1871 census reported at least 1,500 acknowledged prostitutes.[24] In order to mimic the more controlled environment found in cantonment quarters, the Government of India asked the Government of Bombay to limit the Act to women who consorted with Europeans, in 1884, but to no avail, because, as the Government of Bombay replied, there was "no particular class or number of prostitutes whom only soldiers and sailors visit[ed]" and these women were not confined to "any particular part of the city" (HD 1884, Sanitary, December 38–40).

The medical practitioners responsible for CDA enforcement also had an inadequate grasp of its financial complexities. The sanitary commissioner's 1876 budget proposal for reintroducing the Act (after it was temporarily suspended) was astonishingly spare: he divided Bombay into three registration areas, each with a temporary hospital built of bamboo or palm leaf mats. Each registration area would have only one European inspector attached, whose duty it would be to report all brothels and all prostitutes to the health officer for entry in the general register and to order the prostitutes to appear once a week at the examination office, where, if found diseased, they would be detained. He would also apply to the magistrate for a summons against women who failed to attend the examination office or who broke the provision of the Act; he would prosecute them afterward.[25] Three inspectors were clearly inadequate to the tasks of registering and examining (and even potentially prosecuting) all the women who practiced prostitution. In implementing the CDA, the Sanitary Commissioner had effectively provided only for the medical checks of European prostitutes, since the requirement that the doctor be a European indicates that largely European, rather than Indian, women were the ones examined. It was therefore the upper stratum of the male clientele that was being protected from venereal disease, if at all.

These limitations in conceptualizing implementation of the CDA explain the dismal figures we find in Table 1. Figures from major hospitals in Bombay show that not only did the incidence of gonorrhea and syphilis not decline in the years following the first phase of the Acts in 1871; it in fact showed a slight *increase* among European patients, in the year 1871. Among infected Indian patients as well, the first three months of 1871 showed a fairly high rate of infection (748 patients). We could extrapolate that if the same number of patients had been infected over the rest of the year, the figure for the whole year would have been close to 3,000, actually higher than the years before the Act was in operation. Far from proving the effectiveness of the CDA, then, these statistics showed a growing incidence of venereal disease. The years during and after the Act was in operation also showed no major variation, which suggested that the Act itself had no major effect; the only exception was the year 1874–75, when a sudden jump in the number of infected can be observed.

Although the CDA did not appear to affect the incidence of venereal disease, the Government of India continued to place pressure on the city to reinstate the CDA after it was repealed in 1871. Medical and naval authorities were the main proponents of the CDA, and the Sanitary Commissioner publicized alarmist statistics, such as figures showing that, in 1877,

TABLE 1. Incidence of syphilis and gonorrhea among hospital
patients, 1865–1876

Year	Indians	Europeans
1865	1,989	175
1866	2,536	161
1867	2,335	168
1868	2,160	256
1869	2,358	197
1870	2,389	201
1871 (January–March)	748	227
1871–72	2,275	110
1872–73	3,063	148
1873–74	3,726	151
1874–75	4,472	336
1875–76	1,247	—

Source: Parliamentary Papers 1883/50/538–544. For Indians, figures
are from JJ Hospital, with the exceptions of 1874–75 (figures are from
JJ Hospital and Gokuldas Tejpall Hospitals combined) and 1875–76
(figures are from Gokuldas Tejpall Hospital only). European figures
are from European General Hospital.

the largest number of admissions into hospitals for all ships was for gonorrhea and syphilis (RHBBC 1877, 2–3). In 1880, the commander and chief surgeon of HMS *The Beacon,* a ship that had docked in Bombay, complained that after a week's leave, eight of his forty men were stricken with venereal disease. He strongly recommended to the Government of Bombay that a system of police supervision of prostitutes be reestablished (Parliamentary Papers 1888b, 544). Francis Carter, the secretary to the commander-in-chief of the navy, warned that "as Bombay is the head quarters of Her Majesty's ships stationed in the East Indies, the remedying of this evil is a matter of most vital importance in maintaining the ships and crews under the Admiral's command in a state efficient for service" (Parliamentary Papers 1888c, 544). Bowing to such pressure, the new governor, Fergusson, reinstated the Act.

The second phase of the CDA, which lasted seven years from 1880 to 1888, provided wider opportunities for medical and police authorities to implement the law. Yet the police enforcement reports suggest a wide discrepancy between the aspirations of the law and its effects. In the census of 1864, there were nearly 10,000 returns under the classification "prostitute." Yet throughout the time that the CDA was implemented in Bombay, the number of women who registered themselves with the police rarely exceeded 1,500. This figure was much lower than the average of 6,000 to 7,000 women registered every year in Calcutta (Banerjee 1998, 147). Even fewer women were regularly medically examined, as seen from the column on defaulters in Table 2.

Table 2 demonstrates that in Bombay more than four-fifths of the women who practiced prostitution successfully evaded the CDA. The Sanitary Commissioner clearly underestimated prostitutes' aversion to the measures. The premise on which medical authorities functioned was that prostitutes could be forced to behave as the state willed—and it proved unfounded.

HOW THE CDA WERE EVADED

Women who were potential targets of the CDA sought a variety of ways to evade registration and the painful medical examinations. The first approach

TABLE 2. Enforcement of the CDA, 1883–1888

Year and month	Number of brothels	Number of women registered	defaulted	Number of defaulters prosecuted
1882 November	—	—	165	154	
1883 June	265	1,383	290	114 (38 warned, rest fined Rs 5 or Rs 10)
1884 March	273	1,412	356	83 (25 warned, 1 imprisoned)
1885 January	287	1,508	382	110 (74 fined, 36 warned)
1885 July	285	1,502	410	109 (47 warned/fined, 1 imprisoned 14 days)
1886 February	287	1,472	—	180 (74 warned, 92 fined, 2 imprisoned)
1886 July	291	1,498	—	207 (102 fined, 44 warned, 6 imprisoned)
1887 January	296	1,469	351	241 (4 imprisoned)
1887 July	291	1,490	—	173 (70 fined Rs 1– Rs 150, 1 imprisoned)
1888 February	246	1,431	266	184 (3 imprisoned)
1888 October	—	1,479	—	202 (5 imprisoned, 65 fined)

Sources: Reports of the Working of the Contagious Diseases Act, 1883–87.

was to deny being a prostitute by claiming a married status and producing a certificate of marriage when summoned by magistrates. The newspaper *Rast Goftar* reported that nearly 400 women in prostitution formally contracted marriages within a few months of the Act being in effect (August 21, 1870). For instance, just a few days after being caught providing sexual services for money, one woman named Jumna produced before the court both a *Cazee*'s (judge's) marriage certificate and the man she had married (GD 1887a, 171). Another common strategy that women used was claiming the legal status of a mistress or a "kept woman." A woman named Cassee, who was summoned for being an unregistered prostitute, brought forward a "youth who said he was keeping her" (GD 1887a, 174). The magistrate dismissed the cases against both Jumna and Cassee. Not only did British administrators exempt wives; they also exempted mistresses from medical checks because they had no wish to antagonize the class of wealthier Indian men who had mistresses.[26]

Dancing girls *(naikins)*, entertainers who were wealthier than the average urban prostitute, also put up a spirited resistance against the Act. Their petitions articulately argued that dancing girls were akin to ballet dancers of the West. One set claimed that since they could be classified alongside the opera dancers of England, "to compe[l] such a class to submit to an inspection of so revolting a character [was] . . . highly oppressive" (GD 1872b, 283). Another set of petitioners confidently declared that they would like to "educate" the newly arrived governor on the "real character" of dancing girls of India and cleverly chose quotes from the 1836 *Oriental Annual,* in which British writers described *nautch* girls as "modest, inoffensive women" who "never in the slightest degree offend[ed] against propriety" (GD 1872b, 249, 274). Most importantly, the petitioners denied having any relations with soldiers, thereby demonstrating their awareness of administrators' aims (GD 1872b, 275, 274).

Some prostitutes used bribes in order to avoid the medical examination. In one case during the first phase of the CDA in 1871, a prostitute paid money to a man impersonating a public servant, who signed her registration ticket and then demanded a princely sum of 50 rupees in addition to her initial payment. The woman, realizing that such extortion was uncalled for, reported him to the police. The police then investigated the case by using her to frame the man. A police constable accompanied her to the man's house the next time she had to have her ticket signed, with a 50-rupee note that the police had marked to serve as evidence. When she returned after getting her ticket signed and without the money, they prosecuted the man for impersonating a public servant and for extortion (GD 1871b, 165). This episode reveals the resourcefulness employed by women to evade medical examinations. This woman's confidence in approaching the police to report the extortion is also striking. The CDA occasioned many encounters with the police, making them familiar enough figures to seek out when needed. Also, in 1871, a pattern of criminalizing all prostitutes had not yet become entrenched. As discussed in chapter 5, prostitution had until recently been considered a regular, rather than a disreputable, profession.

Those women who were unable to use tactics such as bribes, marriage certificates, or petitions locked themselves up in their rooms to avoid medical examinations. Dr. Knapp, medical examiner in charge of implementing the Act, on three occasions broke open the locks of brothel rooms when he suspected that prostitutes had hidden themselves inside (*Jam-e-Jamshed,* May 26, 1870). Some women fled temporarily to Bandra, to the north, as the Act was not in force there. The railway fares between these two places were cheap, and women traveled to Bombay by trains at night to practice prostitution.[27] When police visited brothels on night duty, women covered for each other, denying that unregistered women were prostitutes, instead calling them "friends" and "visitors" to brothels.[28]

Women who absconded from medical examinations continued to work in brothels at night, but the police could only issue them court summonses rather than arrest them on the spot. The women evaded such summonses by shifting from one place to another. One woman named Murriam told the court that "she was sick and unable to attend" her summons (GD 1887a, 179). She ignored four summonses, and when the police finally issued a warrant to arrest her, she was found "nicely dressed" in "one of the most renowned brothels for soldiers and sailors" in Hanuman Lane (GD 1887a, 180). Even when women were caught and convicted by magistrates for evading the Act, they refused to register themselves and submit to regular medical examinations (GD 1887b, 173).

It is remarkable that women continued to practice prostitution and resist treatment even when physically ill. There were only a few cases of women who surrendered themselves for treatment at hospitals voluntarily. For instance, in the enforcement reports, figures under the category "voluntary admissions to hospitals" were small: six women in 1883, eight in 1884, one in 1885, four in 1886, six in 1886, and nine in 1887 (RWCDA 1880–87). On the whole, women who were ill did not trust the medical establishment to cure them; it was far too closely linked with the system that penalized them (RWCDA 1887, July).

The medical establishment cited the high number of absconders as a way to explain the failure of the Acts. The surgeon general of Bombay in 1887 declared that it was the absconders who were responsible for the spread of syphilis in Bombay, providing several names and case histories of women who had "worked mischief." He went so far as to attribute an increase in syphilis cases to a single defaulter, Cassee Narayen, who had been "at large" for twenty-eight days (GD 1887c, 152). A police inspector accused a woman named Murriam of being a similar mischief maker because she avoided arrest, and he vigorously complained about Mary Toma, who "infected three soldiers" because she absconded from medical examinations for two weeks (GD 1887a, 179–81). The surgeon general argued that the task of locating and bringing absconders before the law was too heavy for the two police inspectors; he ended his memorandum calling for an increase in the number of policemen enforcing the Act (GD 1887c).

On the whole, the police responded to the problem of low registration for medical examination in haphazard ways. Table 2 indicates how lax police enforcement was: of the women who had initially registered under the Act, several women defaulted, and as the last column shows, few such women were actually caught and prosecuted by the police. On the whole, the police floundered for a means to establish who was a prostitute, and relied mainly on complaints. They seized some women who had contracted second marriages, after being tipped off by the women's enemies (*Satya Watta,* June 2, 1870). They also used the help of "paramours" and neighbors of women and registered prostitutes to get information about defaulters. In Jumna's case, her paramour approached the police with the complaint that she practiced prostitution in his absence. In one case, a registered prostitute named Tuckoo approached policemen on CDA duty, complaining about her neighbor Parbattee being unregistered (GD 1887a, 169–73). The police clearly relied on hostilities within the civilian population for enforcing the law, and civilians also used the CDA as a means to settle personal scores.

Women in prostitution played a hide-and-seek of sorts with policemen: Murriam, for example, moved between six different brothels while evading her summonses (GD 1887a, 179–80). The police appeared to enjoy the chase, and it is telling that they record finding Murriam "nicely dressed" in the brothel where she was finally arrested. They reported this and other cases with almost gleeful detail, making evident the pleasures of policing. Indeed the documents seem to be intended to provide titillating reading. They describe catching couples having sexual intercourse or in a state of nudity, and they detail the elaborate ruses of police to trap their quarries. A good example is the Jumna case, where the police first watched Jumna carefully to establish whether her paramour's complaint about her was valid and then sent in a man undercover as a prospective client. They even gave the man six marked silver coins so that the money could serve as evidence. The police inspector then dramatically entered Jumna's room exactly at the point when the two were having sex. He went on to search for the six marked coins and found them "under the pillow on which she was lying" (GD 1887a, 170). In the case involving Parbattee, her neighbor Tuckoo informed the policemen that Parbattee could be seen through the window of her room having sex with a man. One policeman stood and watched while the other followed Tuckoo to the back door in order to catch Parbattee as she was letting her visitor out. The inspector notes that at the time, Parbattee was "in a state of nudity" and that her sexual partner was "in the act of dressing himself." He goes on to narrate that, instead of covering herself, Parbattee "shamelessly sat down in the *mhoree* or bath room and washed herself" in full presence of the police and others (GD 1887a, 172). Parbattee's bathing, which to the police appeared to be "shameless" behavior and could well have been a sign of her insouciance, may on the other hand have been her way of indicating to the police that she practiced personal hygiene—something that she imagined they wanted to see, given the emphases of the CDA.

Magistrates often asked for indisputable proof that women were prostitutes, and police construed this requirement—perhaps too readily—to mean catching a woman in the act of illicit sexual intercourse. The titillating details that the police provide in records are justified as evidence collected to convict women. The terms of the law also incited other pleasurable engagements—rules 27 and 28 specified that the police had to search the brothels by night in order to look for unregistered women. In creating such enticing prospects for police functionaries, the state displayed a clearly pornographic imagination. The working of the CDA expressed, in Foucault's (1979) terms, the productive logic of prohibitions: the rules intensified police fascination with prostitutes, and women's resistance provided occasions for greater police engagement.

Although women in large numbers escaped medical inspections, prostitution on the whole became a much more orderly institution under the CDA. The brothel became the preferred organizational form of commercial sex, for it allowed for easier regulation. There was a rise in the number of registered brothels in Bombay between 1883 and 1887 (see Table 2, the column for number of brothels). Brothel keeping became a protected activity: the prosecution of brothel keepers for offenses related to law and order dropped drastically under the CDA. According to police reports between 1860 and 1869, at least thirty persons were prosecuted every year for brothel keeping. However, when the CDA was in effect in 1870 and 1871, the number dropped to nine and three persons respectively; in the second phase of the Act (1880–88), there were no convictions of brothel keepers at all (ARSCB, 1860–84).

Such leniency toward brothel keepers was connected to the information collection imperatives of the CDA. Inspectors attached to the medical examination officers had to locate unregistered women, and the easiest way to accomplish this task was to have the women contained within the bounded space of brothels and subjected to the supervision of intermediaries, brothel keepers. Under rules 27 and 28 of section IX of the Act, police had to call upon brothel keepers on a monthly basis to furnish the particulars of each prostitute who had resided in or used any brothel. Since only two inspectors were assigned night duty under the Act, the help of brothel mistresses was often crucial to the success of the CDA.

Nevertheless, even brothel keepers, like brothel workers, were able to escape the mandates of the CDA. Although brothel keepers were supposed to forward a monthly statement showing the particulars of each prostitute to the registration offices, one police commissioner complained that "a great number of brothel keepers never come near the offices in which they are registered and when warned to do so, they emphatically decline and neither do they submit the statements" (GD 1887a, 177). Thus, although the CDA reflected the expanding ambitions of colonial governmentality—with its requirements of information collection, surveillance and punishment—its reach in Bombay was severely restricted by inadequate resources and the ingenuity of those it targeted.

FISSURES IN THE ADMINISTRATION: POLICE, MAGISTRATES, AND THE GOVERNMENT OF BOMBAY

The increasing problems of enforcing the CDA made evident a disharmony between the different arms of the colonial state, specifically the judiciary, police, and public health administrators. Far from functioning as a single cohesive entity, the different nodes of institutional power of the colonial state contested each other in open and sometimes vicious ways. The medical community, deeply vested in the success of the CDA, sought to have more control in directing its operation. From the outset, it blamed the police and magistrates for any failures, rather than the scope of the laws themselves; in 1881 surgeon general Gilborne declared that "in many cases inefficient police supervision is a main cause of the comparative failure of the preventive system to reduce admission for venereal disease" (RHBBC 1877, 37). Similarly, in 1880 the chief medical officer in charge of the Lock Hospital complained that "unregistered and clandestine prostitution is rife in almost every street in the native town, and yet the police are powerless to bring the women so engaged under surveillance" (RWCDA 1883, June 22). Punitive measures were seen to be insufficient: the chief medical officer complained that the "magistrate deals with (prostitutes) too leniently" (RWCDA 1885, July 9).

As seen from Table 2, the number of prosecuted defaulters who were actually convicted by magistrates was small, and the number penalized (fined or imprisoned) was generally smaller than the number let off with a warning. The magistrates' apparent leniency produced a growing rift with the police. In police reports as well as newspaper reports, police complained that magistrates who tried the women were not harsh enough and imposed only nominal penalties. They bemoaned the fact that magistrates dismissed cases when women came up with last-minute marriage certificates or with men who would vouch that they were their keepers. Police also complained that magistrates demanded evidence that was hard to get in order to convict women; magistrates declined to use the evidence of other prostitutes, who were seen to be "unreliable witnesses."[29]

The magistrate's office in turn accused the police of not being vigilant enough about the problem of prostitution. In mid-1888, for instance, an argument was publicly carried out in the pages of the *Bombay Gazette* between the police commissioner Frank Souter and the acting chief magistrate.

The magistrate was quoted in the newspaper complaining about prostitutes who had set up liquor shops in public areas after the police commissioner had ordered their dispersal from another area. The next day, the police commissioner wrote to the paper, denying that any of the women in the particular shops was ever on the register of the CD Act, and called the magistrate's statement "impulsive and wholly inaccurate" (*Bombay Gazette,* January 31, 1888, 5). Such a public and rancorous exchange bespeaks the frustration in both quarters.

The persistent call of the police commissioner was to strengthen the measures available to the police. His memo to that effect to the Government of Bombay, however, met with a lukewarm response: the acting chief secretary replied that given the public feeling against the CDA, "it [was] impossible to make the law more stringent" (GD 1887a, 189). By 1887, the commissioner of police admitted that

> under the existing state of the law the efforts of the Police to control contagious disease are almost futile—hundreds of women who are known to be carrying on prostitution in the most open manner cannot be brought on the Register because the Magistrates require evidence which it is next to impossible to obtain. I am obliged to admit that the law on this head is at present working most unsatisfactorily in the city of Bombay and unless Government can see their way to strengthening the hands of the Police and Magistrates as regards the working of this Act, the sooner it is abolished here the better—Government would be spared an unprofitable expense and the Police the discharge of a duty which, under existing circumstances, they find it impossible to perform with credit to themselves or to the satisfaction of the Government. (GD 1887a, 162–63).

The police had declared their failure.

RESPONSES IN BOMBAY'S PUBLIC SPHERE

The CDA were introduced in Bombay at a time of efflorescence in its public sphere. If the aim of the formulators of the CDA was experimentation, they found themselves executing it in the wrong era in Bombay. The city was experiencing its first taste of self-government at the municipal level, and the CDA's repeal on two occasions was the effect of furious protests by municipal administrators and widespread discontent expressed in newspapers. The relationship between the city's merchant class, municipal bureaucracy, and intelligentsia explains the vigor of the responses that these laws elicited. In this section, I sketch the formation of Bombay's public sphere and its contribution to the repeal of the Acts.

A municipality that could levy rates and taxes on the residents was first established in 1865. The municipality perceived the governor (of Bombay presidency) and the central government (then in Calcutta) as having too great a control in the city's affairs. It therefore viewed a measure such as the CDA, requiring local funding but servicing largely imperial goals, as a burden. The municipality's first years were already tumultuous because of conflicts over its budget. The first commissioner, Arthur Crawford, had embarked on a series of ambitious schemes to repair and build roads and bridges but had met with resistance from the Indian merchant community, who urged greater financial caution. Crawford's schemes, and particularly the rates he levied to fund them, were so unpopular that there were demonstrations on the streets and debates in the town hall (Dossal 1989). The local intelligentsia made demands for more popular representation in the municipal government, and Arthur Crawford resigned in 1871 (Dobbin 1972; Dossal 1989). The CDA appeared on the scene just as these tensions had begun to escalate. Not only was it a measure decreed by the central government; it was also imitative of a British law. Its prospects were, from the outset, not bright.

Sensing that it could ill afford a law that would drain its revenues and also provoke popular disfavor, the municipality immediately refused to foot the expense of implementing the Act, citing financial, rather than moral, reasons: it argued that since the Act aimed to protect soldiers and sailors, the imperial treasury should bear its burden. After a little over a year, the CDA was suspended (in the midst of the ratepayer agitations) because the Bench of Justices, a body that influenced municipal spending, refused to contribute its share for the following year.[30] This short-lived first phase of the CDA in Bombay was a testimony to the unstable political equation between the local and central arms of the colonial state and the growing political strength of the city's intelligentsia. The presidency governors of Bombay and Madras had long complained about meddling from the central government (Dossal 1989), but now governance at the local level had become even more resistant with the appointing of elected representatives to the municipal corporation. Calcutta, which in contrast to Bombay was itself the node of the colonial administration, experienced far greater central control, and the CDA was enforced without interruption from 1868 to 1888 (Banerjee 1998).

The resistance to the CDA in Bombay emerged from both the municipal administration as well as a native intelligentsia that resented colonial government and its local merchant collaborators. In the eighteenth and nineteenth centuries, dominant Indian merchant families had risen to power through association with the East India Company as shipbuilders, middlemen, and guarantee brokers.[31] There existed a close fraternity between Indian and British merchants going back to the 1836 setting up of a chamber of commerce that lobbied for the needs of Bombay at the central government in Calcutta. The first English newspapers also stood for the interests of merchants and had Indian proprietors. The government symbiotically granted Indian merchants its security, while it also depended on their goodwill and assistance. As a result, the first Indians in Bombay's public life were merchants: in the 1830s, some were granted the right to sit on the grand jury, soon were made justices of the peace, and became directly involved with municipal administration in the 1860s (Dobbin 1972; Dossal 1989).

The setting up of cotton spinning and weaving factories in the 1850s and 1860s initiated changes in this political makeup. This period of industrial ascendance coincided with the American Civil War, when the world cotton market shifted from New Orleans to Bombay. Artisans and workers from areas of India as far away as Hyderabad flocked to the city, and from a population of 234,032 in 1833–34, the city's numbers more than tripled to 816,562 in 1864 (*Census of the Island of Bombay 1864*, i, ii, vi). Around this time, a middle-class intelligentsia emerged to challenge the influence of merchant classes. This social class drew on new opportunities in Bombay for education and administration. The first English schools and college in western India were set up in Bombay, and the city witnessed the growth of a cadre of Indian government servants, schoolmasters, and lawyers, mostly drawn from Brahmins. They formed a self-styled Marathi and Gujarati middle class that pitted itself against the merchant aristocracy and grew in political influence largely through the role of newspapers, reformist groups, and public campaigns for greater political representation (Dobbin 1972). It was particularly through the vernacular press that members of this social class railed against the government, since they were unable to get a

48 A FAILED EXPERIMENT?

hearing in official debates. The second phase (1880–88) of the CDA in fact coincided with the proliferation of the vernacular press: the number of newspapers in 1870 was twenty-two, in 1880 it was twenty-seven, and by 1885 it had jumped to forty-three.

In this burgeoning public sphere of Bombay, opinion rapidly condensed against the CDA. During the two phases of the Act (1870–72 and 1880–88), articles in Marathi, Gujarati, and English newspapers expressed immense suspicion of the government's intent and derided the effects of the law. Indian reformers submitted petitions urging the repeal of the Act and protested police initiatives that relocated prostitutes in the city. So highly charged was the political atmosphere in Bombay that even before the Act was enforced, a newspaper accused the government of trying to extort money from the public under the guise of checking immorality (*Vritta Prakash*, April 25, 1868). As soon as the Act was put into effect, *Native Opinion*, a widely circulated Marathi newspaper edited by V. N. Mandlik, prominent member of the Bombay Association,[32] wrote about the legislators: "Their object seems to be to import into this country as many of the laws of England as possible, without ascertaining whether they are required here, and whether their introduction will be beneficial or otherwise to Indians in their present circumstances. Their measures are passed, not after a careful and mature consideration, but as experiments" (*Native Opinion*, May 22, 1870). *Jam-e-Jamshed*, the leading Parsi newspaper representing commercial interests, made the argument that the costs of the Act should "fall upon those for whose benefit the measure is intended. There should be a provision for levying fees on prostitutes, to make the Act self-supporting" (December 13, 1869). It also claimed that the Act was irrelevant to the local population who "as a rule married early in life and . . . [lived] an honorable life" (November 17, 1870). The *Bombay Chabuk*, a Gujarati biweekly, printed the complaint that for a municipality that was financially unable to undertake the vaccination of children from smallpox, "providing fornicators with safe objects of their immoral and sinful desires" was unacceptable (August 24, 1870). Overall, in Bombay's vibrant public sphere, the CDA was viewed as an unnecessary imperial imposition.

Once the Act came into effect, protests about the nature of the medical examinations themselves also grew. *Native Opinion*, for example, declared that the examinations "outrage[d] the modesty of females for the convenience of males" (January 8, 1871); the injustice of targeting only women while the disease was spread by both men and women was also noted (*Native Opinion*, May 22, 1870; January 7, 1871). However, opposition to the CDA was mounted not on behalf of prostitutes' welfare as much as on fiscal grounds. On the whole, prostitutes did not enjoy great sympathy among the classes represented by the newspapers. Sentiments such as the following in the Gujarati biweekly *Bombay Chabuk* were common: "The wretched women, who are often driven by want into this shameless and vile profession, are deservedly regarded with contempt and loathing" (April 22, 1868). *Dnyan Prakash*, a Marathi daily, urged the implementation of the Indian Penal Code sections that abolished the sale of girls, as "it [was] much better to prevent innocent girls being brought upon prostitution than to make laws to prevent the horrible contagion that these vile women spread" (November 6, 1869). Prostitution was seen as a corrupting profession, and once women entered it, they were treated with revulsion.

Newspaper articles indicate that the operational failure of the Act became public knowledge very quickly: by June 1870, half a year into its functioning, the Marathi weekly *Satya Watta* proclaimed that "the object of the Act had been defeated" because many prostitutes left the island of Bombay for surrounding areas before the Act was enforced. The 1871 decision of the Bench of Justices to discontinue municipal funding for the Act was lauded in the press.[33] When the Act was reintroduced in 1880, it was greeted with dismay by an even more vociferous press. *Indu Prakash*, a reformist Anglo-Marathi weekly, was highly skeptical of the rationale for its reintroduction and the "statistics paraded to show that soldiers are suffering terribly from the vile disease" (January 13, 1881). *Native Opinion* blamed the local government for not standing up to imperial policy, remarking that they had no "individuality" (February 6, 1881). The same newspaper also showed awareness of the growing movement against the Acts in England, declaring: "What is condemned as most degrading and immoral in England and Europe cannot be looked upon in any other light by the people of India" (July 24, 1881).

Newspapers vigilantly followed the operation of the Act through the 1880s. They reported at one point that out of 200 women detained in Bombay's Lock Hospital, only 90 were found diseased, calling for the punishment of medical examiners.[34] By 1888, the tone taken by newspapers was explicitly seditious: "Government have discovered a nice way of turning the mothers, sisters, wives and daughters of Natives into prostitutes, and it would have been better if India had not given birth to sons quietly hearing of such disgraceful and cruel conduct of Government officers" (*Vartahar,* May 20, 1888); and "we do not feel the least fear to style the British Government the King of Vices" (*Pratod,* May 21, 1888); and this most overtly nationalist exhortation: "Aryans look how your women are oppressed in your holy land, how your religion is neglected, and how many sinful deeds are done under sacred British rule! Rise! Only the National Congress is fit for this work" (*Rajyabhakti,* May 31, 1888). With so little support from local government, intelligentsia, and collaborators, the second repeal of the CDA in 1888 was imminent.

The final push for repeal came from the organized movement in Britain led by the Ladies National Association and its leader Josephine Butler (Walkowitz 1980; Burton 1994). Although this group had "little direct contact with Indian women living in and around military cantonments" (Burton 1994, 155), they viewed developments in India as crucial to their moral purpose and the health of their own movement. After the repeal of the Acts in Britain, this organization turned its sights on repealing the CDA in India as a means to sustain its own considerable momentum. Within two years of repeal in Britain, it helped effect a parliamentary repeal for India as well.

THE AFTERMATH OF THE CDA

The medical regulation of prostitutes did not, however, disappear immediately and continued in varied, albeit less visible, forms. The Bombay government admitted that medical checks and licensing were carried out in months even after the repeal of the Act.[35] In some cantonments in other parts of the country, administrators did not even know that laws had changed and continued with the system in place (Kitchener 1912, 78). The aftermath of the CDA revealed how the interests of colonial military officials and metropolitan administrators diverged: while the latter were subjected to greater liberal pressure from anti-CDA groups, the military officials believed that the repeal of the CDA was a mistake. During the 1890s, antagonism grew between missionaries who opposed state-regulated prostitution and military and medical officials who believed the system to be beneficial. Kate Bushnell and Elizabeth Andrews, two missionaries delegated by the British Commission for the State Regulation of Vice, undertook a highly publicized fact-finding trip to various cantonments in India in the early 1890s. They found that military prostitution continued to be so acceptable that at one point the quartermaster general in India advised all commanding officers that women supplied to brothels should be "sufficiently attractive."[36] They presented such evidence of the continued regulation of prostitution at hearings in the British Parliament (Parliamentary Papers 1893–94). Such reformist activism led to a series of amendments of the Cantonment Code in 1895, which declared brothels illegal and kept medical checks voluntary. Within two years, however, this amendment was revoked under the influence of the secretary of state to India, Lord George Hamilton, an avid supporter of regulation.

The course of the CDA in Bombay reveals not just the peculiarities of the city's political climate but also inherent problems in the colonial project of regulation of prostitution. My reading of the CDA as a failure underscores how the medical framework underpinning this project was misguided in an urban context. The parsimony inherent in the CDA's experimental outlook created the conditions for its own failure in an urban area. The one-sidedness of the experiment—seeing only prostitutes as disease carriers and soldiers as a vulnerable population—also undercut the aim of eliminating venereal disease. The police enforcing the Act buckled under an unrealistic responsibility, and the attempts to actualize this flawed law deepened fissures within the administration. The tension between detractors and proponents of the system of regulation continued into the first decade of the twentieth century until a new concern arose to displace the terms of the debate: the trafficking of women from Europe to the colonies.

Racial Stratification
and the Discourse of Trafficking

In reconfiguring Foucault's history of sexuality, Ann Stoler (1995) notes that any nineteenth-century apparatus of sexuality has to be understood via the imperative of managing whiteness, and that colonial governmentality was fundamentally shaped by the threat of racial disorder. This insight is key to understanding the enforcement of the CDA. While state control of Indian prostitutes proceeded in an unwieldy fashion in the 1870s and 1880s under the Contagious Diseases Acts, the same era nonetheless inaugurated an intense police surveillance of European prostitutes. Indeed, the one dimension of the CDA that met with success in Bombay was the spatial allocation of prostitution along racialized lines. With Bombay's rise as a prominent seaport in the late nineteenth century, its brothels began to service sailors and receive women from distant parts of the world; it joined a sex trade circuit spanning cities in Asia, South America, and Africa (Guy 2000; Hershatter 1997; Hyam, 1990; Levine 2003; Van Heiningen 1984). In such a context, the CDA introduced an orderly system for overseeing a racially stratified sexual order. The system continued well into the 1920s and 1930s, when it was entrenched by the discourse of antitrafficking.

In Europe and North America, the turn of the twentieth century was marked by a moral panic about white women being transported to brothels in colonies.[1] This panic was expressed first through the idiom of "white slavery" and then through laws against "trafficking." The antitrafficking measures in Europe and North America such as the 1910 Mann Act gained emotive weight from the image of violated white women. This image did not, however, translate easily in Bombay's context. Not all brothel workers who came to Bombay had been deceived, nor were they all ingénues whose sexual purity had been stolen. As I will show, the assumptions embedded in antitrafficking discourse in fact enabled Bombay police to sustain a racially stratified sexual order. I argue that while the idiom of antitrafficking demonized third-party procurers who trapped unknowing women and carried them across oceans, the locus of coercion for European brothel workers in Bombay more often lay elsewhere, in the restrictive protection they received from police and brothel keepers.

In the first section of this chapter, I explore the spatial and social location of European prostitutes: their role in defining the city's red-light area, allaying colonial administrators' fears about interracial sex between British men and Indian women. In the second section, I stress the relations of coercive protection that kept European brothel workers within their assigned social and physical spaces. In the third section, I show how this structure of coercive protection was paradoxically consolidated, rather than undermined, by the League of Nations conventions on trafficking in the 1920s.[2] Antitrafficking conventions encouraged a highly selective form of police enforcement: a focus on cross-border trafficking, an attendant neglect of internal trafficking, a legalistic emphasis on third-party procurers,[3] and concern only for victims with no prior history of prostitution. I close the chapter by comparing the enforcement practices of police with those of local social work organizations, in order to highlight the gaps in antitrafficking measures.

A RACIALIZED SEXUAL ORDER

Bombay was one node in a sex trade circuit that spanned several port cities such as Buenos Aires, Cape Town, Hong Kong, Singapore, Cairo, and Shanghai (Guy 1991; Hershatter 1997; Levine 2003; Van Heiningen 1984). Bombay's port grew in importance in the world cotton trade after the 1860s: the Civil War in the United States (and the consequent interruption in cotton production) led to an increasing demand for cotton from India; railway lines connecting Bombay city with rural districts were laid down; and the opening of the Suez Canal in 1869 increased steamship communication with Europe (Kosambi 1985, 35). Although other seaports in the subcontinent such as Madras and Calcutta also had European brothels, Bombay's large European population,[4] and its geographical location on the west coast made it the preferred point of entry for those who recruited and supplied workers for brothels throughout, and sometimes beyond, South Asia.[5] Table 3 provides a comparison with some other cities of the Indian subcontinent. It shows that in 1912 Bombay was home to more than twice the number of European prostitutes as Calcutta.

In Bombay, the category of "Non-Indian Asian" prostitutes referred largely to Japanese brothel workers. Although their numbers were large,[6] Japanese prostitutes drew far less official attention than European prostitutes. They were exempted from the kind of surveillance that affected European prostitutes, largely because of the role that the Japanese consulate seemed to play in their lives. Indeed they functioned almost like a diplomatic enclave, living in a separate quarter in Kamathipura, with customers who were principally Japanese residents and sailors (HD 1932, 16). The Japanese consulate reported quite rosily that "they were not exploited" and that many of the women "enjoy[ed] rather happy and comfortable private lives and even devot[ed] their spare time to mental and physical development" (HD 1932, 16). The consul-general had the power to force Japanese steamships to take such women back to Japan but rarely used this power. Because these women posed less threat of racial disorder, Japanese brothels were far less often mentioned in police and missionary records than European ones.

The presence of European brothels in Bombay can be explained as a resolution of three distinct imperatives for colonial administrators: providing

TABLE 3. European and non-Indian Asian prostitutes in cities of the Indian subcontinent, 1912

City	Number of prostitutes	
	European	Non-Indian Asian
Madras	6	8
Bombay	126	100
Calcutta	50	—
Rangoon	17	168
Karachi	6	20
Poona	9	9
Lahore	20	0

Source: Home Department 1913, Judicial A, *Legislative Notes at the All-India Level,* July 273–289, 221.

sexual recreation to British soldiers and sailors, preventing interracial sex, and preserving British national prestige. European women who first arrived in Bombay in the 1860s largely worked in brothels that served British subjects. Strong strictures against interracial sex in the late colonial period encouraged the rise of such brothels. As in other colonies, the increasing pervasiveness of a biological construct of race meant that preserving racial purity and preventing miscegenation became a crucial political project (Cooper and Stoler 1997; Stoler 1995). The distinctions between Indian and British people were defined in increasingly rigid terms, and medical justifications against miscegenation became common, with the typical warning against interracial sex being that "diseases passed on from one race to another (were) always more severe" (Kitchener 1912, 60). As described in the previous chapter, Indian women were increasingly framed as part of the disease-bearing surroundings that constantly threatened the British presence.

Social and demographic changes in the British population in India also accounted for greater racial distancing. English women began to travel independently to India in greater numbers in the late 1800s, and they were carefully monitored because they were seen as vulnerable to sexual violation by Indian men (Enloe 1989). After the Revolt of 1857, when Indian troops staged an uprising that contributed to the collapse of the British East India Company, a new class of poorer Englishmen entered cities, primarily made up of the East India Company's disbanded army. Colonial administrators viewed them as unruly and likely to disturb the public peace; one chronicler of the period referred to them as the "loafer class" (Smith 1879, 317). Threatened by more adventurous white women, a white underclass, and evidently mutinous Indians, the settled British population policed racial boundaries ever more strictly.

Although the tolerance for interracial sex declined, brothels remained a staple feature of colonial rule. Even after brothels were banned in Britain in 1885, they continued to be tolerated in India, as in Hong Kong and Singapore (Levine 2003), because of the perceived need for recreation for the overwhelmingly single British servicemen and sailors. As the number of sailors visiting the city increased, an organized system for directing sailors from ports to licensed brothels emerged, approved by the chief medical officer of Bombay (Government of Bombay 1885). This system continued into the 1920s, when social workers reported that sailors coming ashore were driven straight to brothels (HD 1921a). Brothels even catered to specific shipping lines, assigning pimps to wait at dock gates to escort sailors (GD 1927–28b, M130).

Although British administrators condoned brothels, they tried to ensure that brothel workers were not British, as that could reflect poorly on British womanhood (Hyam 1990; Levine 2003). English women who came to India to find husbands but turned to prostitution were decried as "scandals to the nation" and punished or sent home (Kincaid 1973, 43, 44). The injunction against British women "openly ply[ing] this trade" rang clear in legislative discussions (HD 1913b, 221). Thus, although white prostitutes were preferred for racist reasons, British prostitutes posed problems for the national prestige of administrators.

The separate dictates of racism, British national prestige, and sexual recreation for British soldiers and sailors were resolved by the tolerance of non-British European prostitutes. While British prostitutes were deported, women from other European countries—such as France, Germany, and Italy, and particularly Poland, Austria, Romania, and Russia—were allowed to reside in Bombay.[7] Many of the European women had been brought to the city by networks of suppliers who transported them to brothels in colonies. Their specific countries of origin are mentioned in various records: census tables (Government of India 1921), CDA enforcement reports (1880–87), questionnaires sent out by the Prostitution Committee in 1920 (HD 1921b), and annual antitrafficking reports sent by the police (1925–38) all list European birthplaces and nationalities of prostitutes. The signatures listed in the petitions that prostitutes sent to the police are also revealing: names such as Polsky, Puritz, Prevenziano, Greenberg, Erlich, Feldman, Stern, which suggest Polish, Russian, Italian, and German origins (GD 1887b, 372). Most obvious is a list that the Government of Bombay drew up when the First World War broke out, which identifies German and Austrian prostitutes as "enemy" subjects (Political Department 1915). Thus, although the term "European" was used in colonial India generically to include Britons, in this context the European women who consorted with British men had specifically Continental origins.

This racialized sexual order was acknowledged in formal terms: Stephen M. Edwardes, police commissioner of Bombay from 1909 to 1917, declared that without European prostitutes there would be "increasing resort to Indian women," a possibility which "could not be regarded with impunity by those responsible for the general welfare of India" (Edwardes 1983, 81).

As he explained it, "The growth of European populations, and the government's disapproval of liaisons with Indian women made authorities accept European brothels as a necessary evil. No direct steps were taken to curb [them]" (85).

This official tolerance for European brothels ran counter to trends in the metropolitan British state, where organizations such as the Ladies National Association had mounted successful campaigns in the 1880s to repeal the CDA, abolish regulated prostitution, and ban brothels (Burton 1994). The colonial state had a greater interest in regulating interracial sexual recreation than the metropolitan state: brothels remained legal until the 1930s, and informal registration and medical checks of prostitutes continued into the 1920s in Indian cities (Burton 1994; Levine 2003). Yet it was incumbent on British colonial administrators to distance themselves from European brothels in order to ward off political controversy. Colonial officials symbolically achieved such distancing by selectively highlighting the Jewish background of European prostitutes. In his description of prostitution in colonial India, Edwardes repeatedly referred to "the preponderance of Jewesses in the brothels of Indian coast cities" and the "Jewish pimp" (1983, 79). At a 1921 League of Nations conference, he asked the representative of Jewish Associations why their "co-religionists" formed the "majority of the procurers and 'fancy men'" who visited Bombay (HD 1922, 12).

While many among the traffickers and the trafficked were undoubtedly Jewish, the anti-Semitism prevailing in Europe inflated the Jewish presence in the sex trade (Bristow 1983). Edwardes's characterization pointed to the subtext of Jewish criminality that was popular in Europe at the time. This subtext obscured the sociohistorical explanations for Jewish participation in the sex trade, such as the widespread dispersal of Ashkenazi Jews in the 1880s because of Russian pogroms, the collapse of economic and social structures in the Ghetto, and religious laws that were unfavorable to widows and conducive to fraudulent marriages (Bristow 1983; Guy 1991; Levine 2003; Marks 1996; Mirelman 1990).

The actual religious or ethnic identities of European prostitutes in Bombay are perhaps less important than the official insistence that they were "less white" because they were Jewish or Eastern European. While many among the traffickers and the trafficked were undoubtedly Jewish, the prevailing anti-Semitism in Europe inflated the Jewish presence in the sex trade (Bristow 1983). Edwardes called the term "white slave traffic" a misnomer in the Indian context because the women "were chiefly of Eastern European origin"; he displayed an Anglo-Saxon notion of whiteness and conflated Eastern European nationality and Jewish religion (Edwardes 1983, 77). Officials in Bombay also drew on the British ideology of Jews as "foreigners" (77), which had been heightened in Britain after the Russian pogroms (Marks 1996); in doing so, they simultaneously configured themselves as a legitimate, settled population. Ultimately, the system of sexual recreation for sailors in Bombay city depended on the varied foreign nationalities of the women.

THE RISE OF A RED-LIGHT ENCLAVE

Although European prostitutes' intermediate racial stratum and outsider status provided a neat resolution of political imperatives, the women had a volatile social presence that required regular police attention. They first settled in Kamathipura around the middle of the nineteenth century. In the 1864 census, Kamathipura had the second-largest female European population of women, at 224, after Colaba, which had 408 (*Census of Bombay* 1864, 94). While the concentration of European women in Colaba may be attributed to the army quarters located there, the large number of European women in Kamathipura, which was marked as part of a native town in the early 1800s (Kosambi and Brush 1988), can be attributed to brothels set up there. Although Indian brothels were also to be found in this area, European brothels became so conspicuous that by the 1880s a principal street in Kamathipura called Cursetji Suklaji Street was described as *safed galli* (white lane) (Edwardes 1923, 85–89).

Kamathipura was not a particularly large area—it stretched one third of a mile north-south and about half a mile across at its widest point. It consisted of a series of narrow numbered lanes, bounded by traffic arteries, Grant Road, Duncan Road, Falkland Road, Foras Road, and Bellasis Road. Why Kamathipura became the site of European prostitution is not immediately obvious. In early descriptions of the city, it was demarcated as a "native town," or an area where Indians, and not Britons, lived (Government of Bombay 1864, 94). It also did not border Bombay's dockyard or the garrison. It did, however, have major roads linking it to the docks, such as Babula Tank Road, and it also lay close to the Byculla Club and the European residential suburbs of Byculla. Duncan Road, the eastern border of Kamathipura, constituted the major thoroughfare leading to the fort from Byculla.[8] Thus Kamathipura was both accessible and sufficiently set apart from work and residential areas of Europeans in the city.

Kamathipura was also unattractive to elite Indians because of its caste makeup. The area Kamathipura owed its name to Kamathis—artisans and construction workers who had migrated from Hyderabad at the turn of the nineteenth century. In the 1860s, Arthur Crawford, the first municipal commissioner, also directed municipal sweepers to live there. The low caste of such residents, apart from its Kamathi inhabitants, made it cheaper for leasing by brothel owners. According to one landlord named Beebec Vaziram, the sweepers led "disorderly lives" and so "no respectable person would live there" (GD 1888a, 227, 229). Ultimately, this landlord leased houses out to Italian and German prostitutes. Jewish cemeteries appeared in this area by the 1870s: one on Grant Road just south of the numbered streets of Kamathipura, and another at the intersection of Bellasis Road and Duncan Road, the northeastern corner of Kamathipura.

That Eastern European prostitutes adopted an area occupied by outcaste sweepers was indicative of their own position on the social scale: these women were clearly outsiders, belonging to neither the stratum of rulers nor the ruled. Their profession placed them outside the limits of respectability, and their Eastern European nationalities made them less appealing neighbors to the settled British population. Kamathipura thus became a site where people of a lower "moral" and economic status converged and lines of racial difference faded, unlike the rest of segregated colonial Bombay.

It is through the public campaign of Bombay residents calling for the enforcement of segregation rules in the CDA that Kamathipura came to be the established prostitutes' quarter of the city. Middle- and upper-class Indians rallied around the CDA rule that allocated European prostitution to fixed zones in the city. During the first phase of the CDA, the police commissioner had removed several European brothels from principal thoroughfares, and the residents of respectable neighborhoods wished to see such measures continue. A long dispute over where to locate European prostitutes occurred in the 1870s and 1880s, with residents of various neighborhoods vying for influence over the police commissioner's decisions. In 1872, for instance, even after the CDA had been suspended in Bombay, residents of Girgaum wrote a petition to the governor in council asking for the removal of prostitutes from Girgaum Back Road, citing the proximity of schools and churches. They complained that European prostitutes were particularly offensive, unlike the Indian prostitutes, who catered to working-class men (GD 1872a, 105–7).

Such attempts to shift prostitutes sometimes met with resistance, and the case of Cursetji Suklaji Street is a striking example. When Governor James Ferguson decided to move prostitutes from Duncan Road, which had become too "public" a street, to Cursetji Suklaji Street, protests arose from residents, particularly those in the Bohra community who had a meeting place in the vicinity, and from a group who called themselves the "respectable poor."[9] In 1887, in a concession to the Bohra community, police commissioner Frank Souter ordered the removal of European brothels from Cursetji Suklaji Street, arguing that this street had also become a thoroughfare. The dispersal of European prostitutes from Cursetji Suklaji Street across the city to other areas drew a chorus of complaints from residents of those areas. A number of signed petitions from the residential neighborhoods of Fort, Khetwadi, and Chowpaty were sent to the police commissioner, and complaints were published in newspapers about respectable areas now being "infested" by prostitutes (GD 1888b, 47).[10] Some European prostitutes also wrote directly to the governor in council, complaining about their arbitrary relocation by the police commissioner (GD 1887b, 370). Landlords of brothels on Cursetji Suklaji Street, who sought to have their prostitute tenants back for the high rents they paid, also orchestrated a petition campaign refuting the claims made by the Bohra community about disturbances caused by prostitutes (GD 1887b, 362–69). A petition from "native prostitutes" in Koombharwadwa, an area adjoining Kamathipura, claimed that European prostitutes were welcome in this neighborhood because they brought peace and order (GD 1888c, 83–87).[11]

The Government of Bombay finally had to arbitrate when it appeared that the police commissioner was not paying heed to widespread public opinion. The acting chief secretary of the Government of Bombay faulted the police commissioner's dispersal of prostitutes from a fixed zone and reversed the policy. The *Indian Spectator,* an English publication, bragged that the decision occurred due to the "perseverance of those who fought for public decency . . . and was . . . a triumph of public opinion to which the Press contributed largely" (May 20, 1888). A cartoon in *Parsi Punch* showed a European woman dancing with joy—"Hooray! Three cheers for the discomfiture of the Police Commissioner"—and wrote approvingly of the decision of the Bombay Government to reverse the police commissioner's policy (May 20, 1888). It came to be settled, then, that the majority of Bombay's respectable inhabitants preferred to have European prostitution confined to a clear zone.

Between the 1880s and 1920s, Kamathipura took shape as the assigned red-light zone of the city. Kamathipura's changing role in the spatial organization of prostitution in Bombay is shown in Table 4. The table tracks the distribution of both Indian and European prostitutes in Bombay between 1864 and 1921, as culled from census figures. The table displays several noticeable features of the spatial segregation of European prostitutes. First, there are vastly greater numbers of reported prostitutes in 1864 compared to 1921. I explore this point in greater depth in chapter 5, when I analyze census figures and trace the effects of criminalization on prostitutes. Second, there is a progressive clustering of prostitutes into fewer and fewer city sections: in 1864, there were eight city sections with 500 or more self-classified prostitutes; in 1921, there were only two such sections, Kamathipura and Khetwadi. By 1921, Kamathipura had the highest concentration of prostitutes, and a 1917 guide to the street names of Bombay remarked: "Kamathipura is commonly used to denote the prostitutes' quarter . . . Grant Road and Suklaji Street (are) names which connote a good deal more than geography" (Sheppard 1917, 84). "Every subaltern and soldier in the British Army from Cape Wrath to Hong Kong knows of 'Grant Road,'" noted a Royal Army Medical Corps official in 1921, adding that it was the "first place of interest" they went to see when visiting Bombay (HD 1921b, 18).

The puzzling aspect of Kamathipura's notoriety is that it was not the only area to which prostitutes were confined, as the table shows. The figures for both 1864 and 1871 show a concentration of prostitutes in other parts of Bombay highly populated by working- class Indians, such as Market, Oomburkharee, Phunuswaree, and Girgaon. Figures for 1901 and 1921 also indicate that there were areas other than Kamathipura in which prostitutes lived in large numbers: Khetwadi, Phunuswaree, Girgaon, and Tardeo, two of which neighbored Kamathipura and had a high concentration of mill workers, as described in chapter 5.

Although Kamathipura was not the only area with a concentration of prostitutes, it was, significantly, the one where European prostitutes first

TABLE 4. Distribution of prostitutes in Bombay city, 1864, 1871, 1901, and 1921

Section of city	Number of prostitutes			
	1864	1871	1901	1921
Bhooleshwar	585	86	46	4
Byculla	—	14	9	13
Chaoputee	116	89	54	193
Chukla	36	136	87	28
Colaba	4	—	—	—
Dhobeetulao	826	76	65	1
Dongree	143	36	5	—
Esplanade	1	—	—	—
Fort, Southern	—	—	6	—
Fort Northern	12	—	—	—
Girgaon	1,044	223	175	289
Harbour	2	—	—	—
Kamathipura	610	94	207	896
Kharutalao	130	46	131	2
Khetwadi	356	58	350	779
Kumbarawara	498	89	223	11
Mahaluxmee	—	1	4	—
Mahim	30	5	6	—
Mandwee	458	26	—	—
Market	1,701	114	42	1
Mazagaon	5	55	3	2
Oomburkharee	1,583	31	4	—
Parell	36	5	1	—
Phunuswaree	1,323	356	328	316
Seoree	7	3	7	—
Seo	—	3	5	—
Tardeo	10	82	2	1
Walkeshwar	19	17	15	—
Wurlee	1	6	12	—

Sources: Census of Island of Bombay 1864, table 60, 84; Census of India 1921, vol. 9, part 1, section 20.

Note: This table was compiled using figures from tables in different census reports. Not all census reports provide information about prostitutes, hence the jump from 1871 to 1901.

resided and then were allocated. Police aggressively "herded together" European prostitutes into the area. According to a nationwide report on prostitution, if women attempted to leave this area, "police action [drove] them back into it" (HD 1920, 24–29). The same report concluded that "allocation [had] frankly been adopted as the best method for dealing with [prostitution], and police action [was] . . . set in motion against brothels springing up in all places" (HD 1920). There were no parallel efforts to locate Indian prostitutes in just one area. Only European brothels registered in the colonial state's gaze, and Kamathipura was labeled the prostitutes' zone. Thus, European prostitutes came to define the contours of the neighborhood that remained infamous until today as the city's red-light district.

COERCIVE PROTECTION

While the surveillance of prostitutes was a standard feature of state regulation under the CDA, the level of precision in archival information about European prostitutes even after the end of the CDA era in Bombay is striking. In her study comparing sites in Asia and Australia, Levine (2003) finds that attention to Jewish prostitution was stronger in India than other Asian colonies, and "especially" so in Bombay (224). Officers above the deputy inspector grade, who were usually of British origin, considered themselves privy to the goings-on in European brothels long after the repeal of the CDA.[12] The police force maintained larger numbers of European officers in order to meet the requirements of policing European prostitution; for instance, even under a tight budget and despite the relatively fewer European prostitutes, Police Commissioner P. A. Kelly requested that at least one of the two new officers assigned by the government to enforce prostitution laws should be European (HD 1936). Police commissioners showed themselves to be familiar with names of individual brothel workers: in 1930, the commissioner uncovered a case of visa fraud when he recognized that a French prostitute who previously lived in Bombay had altered the spelling of her name from "Indree" to "Andree" in order to reenter India (HD 1930, 4). A Romanian woman was denied permission to visit Bombay in 1928 because the commissioner knew her to be a prostitute (HD 1928a, 18). Similarly, in a 1931 report, a French woman, Mona Bourilly, was denied a visa for India because police knew that her reference, Henriette, was a prostitute (HD 1931, 67). This intense individuation of

European prostitutes, given the relative absence of personal information on inmates of Indian brothels, is striking.

The most obvious evidence of police surveillance of European prostitutes is their careful registration records, which stand in contrast to the vague numbers found on Indian prostitutes. During the enforcement of the CDA, the number of registered European prostitutes never rose above 75, as compared with the average 1,500 registered Indian prostitutes (RWCDA 1880–88). In 1920, the contrast was even starker: only 67 European prostitutes were reported, a tiny fraction of the 5,000 Indian women estimated by the police (HD 1920).[13] While official figures provided for Indian prostitutes were always estimates, for instance "around 4000," even small changes among European prostitutes were noted, for instance from "44" in January 1885 to "46" in July 1885 (Government of Bombay 1885).

Maintaining order in brothels was the key imperative shaping policing activity. The police kept themselves informed of new arrivals and deported prostitutes "guilty of misbehavior" (Edwardes 1924, 80; HD 1920). Bombay police even classified European brothels into first, second, and third class based on their assessment of how well conducted they were and tabulated the number and nationality of women in the three classes of brothel houses. The first class consisted solely of European women living in private houses. The second class consisted of women who solicited in streets, and the third class consisted of women who were grouped along with Japanese and "Baghdadi" women (HD 1920). The police also stayed alert to possible sexual relations between Indian men and European women (Levine 2003). Krishnan's (1923) anecdotal description of the red-light area reveals that European prostitutes sometimes solicited "fair skinned" Indian men, who were mistaken for foreign sailors (63).

The regular record keeping by the police points to the crucial role of brothel mistresses in furnishing information. Although brothel workers may have come forward to identify themselves as prostitutes to the police, it is far more likely that police applied pressure on brothel mistresses to maintain records. As explained in the previous chapter, the CDA laid the seeds of a mutually beneficial relationship between brothel keepers and the police. While the police relied on brothel keepers to assist in medical regulation and ensure order, brothel keepers kept workers under control by using the threat of police retribution. This system became so entrenched in European brothels that it persisted well after the repeal of the Acts. A countrywide police report in 1920 advocated the presence of brothel mistresses as intermediaries:

> Their presence is essential to the due control of women who would otherwise fight among themselves, thieve and require constant police interference . . . She stands as a monitor and guardian between the male clientele and girls of the brothel who belong to a very low class and who would not hesitate to fleece a client of his valuables if there were no "domestic" control . . . If European prostitution is to continue in this country, it seems to me advisable to allow the European mistress. (HD 1920, 24–29)

Thus, the use of nonstate intermediaries to enforce discipline—a common modality of colonial authority—was crucial to the sex trade.

Brothel workers rarely complained against brothel keepers and pimps to the police, because they relied on them for protection *from* the police. In one court case involving the prosecution of a brothel keeper, a brothel worker called her brothel keeper "a friend she was visiting," prompting the magistrate to dismiss the case (GD 1887a, 173–74). Often, brothel workers also relied on corrupt police officers for protection from laws themselves. CDA rules penalized prostitutes who had not been medically checked, as well as foreign nationals without adequate documentation—these were laws that European prostitutes struggled to evade. The police were furthermore important in keeping at bay hostile Indian neighbors, missionaries, and an increasingly intolerant emergent Indian middle class. Brothel workers thus experienced layer upon layer of protection that simultaneously controlled their location and inhibited their movement. The term "coercive protection" best describes these complicated relations between European brothel workers, their mistresses, and the police. Brothel workers were, to borrow the political theorist Wendy Brown's words, being protected by the very power "whose violation [they] fear[ed]" (Brown 1992, 9).

This structure of coercive protection is best demonstrated in the findings of a 1917 police inquiry into the conduct of an inspector. The inquiry revealed that Inspector S. Favel, a member of the investigation wing (CID) and described as the "right hand man" of the previous police commissioner, routinely extorted money and gifts from pimps, brothel mistresses, and brothel workers by threatening deportations. He also collected commissions when brothels changed hands, shared brothel profits, and availed of free sexual services (Judicial Department Proceedings 1917, 195–203). The statements made before the police by Favel's accomplice, five brothel mistresses, and a brothel client describe how policemen visited brothels, oversaw the arrival on ships of new brothel workers, and sometimes even owned shares of brothels; the statements together create a picture of a quotidian relationship between the police and brothel mistresses.

One of the more troubling revelations in the statements is that the police actively prevented women from leaving brothels. For women who sought to escape brothels, police surveillance and blackmail presented a formidable barrier. A clear illustration is found in the statement of D. Meyer, a Manchester-born man who attempted to "rescue" a Russian "girl" named Mary Fooks from 392 Falkland Road, a brothel from which Inspector Favel shared proceeds (Judicial Department Proceedings 1917, 99–100). Meyer wanted to keep Fooks as his mistress, as he mentions "installing" her in a house in Queen's Road, and later "lodging" her in Rope Walk Street. Inspector Favel hounded Meyer in order to interrupt his plan and threatened him with Fooks's deportation; Meyer had to finance Fooks's purchase of brothel shares to avoid that outcome. In order to keep Fooks out of brothels, Meyer had to stay "on the right side of Favel" by plying him with gifts ranging from lengths of Chinese silk cloth to throwing a picnic in Favel's honor when the latter won the King's police medal.[14] Meyer recounts that he even rented Favel a holiday bungalow below market price and also sold him his horse carriage cheaply. Thus, even the financial support of outsiders did not guarantee women escape from brothels.

Women who wished to leave Kamathipura and reside in other parts of the city had to seek Favel's permission, as shown by Mlle Margot's statement that "Favel receive[d] money from girls to permit them to live in the Fort with their 'sweethearts.'" This mistress of No. 6 Grant Road relates with considerable envy that "Lisa Palz" now lived in the Fort area and "practiced prostitution and ran a gaming house" after paying for both those privileges (Judicial Department Proceedings 1917, 99). Even the privilege of appearing in public at the races involved bribing Favel, she explains. Police surveillance not only dogged activities within the brothels but also followed brothel workers to parts of the city deemed respectable.

Inspector Favel does not appear to have been alone in such activities: Mlle Mina, another mistress, mentions that she had the protection of "Mr. Sloane and Mr. Nolan," presumably two other police officers (Judicial Department

Proceedings 1917, 101). Favel's go-between, Mancharam Pitamber, alias Barny, explains that there were others who served in the role of go-between over the sixteen years that he spent as a dressmaker for European prostitutes. Barny also mentions visits by the commissioners and deputy commissioners to avail themselves of sexual services in brothels. He indicates that Favel had enough influence with the commissioner and deputy commissioner to easily engineer a deportation of a brothel worker (Judicial Department Proceedings 1917, 98).

Other historical records corroborate the close involvement of police force superiors with the city's European brothels. The best example is a 1925 letter from P. A. Kelly, the police commissioner of Bombay to the Home Department relating that a brothel mistress brought three Jewish prostitutes who had newly arrived from Cairo to the police station for registration. The deputy commissioner "raised no objections to their going to the brothel" (HD 1925, 89). The police commissioner's matter-of-fact tone indicates that such cooperation with brothel mistresses was standard practice, even in an era when formal registration had ended. The same letter also contains a revealing example of cooperation with procurers. It describes a man named A. Katz, who was mostly likely a procurer, as he was "known to be a friend of the mistress" of the same brothel, and who arrived with the three women from Cairo. The police commissioner, however, relates that he "found no grounds" for deporting the man and notes that the man "was found to be making bona fide attempts to start a respectable business in Bombay" (HD 1925, 89). Similarly, in 1936, the police reported that Jean Baptiste Andreani, "a Frenchman suspected of trafficking," arrived in Bombay from Europe in January and returned in May without being prosecuted (Political Department 1936). That same year, two women, Erma Edith Contin and Marie Josephine Bottai, entered Bombay, registered as prostitutes, and went on their way. Thus, even after laws banned procuring women for brothels and registering of brothel workers, police continued to foster European prostitution in Bombay.

The complex, tentacular control that the police wielded produced few opportunities for prostitutes to break away from brothels. Even rescues by outsiders were only possible with police permission; the police worked hard to keep women within the bounds of Kamathipura. Brothel workers clearly could not rely on the police to counter abuse suffered at the hands of pimps, mistresses, or clients. Indeed, the fear that police evoked through their threats of deportation and constant extortion reinforced the power of mistresses within the brothels.

This structure of coercive protection is not unique to this stratum or city. Similar relations between police and brothel keepers were observed in Buenos Aires, a key node in the early-twentieth-century sex trade.[15] Julio Alsogaray, a maverick commissar of police, derided what he termed the "trilogy of white slavery"—municipal authorities, police, and traffickers working in tandem (Glickman 2000; Mirelman 1990, 206). As in late colonial Bombay, prostitutes, procurers, and pimps in this city were often characterized as Jewish. What seems to be different in Buenos Aires is the wholesale effort of Jewish reform societies to combat "white slavery" and rescue Jewish prostitutes (Mirelman 1990; Bristow 1983; Guy 1991). The Jewish immigrant population in Buenos Aires ostracized Jewish pimps and brothel keepers, who in turn established a separate synagogue, cemetery, and mutual help society (Mirelman 1990, 206). In comparison, Bombay's local Jewish population identified less with European brothel workers and protested less. In European settler colonies such as Argentina (or in South Africa and Australia), Europeans guarded their reputation more closely and even recuperated "white" prostitutes for marriage by constructing them as victims. Guy (2000) argues that in Buenos Aires, "stories of 'white slavery'" were fueled by the threatened prestige of European settlers (74–76). In Bombay, however, Eastern European prostitutes were clearly marked as outsiders, and it was only when international concern over trafficking reached its peak in the 1920s that it became impolitic to condone European brothels. The next section analyzes the effects of antitrafficking discourse.

WHITE SLAVES AND INTERNATIONAL SLEUTHS

The idiom of white slave traffic—the trade in, and bondage of, white women in prostitution—became dominant in the first two decades of the twentieth century in Europe and North America. It is unclear whether trafficking initially was meant to refer to movement across borders, for the term "traffic" simply meant a trade, or commerce.[16] But much of the traffic that caught the attention of social purity campaigns was that of girls from Europe carried away to colonies, and the term "white slave traffic" grew in use. The cross-national dimensions of the sex trade provoked coordinated action across nations. Following the formation of the International

Society for the Suppression of White Slave Traffic by William Coote in 1899, meetings of country representatives were convened every three years for the next two decades. Member countries signed agreements to keep a watch at ports of embarkation, to repatriate women, and to criminalize abduction and trafficking (League of Nations 1943, 10–11). The problem of offenses committed across the borders of countries was now to be overcome through a harmonizing of laws between countries.

The League of Nations took on trafficking in women and children as part of its mandate in 1920. A permanent committee was set up to collect information, study methods of prevention, and advise the Council of the League of Nations. Representatives were appointed from thirty-three countries, including India (League of Nations 1943, 10–11). It is interesting that India was drawn into this particular internationalist legal regime as a distinct political entity, given its status as a dependent member of the British empire.[17] The contours of the sex trade necessitated its involvement— Indian ports were nodes in the trafficking circuits that imperial reformists sought to disrupt. Therefore, like other participating nations, India had to submit annual reports on the enforcement of antitrafficking measures. As Bombay city was the central destination for traffickers in India, the Government of Bombay was the central authority implementing the international conventions of 1904 and 1921. The Government of Bombay now put pressure on the police to enforce the new conventions.

The discourse on trafficking set up a prototypical victim: the needy young girl who was enticed away by promises of respectable work, adventure, or marriage. In a book touted as the official weapon in the "great war against white slavery," the American antitrafficking advocate Clifford Roe (1911) compiled anonymous narratives of girls abducted by fraudulent means, lured from homes and trapped in distant cities by men and women who hunted them. The girls were typically portrayed as being younger than age twenty, naively trustful of strangers, and of peasant or small town origins (Roe 1911, 105).

Such images of the ingénue were not easily applicable, however, to European brothel workers in Bombay city. Social purity crusaders, such as the English missionaries Alfred Dyer and Reverend R. H. Madden, had attempted to characterize European brothel workers thus in the 1880s but had met with little response.[18] For instance, when Dyer tried to bring Bombay's white brothels to the attention of Europeans in 1882, the Brussels press dismissed his story as an isolated case (Roe 1911, 399). European prostitutes themselves often resisted the overtures of purity crusaders. In 1894, when missionaries in the vicinity of Cursetji Suklaji Street petitioned the police about their "immorality," European prostitutes complained to police of the annoyance caused to *them* by missionaries and requested that missionaries be warned against interfering with their private rights (HD 1894). Although the Salvation Army regularly printed information on how to escape brothels, directed to (presumably European) prostitutes, in the English-language newspaper *Indian Social Reformer,* its officers acknowledged that rescues were "difficult" since "many" desired to remain in prostitution for its money (*Indian Social Reformer* 1921a, 836).

A discrepancy existed between the rhetoric of trafficking and the conditions under which brothel workers lived. Whether or not they were deceived in traveling to Bombay, it is quite clear that European brothel workers' material conditions in the city were fairly secure relative to others who practiced prostitution in the city. A doctor who treated venereal diseases in the red-light area reported to the Prostitution Committee of 1920 that "foreign" prostitutes earned on average 1,500 to 2,000 rupees per month (HD 1921c), a sum that could buy a horse carriage, or "a summer rental of a bungalow" (Judicial Department Proceedings 1917, 100). The brothel mistresses' written statements in the Inspector Favel inquiry give insight into how well established and prosperous some European prostitutes and mistresses were. Many brothel workers were able to save up enough money to own shares in brothel houses, and many leased houses from landlords.[19] Pairs of women shared the risk and costs of running brothels: the average half-share cost anywhere from 7,000 to 10,000 rupees in 1908. Brothels were profitable corporate entities: their value rose over time, as in the case of 392 Falkland Road, whose half-share value rose from 7,000 rupees in 1909 to 11,500 rupees in 1917 (Judicial Department Proceedings 1917, 102). It is not clear how much money the average European brothel worker charged per customer, but she could earn anywhere from 30 rupees to 300 rupees a day (HD 1921b, 27). It far exceeded the 2 to 3 rupees earned per day by lowest-rung Indian brothel workers (HD 1921b, 27), who charged 3 to 4 annas (a quarter rupee) per customer.[20]

The relative material security of European prostitutes allowed Bombay's police to cast them as exceptions to the discourse of trafficking. In official reports, police presented European prostitution as an unremarkable and justifiable practice: "Apart from the ethical aspect of the whole question of prostitution," one report reads, "there is nothing to offend the eyes or sensibility of anyone" (HD 1920, 24–29). According to S. M. Edwardes, European prostitutes entered the "profession" of their own free will, after serving an "apprenticeship" in Europe, Constantinople, or Egypt. Whereas prostitution was a "hereditary caste" for Indian women, European prostitutes were "fallen women" whose "weak morals" had led them into vice (Edwardes 1983, 77). In his view, character flaws such as love of extravagance and carelessness with money made European women vulnerable to debt. The cycle of debt from which they were unable to break free was seen to bring them to India and keep them in prostitution (79).

In various ways, Bombay police declared that European prostitutes in Bombay were not worthy victims of trafficking because they lacked the prerequisite sexual purity. Whereas U.S. courts applied white slavery laws even when the transported woman was a confirmed prostitute (Haag 1999), for Bombay's police, evidence that a woman was a prostitute before arriving in the city was enough reason to deny the case as one of trafficking. Consider, for instance, the following remarks contained in a 1926 police report of enforcement of antitrafficking measures:

> French girl, inmate of brothel, returned to France in 1925. Came back to Bombay in Autumn bringing with her younger sister. Both found living in the same brothel. In March 1926 another French girl who came out as a lady's maid to a French lady on the same boat became friendly with elder sister and was found in same brothel in March. Police took no action re: younger sister as she had been in the life in France. Police are trying to put pressure on the lady's maid to return to France. (HD 1926c, 85)

It is significant that the police only targeted the "lady's maid" as a trafficking victim because she had not practiced prostitution prior to her arrival in Bombay. The report also indicates that brothel workers themselves saw enough merit in their work to actively draw in family members and others of a similar class background. Recruiting for brothels did not occur only at the hands of wily strangers, as the discourse of trafficking presumed.

Police regularly dismissed cases that did not reach the required level of pathos. In an 1887 court case, a woman named Rosa Schweitzer tried to initiate police action against the man who brought her to India. In an effort to prove his work as a trafficker, she related that "L. Lefflauski . . . brought 2 [other] girls to Bombay—one German, and the other a French girl." She also related that she was "assaulted by him because (she) refused to go to Europe to bring fresh girls" (HD 1888a). Rosa reported her assault to the police and a court summons was even issued to Lefflauski. The court later dropped her case on the grounds that Rosa was not "a minor" or young enough to qualify as a true victim, and her "abduction (if any) had taken place outside India" (HD 1888b). In the words of the secretary of the Judicial Department, "Before (she) had reached this country (she) had learned by experience the life (she was) intended to lead" (HD 1888a).

The only worthy trafficking victim, it seems, was young and virginal. A 1920 national report on prostitution in Indian cities concluded that all the foreign prostitutes in Bombay "were prostitutes in their own countries . . . long before their arrival in India, and if any of them were victims of the 'White Slave' traffic, they have been so victimized long before their arrival in India. The 'White Slave' traffic as known in Europe is non-existent in India" (HD 1920, 24–29). In 1932, the police reported to the League of Nations that "if a girl comes to Bombay who has already been seduced or been a prostitute then we leave her alone . . . no European woman had been allowed to stay as a brothel inmate during the last years who was not already, on her arrival, a prostitute" (HD 1932, 17). This perception, importantly, was not consistent with how the League of Nations viewed the problem of trafficking. In a 1930 report by Experts of the League of Nations, the French representative acknowledged that "the traffic in women of European races [was] mostly a commercial trade in prostitutes" but went on to declare that the League of Nations' aim was to ensure that "no prostitute could exercise her profession in a foreign country" (HD 1929–30, 16). The Jewish Association for the Protection of Women, which regularly reported its rescues to the League of Nations, focused on all women found in brothels, not just those who had no previous links to prostitution. Thus, Bombay's police chose to interpret antitrafficking conventions in ways that allowed them to shore up their relations of protection.

Local social work organizations and missionary groups provide an interesting counterpoint to the positions taken by the police. The records of organizations such as the Bombay Vigilance Association and Christian missionary groups such as the League of Mercy and the Salvation Army present a more alarmist picture of European prostitution. These groups took a close interest in monitoring trafficking and placed a quasi-competitive pressure on the police. The Bombay Vigilance Association, with a managing committee consisting of prominent Indian reformists such as Kanji Dwarkadas and Chunilal Mehta, set out to help police enforce the 1923 Bombay Prostitution Act (HD 1927a). Officers of the Salvation Army, the long-established missionary agency, visited brothels on safed galli in Kamathipura "once a week" seeking rescue cases (*Indian Social Reformer* 1921b, 140). The League of Mercy, headed by the Bishop of Bombay and run mostly by British women, exclusively sought to rescue European and Anglo-Indian girls who worked in brothels and ran a shelter in Bombay for them. The group hired a "rescue worker" trained in England and repatriated women independently of the police (*Indian Social Reformer* 1922, 5). Directed by stringent notions of "moral hygiene" that drew on Victorian, Christian, and Brahminical ideologies (Whitehead 1996), these organizations zealously identified gaps in police responses.

In 1923 for instance, the League of Mercy returned seven girls and two children "to England"; a mother and two children "to Africa"; two girls "to Ceylon" (HD 1924, 15). In the same year, the police report mentioned only the deporting to Russia and Poland of two women who had been practicing prostitution. In 1927, the League of Mercy repatriated to Czechoslovakia a girl "found living with a Parsee . . . in a diseased condition," while the police report for that year mentioned no repatriations (HD 1928a, 53). The League of Mercy's higher repatriation figures were driven by a strict code of women's honor that suspected any woman who traveled alone: in 1926, among the several English girls the group sent back was one who had simply arrived in Bombay "to marry a man she had never seen" (HD 1927a, 69). In 1925, the Bombay Vigilance Association directly petitioned the Government of Bombay to "remove foreign prostitutes" from Bombay using the 1864 Foreigners' Act, which allowed the government to deport non-British subjects suspected of criminal activity. The police commissioner refused, arguing that it would be a "serious mistake" and a "change of policy for the Government," which had not outlawed brothels. He further noted that "foreign brothels . . . [were] far superior in every respect to the Indian brothels" and that Indian brothels should be the first to be closed, hinting that this primarily Indian association focused on Indian brothels (HD 1925a, 8).

Moral reform organizations included within their purview the extensive trafficking between Indian provinces, a phenomenon ignored by the police.

The Bombay Vigilance Association's records indicate that many Indian girls and women were lured to the city by deception: its 1928 report mentions that among the fifty-four trafficked Indian women and girls, four had received promises of marriage and eleven had received promises of employment, thirteen were either "seduced" or kidnapped, while the rest were dedicated by their parents to temples or considered prostitutes by caste (HD 1928a, 47). Its 1929 report similarly mentions false promises of work made to girls, particularly jobs as mill workers and *ayahs* (nannies) (HD 1929a, 47–49). In its 1927 annual report, the Bombay Vigilance Association explains that women who called themselves "employment agents" often procured girls for brothels (HD 1927a, 102–3). In government reports each year, however, the section on "employment agencies" remains blank, with the police typically declaring that "no such agencies have come to light" (HD 1927a, 51; HD 1929a, 87; HD 1930, 65). Although police refused to attend closely to trafficking between Indian provinces and sometimes even refused to classify the phenomenon as trafficking, the cases detailed by social reform organizations give a fuller picture of how such intraregional movement occurred.

In order to make the competing voices of social reform organizations less audible, Bombay police strictly limited the parameters of the term "trafficking." They held to a very literal understanding of the 1910 antitrafficking convention and declared that trafficking involved a third party transporting the victim to a brothel or client. This definition of trafficking enabled Bombay's police to minimize the scale of the social problem that they monitored. Therefore, although the Bombay Vigilance Association reported that fifty-four girls or women were trafficked from other parts of India to Bombay in 1928, and sixty-five in 1929, the police commissioner argued that this information was not worthy of reporting to the League of Nations because the cases were "found not to fall under Articles 1 and 2 of the 1910 Convention," which emphasized cross-border movement (HD 1928a, 47; HD 1929a, 47, 61). Bombay's police also held to the 1910 convention definition that trafficking involved a third party transporting the victim to a brothel or client. This definition neglected cases where no third party was involved, such as when brothel mistresses were themselves procurers. The moral reform groups, for the most part, deferred to this legal definition. The League of Mercy, for instance, regularly opened its annual reports to the League of Nations on the diffident note that it had few cases of "real trafficking" to report.

Since trafficking implied that the shipping of prostitutes across countries was the crux of the problem, and as the focus of the discourse rested on third parties, police attention was centered on the figure of the foreign pimp. The police seemed to fancy themselves international sleuths, and each of their annual reports submitted to the League of Nations opens with one or two colorful cases dealing with foreigners and demonstrations of their widening circuit of connections with police and consulates in distant cities. The "extraditions" and "repatriation and deportations" sections of the police report abound with unwarranted and sometimes voyeuristic detail about pimps. The 1927 arrest of Luciano la Rosa, labeled a "well-known international pimp" by the police, is described carefully right down to the "obscene photographs" of a "semi-nude" woman found in his possession (HD 1927a, 31). In 1925, the police explain that they followed the activities of a newly arrived man from France who described himself as a photographer but who two days later took his wife to a brothel. The police claim that they arrested the man but that the French consul intervened and urged them to release him (HD 1925a, 7).

Under pressure to demonstrate that they were complying with the League of Nations conventions, but unable to come up with examples of deportations every year, Bombay's police turned to reporting "suspicious aliens" and "suspicious cases." In the 1928 report, they explain with excitement that they coordinated with police in Marseilles, France, to monitor the movements of four French women who had set sail for Bombay. The women ultimately avoided coming to Bombay, but this fact did not stop the police from reporting the case to the League of Nations. Similarly, in 1929, the police communicated with the British passport control officer in Paris to deny permission to Gaston Guillon and Marie Amandine Poinet to arrive in Bombay. This pair claimed to have been in the hairdressing business in Brazil for fifteen years before they set sail for India via France. Bombay's police sought to display their grasp of the sex trade by explaining that personal grooming establishments such as "massage" and "manicure" services were often a mask for "disreputable businesses" (HD 1929a, 11–12).

The police also occasionally deported foreign prostitutes in token, and often misplaced, measures to show their resolve. As with the deporting of pimps, the further away the origin of the women, the better the police felt they were doing their job. The 1924 report mentions that the police deported a Polish woman "who had been practicing prostitution in Singapore and

Penang" (HD 1924, 13). In addition, a Russian woman who admitted to carrying on prostitution in Shanghai, Hong Kong, and Japan since 1918 was also forced to leave the city. The police related the previous history of the women with fanfare, as if this were somehow indicative of their own competence (HD 1926c, 85).

More often than not, police records reveal great leniency in regulating the inflow of European women. In 1930, although the police commissioner initially recommended against granting "Miss Valerie Trdliova" a visa because her sister in Bombay had been a prostitute before she married, he relented when the determined Trdliova reached Pondicherry and applied again for a visa, and he recommended that she be permitted to enter Bombay (Political Department 1931, 2). The name "Maithe Pincell" appears in police reports for two years in a row as someone who "continue[d] to reside" in Bombay despite the authorities' knowledge that she had entered the country on false pretences in order to prostitution (Political Department 1936; Political Department 1937).

Rare were the cases that actually conformed to the dominant narrative of trafficking. The one notable example in the records is that of a man who came to Bombay on the "pretence of getting his wife out of a brothel" but whose purported wife "refused and said [the] man had put her into brothel life and merely wanted to get hold of her to live on her again" (HD 1926c, 85). At her own request, the woman was deported to Russia. Oddly, this case is not highlighted in the main body of the report submitted by the Bombay Government to the League of Nations, even though it bears all the signs of a rescue, with the appropriate duplicitous, and foreign, villain.

On the whole, it is clear that Bombay's policemen were quick to dissociate the phenomenon they encountered from the one decried in Europe and North America. The discrepancy between annual reports of police and social purity groups confirms the overall police interest in sustaining the sex trade. Their insistence that European prostitutes in India were not victims of trafficking perpetuated their own relations of coercive protection. The idiom of trafficking in turn allowed them to minimize the problem of coercion in brothels while expanding the possibilities for police corruption. The threat of deportation became a potent weapon to use in extracting money from brothel workers and pimps. Thus, the language of trafficking gave rise to specific emphases and omissions in the official approach to European prostitution in Bombay. The relations between police and long-standing European brothels, meanwhile, were not challenged in serious ways.

CONCLUSION

The colonial state in Bombay utilized laws such as the CDA and antitrafficking conventions to facilitate and formalize access to European prostitution. Although the number of European brothel workers was small, this chapter demonstrates that they were crucial to the colonial aim of managing interracial sex in Bombay. The women's status as outsiders explains their settling in Kamathipura, an otherwise odd choice for white women in the racist colonial order. Their non-British status also explains the surprisingly open complaints against them by Indian residents. They were closely counted, their whereabouts were publicly debated, and their presence altered the spatial configuration of prostitution in the city. That part of Bombay in which they lived continues to be defined as Bombay's red-light area.

European women probably came to Bombay knowing they would work in brothels, but their ability to leave the trade if so desired was strictly curtailed. I have focused on the specific kind of coercion that curtailed such mobility: relations of control in which those who were supposed to protect brothel workers from abuse were also the ones who benefited most from their work; and those who were supposed to be a site of recourse were vested in the continuation of brothels. European women in brothels were set apart from the rest of the city's brothel workers, subjected to disciplining and surveillance by police and brothel keepers, their lives geared toward servicing a foreign population. This dynamic was threatened only marginally by the advent of antitrafficking discourse and, as I have argued, was intensified by the new power vested in the hands of police.

The discourse of white slave trafficking, with its emphasis on cross-border movement and the prerequisite purity of its victims, allowed police to enforce measures selectively and often entirely bypass those who lived within less visible cages of coercive protection. The procuring and abduction of Indian girls into prostitution went largely unnoticed, while foreign pimps populated the pages of police reports to the League of Nations. As the reports of local moral reform organizations indicate, Bombay's police willingly constricted the definition of trafficking and thus enabled European prostitution in Bombay to survive these international legal measures.

The policing practices discussed in this chapter exemplify an important feature of colonial governmentality: the vector of race crucially delimited the scope of the state's reach. Two constituencies coexisted within a single geographical area: Indian prostitutes, who were presumed to be under the watch of Indian reform groups, and European prostitutes, who were exclusively the domain of European police officers. Rather than functioning as a uniformly oppressive entity, the colonial state only presented the appearance of universal surveillance.

chapter 4

Akootai's Death:
Subaltern Indian Brothel Workers

In the early twentieth century, Kamathipura became home to large numbers of Indian women in prostitution. Although European prostitutes, with whom the police socialized, were the hypervisible identifiers of this area in the official imagination, Indian women housed in Kamathipura's brothels far outnumbered such women. The colonial state viewed Indian prostitutes in these spaces as a de-individuated mass and with a certain willful blindness. It carefully monitored and fostered the presence of European prostitutes but exempted entire strata of Indian women from its coercive protection. This chapter brings to the foreground questions that were sidestepped in police records: What kinds of lives did Indian women in prostitution lead? What relationship did they have with the state?

Addressing such questions entails engaging with the subalternity of Indian prostitutes. When Gayatri Spivak (1988) famously declared that "the subaltern cannot speak," her comment was directed principally at Subaltern Studies scholars who spoke on behalf of the "small voices" in South Asian history; she warned that subalterns, by definition, could not represent themselves in official sources and that their voices, even in Subaltern Studies writing, were already altered by the aims of those who represented them.[1] This feminist caution for greater reflexivity in scholarly practice has traveled widely, often to contexts distant from subaltern studies. In this chapter, I would like to revisit the question of how subalterns speak and are spoken for, by focusing on the case of a murdered prostitute whose death produced larger-than-life effects. Using statistical and narrative sources

[handwritten: Chapter question]

representing urban prostitutes in colonial Bombay, I will reconstruct details
of this brothel inmate's life and then contextualize the case within more general narratives about Indian brothels and the steady criminalization of prostitutes. While agreeing that it is never possible to fully access prostitutes'
voices, I will nonetheless engage in a mode of information retrieval that
allows an analysis of the relationship between the state and prostitutes.

Urban Indian prostitutes may be considered classic subaltern figures inso-
far as they were aligned in an oppositional relationship to both colonial
and elite nationalist groups. Reviled in Indian nationalist and British colonial history writing, they symbolized the ills of urbanization and even the
subjugation of India—Indian legislators viewed prostitutes as the nation's
shame, associating female purity with the nation's honor. Prostitutes also
figured in colonial police records relating to arrests and imprisonment, as
well as in residential campaigns to "clean up" neighborhoods; city administrators and residents welcomed laws that could either ban prostitution or
banish it to a defined area of the city. Despite, and perhaps because of, the
marginal social status of prostitutes, official sources such as police files, census and survey data, and high court trials sporadically provide rich, chilling
details about them, indicating the social reformist zeal in targeting this population, "whose conditions of life were a source of moral and material danger to themselves and to others" (Asad 2002, 79).

Subaltern studies assumes that the recovery of subaltern voices is arduous
because such voices were often inaudible to official record keepers. When
it comes to Indian prostitutes in Bombay, however, the methodological
difficulty lies not in the paucity of information but instead in the unsym-
pathetic forms of official attention that they received. The criminal or near
criminal status (depending on prevailing legal currents) of prostitutes meant
that the state rendered them permanently dubious personages. Their ability
to represent themselves was strictly curtailed. Social welfare organizations,
meanwhile, approached this constituency as a homogeneously tragic group,
visible only through a lens of pity. The voices of prostitutes, for the most
part, remained undocumented, and prostitutes rarely emerged as concrete
people, with aspirations, difficulties, and pleasures, who had to often risk
their lives in order to earn a living.

The dilemma for feminist historical research thus becomes how to interpret the available official records on prostitutes. The motives of the official
authorities who constructed records about prostitutes must be foregrounded

even as any information is retrieved. My aim in this chapter is to grapple with two kinds of sources—court and sociological survey records—and to make explicit what they tell us about Indian prostitutes circa the 1920s. This chapter is thus organized according to the type of sources used to address questions about Indian brothel life. The first section focuses on testimonies from a 1917 High Court trial of a brothel keeper for the murder of a brothel worker, Akootai. The widely circulated details of this case contributed to the subsequent abolitionist climate in Bombay; the case is often referred to as the "Duncan Road murder case" in social workers' reports and newspaper articles. The court testimonies in this case provide a glimpse into the living circumstances in brothels. Relying on the testimonies of other brothel workers, I reconstruct the details of the case from the perspective of the murder victim, Akootai.

The second half of the chapter explores the question of how typical a brothel inmate Akootai was. I turn to sociological data on brothels in Bombay to address this question: I review questionnaires and tables produced by the Prostitution Committee formed in the wake of the 1917 trial. This committee was composed of representatives of social welfare organizations and the police, and it combined questionnaire, observation, and census data. I also look at records of organizations devoted to combating trafficking. The general information on women's background and living conditions within Indian brothels provides a vivid confirmation that Akootai's life was not an anomaly.

THE DUNCAN ROAD MURDER TRIAL

Although Indian prostitutes rarely represented themselves in official records, the 1917 High Court murder case, *Emperor v. Syed Mirza,* is something of a stunning exception (HD 1917a). It contains witness statements made by numerous brothel workers before the presiding magistrate. Their transcribed voices convey a remarkable clarity, although their accounts were undoubtedly mediated by translation into English, and probably amplified for shock value. The voluminous statements, with details about how long they worked in the day, how much they earned, and what their relationships were to each other, make it clear that the prosecutors and presiding magistrate were deeply interested in exploring the milieu of brothel life. The specifics of the murder, including the victim's failed attempt at escaping the brothel, and the gory methods of torture that her murderers used, all incited intense public voyeurism. I came across the witness depositions when paging through the indices of annual police records and was unexpectedly moved to tears—within the hushed confines of the archives—by the poignancy of the murder victim's story. The circumstances of her death became an occasion for thinking about the possibilities and limitations of such a life.

I will begin by recounting key details of the case.[2] The murder victim was a brothel worker named Akootai, and the accused were her brothel keepers Syedkhan Mirza and his two accomplices Gangabai and Gomtibai. These brothel keepers supervised five women totally: Akootai, Phooli, Moti, Paru, and Jijabai. They did so in three rooms in a building on Hajam Lane in the Duncan Road area. Tarabai, an older woman, cooked for them all. The brothel keepers also rented space in a house across the street, in which they, along with the six women, slept and ate their food. The neighborhood consisted of several multistoried buildings in which groups of rooms were rented out as brothels. The rooms that Akootai and others worked in were on the ground floor of their building; their barred windows in front gave them the appearance of being cages. People on the street could view the women inside through the bars. The brothel workers used the verb "to sit" (in translation) to refer to their main activity of awaiting and servicing clients. Akootai thus "sat" in her compartment with Paru, while Phooli and Moti shared the adjoining compartment and Jijabai, Tarabai, and Gomtibai sat in the third room.[3] Phooli, Moti and Paru, who were more heavily supervised than Jijabai, provided the lengthiest witness statements. Their statements corroborate the details of Akootai's death quite consistently.

The story, as told by various witnesses, goes like this. For a number of days prior to Akootai's death on February 20, 1917, Akootai had been stricken with venereal sores. According to Paru, who shared Akootai's room, Akootai had a swelling and burning sensation in her genitals that prevented her from sleeping at night and caused her to doze during the day. The pain and exhaustion made it difficult for her to accept customers. For some four or five days she had refused several customers, often running into altercations with them. Meanwhile, Paru took on customers whom Akootai had refused. Akootai's refusals irked her supervisors Mirza, Gangabai, and Gomtibai, and they repeatedly assaulted Akootai for turning men down. They also attempted to get rid of the problem of the venereal sores on their own: on two occasions, they tied Akootai to the bed and gagged her

while applying lunar caustic, a chemical used in the treatment of gonorrhea, to her genitals. They assumed it would either burn off the sores or numb the pain. When she cried out, they punched her and pinched her genitals.

By the evening of February 16, Akootai had been through days of such pain. After accepting three customers, Akootai finally refused her fourth customer. When the customer complained, Gomtibai, her supervisor, suggested that he "sodomize" Akootai instead. Akootai reacted with such strong fear to the suggestion that the man changed his mind and decided to leave. Akootai's protests were so strong that the man left without asking for his money to be returned. This is a detail that almost every brothel worker—Phooli, Paru, and Jija—mentioned and it indicates their eagerness to dispel any blaming of Akootai for the events that followed.

[handwritten margin note: man left w/o asking for his ？ back]

Although Akootai's refusal had not cost the brothel any money, Gomtibai proceeded to hit Akootai repeatedly with a wooden stick and a large iron nail. It was this beating that apparently drove Akootai to desperation: when Gomtibai next went to the toilet, Akootai attempted to escape the brothel. She told the woman holding the key to her compartment, Tara, that she had a customer waiting outside. When let out, Akootai ran down the dark lane. Tara cried out an alarm, and Mirza and two male neighbors set out after Akootai immediately. They caught her before she got very far.

That night, Mirza, Gangabai, and Gomtibai tortured Akootai as a punishment for her attempted escape and as a warning to other brothel inmates. They assaulted Akootai with their fists, a metal yard measure, and a curry stone;[4] they branded her with lit matches and made her bathe in scalding water. They removed her clothes and pulled her hair. Her cries for mercy could be heard by everyone around. By the next morning, her ribs were broken, she could no longer walk, and she was breathing heavily and hardly able to speak. Jija noted that the only words she heard from Akootai at that point were "I will not run away now." Late into the afternoon, Gangabai and Gomtibai continued to beat Akootai, forcing her to eat onion skins and denying her food and water. When Akootai asked, at one point, for soda water to quell the burning in her stomach, Gangabai handed her a glass of urine instead. She then fell unconscious. Gangabai tried to force-feed her liquor to revive her, but to no avail, and Akootai died soon after. When Mirza arrived on the scene, he took stock of the situation and immediately began to arrange for her burial. He circulated instructions to the others to say that Akootai had died of venereal disease and rheumatism.

He ordered material for wrapping her corpse and hired men to come in to carry her corpse to the morgue.

He was just leaving the brothel behind the men carrying out Akootai's corpse when Vithoo Jagoji, a police *hawaldar* (constable) who lived in the Two Tanks area close to the brothel, sighted them. As Jagoji related it, he and his police companion were walking through Hajam Lane when they noticed a wrapped corpse being carried out of a brothel, followed by a man. When the man following the corpse (Mirza) suddenly turned around and started walking in the opposite direction, the policemen grew suspicious. They stopped to question the man and ordered the corpse bearers to carry the corpse back to the brothel for investigation. Following information provided by others in the brothel, the police called in their inspector to the scene and took the man, Mirza, to the police station for questioning and also arrested Gangabai and Gomtibai. The police inspector sent the corpse in for a postmortem, which later stated that broken ribs were the likely cause of Akootai's death, and that the body was marked by severe bruises, welts, and caustic burn marks.

This case raises several questions. Was this incident an anomaly? Did the brothel keepers intend to kill their worker or was it a case of disciplining gone awry? What drove Akootai, in particular, to try to escape? And while this official record was structured to elicit condemnation of the killers and sympathy for the victim, is there a way to recuperate a sense of Akootai and her fellow inmates as anything other than undifferentiated victims?

Some of the statements from Akootai's companions in the brothel suggest that the brothel keepers had used similar methods to discipline all the women. Phooli mentioned that Mirza and Gangabai made the brothel workers drink his urine if they refused to submit to customers; she had been forced to do so twice. All the workers stated that the brothel keepers assaulted them every second or third day if their earnings fell below expectations. Moti mentioned that Mirza once dislocated her right elbow. The threat of being beaten with a curry stone, it appears, drove her to accept even low-paying customers. Akootai was regularly beaten for not submitting to customers. Her punishment in this case was clearly meant to be an example to others: the brothel keepers brought all the other inmates up to the room where they were beating Akootai with a curry stone and yard measure, threatening that they would treat the others similarly if any of them tried to escape. When Moti began to cry upon witnessing Mirza hitting

Akootai with a stick, Mirza hit Moti as well and removed all her gold ornaments. He told her that it was a way to prevent her from running away. Thus this episode was part of a string of violent incidents aimed at keeping the brothel workers afraid of their supervisors.

Phooli, Moti, Paru, and Akootai were effectively prisoners in the brothel—they were locked in the barred rooms on the ground floor, where they received customers during both day and night. They slept five to a room and under lock and key; they were even accompanied to the toilet. They saw about nine men per night, although one of them claimed she saw up to fifty men a day.[5] They charged about three to four annas (a quarter rupee) per customer and earned about three rupees a day for their brothel keeper. Mirza in turn paid only three rupees in rent per day for his brothel, according to his rent collector.[6] Gomtibai confiscated all the earnings of the women; the boarding, clothes, and ornaments were all that the inmates considered their reward.

The brothel workers in turn highly cherished their clothes and ornaments: Phooli quite piteously explained that Mirza used to buy ornaments for the brothel workers because there was no one else who could buy them for them. Jewelry, which in South Asian society has served as not only a means of beautification but also a repository of saved wealth, was hence perceived by the brothel workers as an appropriate type of reward, however meager. Akootai's neighbor Phooli was able to recount exactly the number and type of ornaments—bangles, necklace, nose ring, anklets—that Akootai wore when she tried to escape the brothel. The locks on compartment doors also loomed large in the brothel workers' lives: when shown three locks on exhibit, Phooli was able to identify the lock used for Akootai's compartment, for her own compartment, and that for another inmate. Even in their brief interactions outside the brothel, the inmates continued to fear their brothel keeper: Moti, another neighbor of Akootai, recounted that when she went to a bonesetter to nurse an elbow that Mirza had dislocated, she told the bonesetter that the injury had occurred because of a fall, not Mirza's assault.

How did Mirza maintain such a high level of control over the brothel workers? One source of his power was his alternate activity as a moneylender. The witnesses' accounts provide insights into their perceptions of his power. Phooli, Moti, and Paru each believed that they were bonded to Syed Mirza because of the money they had borrowed and because he had taken their thumbprints when they entered the brothel. Phooli came under his control because of twenty rupees she had borrowed from him—Mirza's brother had brought her to this brothel to pay it off. She had remained there for seven months. In Paru's case, Mirza paid off her debt to another man when she began working in his brothel; she had been enticed away from another brothel on Duncan Road by Mirza's brother, who claimed he would keep her as his mistress. Moti was sold for fifty rupees to Mirza by a former paramour.

It is a measure of the terror Mirza wielded that various witnesses remained fearful about their debts to him even when testifying in court. Lingabai, who worked in another brothel, ended her statement with the unsolicited information that she had borrowed "5 rupees from Syed Mirza at the rate of 4 *annas* as interest per month per rupee" and that she had "paid the amount off 8–15 days before getting the liquor for Gangabai." Naikoo, a cousin of Akootai, repeated in his testimony that he "had paid Mirza off" and that "he no longer owed him any money."[7] The recurrent references to money owed and repaid indicate the crushing weight of debt in their lives. The witnesses seem to have been worried that the court would hold them liable for their debt and hence be sympathetic to the moneylender. Their fear that being indebted would justify the violence against them speaks volumes about the prevailing regime of debt they lived under.

Mirza exerted control over his brothel workers in less direct ways as well. The familial relationship he shared with the other supervisors Gangabai and Gomtibai contributed to the tight discipline within the brothel. Although the brothel inmates referred to Mirza and Ganga as a married couple, the latter's sworn testimony indicates that they were not officially married. Gangabai was Mirza's wife by a *nikah* (Muslim customary ceremony), and although she belonged to a Hindu caste by birth, she was also given a Muslim name as a sign of her new status. Gomtibai, whom everyone referred to as Gangabai's daughter, belonged to a different caste from Gangabai (and was thus likely to have been adopted by her) and was also given a Muslim name. While such adopting of Muslim identities was common among dancing girls and hijras, because being Muslim assured one of a decent burial regardless of caste or class (Edwardes 1910), in this instance it is also indicative of their intimate relationship with Mirza. Despite their lack of official status as a family, these characters present an egregious version of the brothel run as a family business. The brothel rooms were rented in Gangabai's name, and hence Mirza was her partner in running the brothel. The brothel workers lived and slept in the same room with them as if they were a single household and accepted their authority as they might have a parent's. The brothel workers also shared siblinglike relations because of their enforced closeness. As seen from their consistent and sympathetic descriptions of her torture, the brothel workers were clearly close to Akootai, as she had been at the brothel longer than any of them, for two years. Indeed, the name "Akootai" combines the word for "older sister" in two languages—*akka* (from Kannada) and *tai* (from Marathi).[8] Perhaps she became their elder sister by virtue of being in the brothel longest, before their arrival. In other words, familylike relations reinforced structures of obligation and domination in this brothel (Tambe 2006).

There is one anecdote in the testimony that provides an added dimension of complexity to Akootai's personality and family life. Akootai's cousin Naikoo, who visited the brothel regularly, narrated to the court that a few weeks before Akootai's death, he had gone there searching for his missing wife. Soon after he found his wife on the third floor, Mirza appeared on the scene and hit Naikoo with a curry stone and told him that his wife had been bought from another man. Naikoo reports that Akootai also appeared at the time and "struck him with a stick," asking him why he had come there. This throwaway line in Naikoo's testimony is a most intriguing fragment that raises several questions about Akootai. Was Akootai upset because Naikoo had sought to reclaim his wife? Was she punishing him for beating his wife, as one of the witnesses insinuated he did? Was she aligning herself with Mirza in delivering punishment to her cousin? Or did she have a prior grievance, such as Naikoo's possibly having sold her to Mirza in order to pay off his own debts? Naikoo realizes that such questions may have occurred to his listeners, for he goes on to declare to the court that Akootai had worked at the brothel for longer than he had known Mirza, and that she had a husband (whose name he had forgotten) in Kela, in Kolhapur state. This declaration that Akootai was married may have been his way of indicating that he had no sexual relationship with her. But for us, it raises other questions. Had Akootai run away from her putative husband? From Naikoo's account, we can gather that she had worked in Mirza's brothel as part of a stable arrangement. Had she managed to survive for two years in this brothel on better terms with the brothel keepers? The length of her stay and her robust behavior toward Naikoo suggest that she may possibly have been on better terms with her supervisors at one point. The brothel keepers' aims could also have been to seriously wound, rather than kill, Akootai. Gangabai, for instance, appeared frightened of Mirza's reaction when Akootai died. She did not explain her role in Akootai's death to Mirza when he arrived upon the scene and found Akootai unconscious. He asked Gangabai, "What have you done?" and Gangabai remained silent.[9] She then lied to him that Akootai had gone to the brothel and received liquor from a customer and she further suggested that Akootai was only pretending to be unconscious.[10] However, when he kicked Akootai and found her to be immobile with her teeth set, he headed off to obtain a pass for her burial from a local municipal official, or *ramoshi*.[11] The *ramoshi* who arrived upon the scene to register the death did not inquire too deeply into the cause of the death and the state of the corpse. Gangabai's dissimulation continued: she declared to the *ramoshi* that the dead woman was a pauper and that out of charity she would pay five rupees for the burial. She even asked Mirza to give the man four annas "for tea," an implicit bribe.[12] Later, when a police inspector and his superintendent visited the brothel house to collect evidence, Gangabai portrayed distress—she quite dramatically dashed her head against the ground and the wall. Her behavior suggests that she was quite fearful about the consequences of her actions. Mirza, on the other hand, remained calm. Even in the aftermath of Akootai's death, he continued intimidating those whose assistance he needed. He approached four Maratha coolies in the neighborhood to carry the corpse and lied to them that Akootai belonged to the Maratha caste (because her Mahar identity would have rendered her untouchable to them). When they insisted on bringing the dead body down to the road for tying up with cloth, he threatened them and said that he had had four corpses taken from upstairs before this. The mention of these four corpses, if true, tells us that Mirza had presided over, if not caused, four other deaths in the brothel.

This case came to light because two policemen happened to pass by the brothel on their way home after duty at night. Such an encounter was not in itself unusual. Constables were often drawn from the class of mill workers who resided in the neighborhood of Kamathipura (Chandavarkar 1998). In this case, Vithoo Jagoji, the policeman who first suspected Mirza, lived in the Two Tanks area, to the immediate southeast of Kamathipura. Indian constables were very much a part of this milieu, sometimes even having paramours working in the sex trade. For instance, an annual police report from 1921 mentions that a constable named Dhunji Deoji was searching for his mistress in the first lane of Kamathipura when he found a dead body (ARPTIB 1921, 5). It is actually remarkable that more such crimes did not get reported. Only six other murder cases of prostitutes can be found in police records from 1860 to 1947, none of them containing as much detail as the Akootai case.[13]

The historical record about this case is rich largely because of the statements provided by the Akootai's coworkers. Although the threat from Mirza's strongmen subdued them in their regular lives, at the time of presenting their testimony before the magistrate they were voluble in their denunciations of Mirza; they were desperate to ensure a guilty verdict. At the end of the trial, Mirza and Gangabai were convicted and executed, while Gomtibai was sentenced to life in prison. Thanks to the detailed and consistent testimonies, Akootai's story figures in official texts as a striking example of resistance to brothel discipline. By turning away customers despite the constant violence from her supervisors, and indeed in trying to escape the brothel, she displayed remarkable spirit. The fact that she died as a consequence of torture is also a testament to her disobedience.

Akootai's murder stands apart from the other six recorded murder cases in that it was the only trial to be reported extensively in newspapers. Newspapers relished in decrying the circumstances of Akootai's death, using hyperbolic phrases such as "reproach to civilization" (*Bombay Chronicle,* April 6, 1917) and "shameful blot on civilization" (*Indian Social Reformer,* April 22, 1917). The *Bombay Chronicle* helpfully informed its public that it had not reported on the "unprintable horrors" of the case because "it would be impossible in a public report to give an adequate account of its entirely unmitigated enormity" (April 6, 1917). It went on to provide quite a few details, nonetheless. The heavy reportage of the Akootai case drew on a prevailing panic about Pathans, the ethnic group to which Mirza belonged.[14] Pathans (also called Pashtuns) drew their lineage from southern Afghanistan and were classified, problematically, as a "criminal tribe" in the early part of the twentieth century in Bombay.[15] Chandavarkar (1998) notes that they were commonly portrayed as greedy moneylenders who forced the wives of debtors into prostitution and engaged in thievery; he reports an entrenched protection racket in which shopkeepers hired gangs of Pathan "watchmen" to protect their establishments from attacks by other Pathans

(1998, 194, 197). The details of Syed Mirza's ethnic background and occupation as a moneylender, and the circumstances under which women joined his brothel confirmed such views; this case convinced many onlookers that the root of the problem was the criminal propensity of a community.

The frequent reporting of this case and the careful transcription of the testimonies indicates its status as a spectacle. From British administrators' point of view, the general meaning that this trial made possible was that large numbers of Indians were wretched and unworthy of the self-rule that nationalists were increasingly demanding. The police administration framed its response in such terms, with police commissioner F. A. M. Vincent declaring that they were "dealing with a class steeped in abysmal ignorance, people whose social and moral fabric is elemental, not to say barbaric"; the police force could not be expected to control this class with its "low state of evolution" (HD 1917a). Instead of providing the means by which cases like Akootai's could be prevented, Vincent tried to illustrate through further examples the "barbarity" of such Indians: a husband who abandoned his wife suffering from rabies at the door of a hospital and a woman who died from burns inflicted by her husband. The urban subaltern, in other words, was plainly undeserving of state resources.

Nationalist reformers used this case to decry the police's ineffectuality and to propose new laws controlling prostitution. They accused the police of insufficient action: D. E. Wacha, who coordinated a call for further investigation into urban prostitution, surmised that similar acts had probably been committed before but not revealed.[16] Newspapers such as the *Bombay Chronicle* noted that Akootai "was only one wretched woman among hundreds . . . many others . . . may even have met with such an end as hers" (April 6, 1917).

To what extent was Akootai a typical brothel inmate of her time? It is possible to address this question by turning to census figures and the report of the Prostitution Committee set up in the wake of the trial. This committee, composed of the bishop and archbishop of Bombay, the commissioner of police, the municipal commissioner, the philanthropist Jamsetji Jeejeebhoy, influential lawyers, medical professionals, army professionals, Salvation Army office holders, and a member of the legislative council, formulated a questionnaire on the scope and scale of prostitution and distributed it to social workers, military administrators, public health professionals, and missionaries (RCP 1922, M7). The main text of their report and the responses to the committee's questionnaires elucidated various features of brothel workers' lives. In the following sections, I analyze its information on the birthplaces, literacy, and caste, health, and living arrangements of prostitutes. When read together, this information suggests that the circumstances of Akootai's life were not unusual.

SOCIOLOGICAL NARRATIVES

ORIGINS AND BACKGROUND

Akootai hailed from Kolhapur state, to the south of Bombay presidency, according to her cousin Naikoo (HD 1917a). Like Akootai, the majority of Indian women in Bombay's brothels were not born in the city in this period. Table 5, compiled from 1921 census figures, shows that of the 2,995 reported female prostitutes, only 460 listed their birth district as being Bombay city. They typically came from regions such as Deccan, Ratnagiri, and Goa to the south and Hyderabad state to the east. It makes sense that the largest number of women came from the Deccan and coastal areas of Ratnagiri and Goa; regular seasonal migration occurred from these areas to Bombay, structured around the availability of farming work (Chandavarkar 1998). At times women came from regions as far away as Kashmir, Punjab in the north, and Bengal in the west. Many of these brothel inmates who, like Akootai, sought to run away from brothels would have found themselves in a city where the languages spoken were not the same as in their birth districts. Brothel keepers were able to wield great control over their workers because of the latter's distance from their birthplaces and social networks.

Census numbers differ in some important ways from the findings of the questionnaires sent out by the Prostitution Committee. Although the census table only lists seven women from Europe, Dr. J. E. Sandilands and Captain J. A. De Souza reported in the questionnaire records that they found 50 European prostitutes out of the 545 women they investigated in 243 brothels (HD 1921a, 348). This discrepancy between census and private survey data underscores the motives of census officials: they were not driven to report high numbers of European prostitutes, as administrators in Britain would have viewed a high number with alarm.

The large number of dependents for prostitutes hailing from outside Bombay in Table 5 suggests that women moved to, and settled in, Bombay

TABLE 5. Birth districts or countries of female prostitutes, their dependents, procurers, and brothel keepers in Bombay city, 1921

Birthplace	Prostitutes	Dependents	Procurers and brothel keepers
Ajmer-Merwara	1	0	6
Arabia	5	0	0
Baroda	4	0	4
Bengal	11	0	0
Bombay city	460	44	106
British districts of Deccan	827	127	43
British districts of Gujarat	68	0	12
British districts of Karnatak	71	0	16
Burma	1	0	0
Central Provinces	39	1	9
China	5	0	1
Cutch	10	0	2
Delhi and Punjab	88	3	8
Egypt	8	0	0
England	1	0	1
France	5	0	0
Goa	510	225	137
Gwalior	0	0	3
Hyderabad State	183	26	9
Japan	45	0	0
Kanara	48	14	13
Kashmir	41	0	0
Kathiawar	53	10	5
Kolaba	51	0	4
Kolhapur	50	8	6
Madras, Mysore, Cochin	16	0	1
Palanpur	0	0	1
Rajputana	38	0	6
Ratnagiri	306	38	76
Russia	1	0	0
Savantwadi	14	34	15
Sind	11	0	5
Thana	4	0	5
Turkey in Asia	17	0	1

Source: Census of India 1921, vol. 9, part 1, section 20, table 3.

with their children. The table also indicates that procurers hailed from similar places of origin as prostitutes, particularly Goa, Ratnagiri, and Deccan. Procurers relied on their personal networks in their birth districts to draw in new women. The Prostitution Committee concluded that procurers bought girls from impoverished parents who abandoned their daughters due to "famine" and the "expense of marriage and dowries" (RCP 1922, M9). Once in Bombay, brothel keepers placed girls and women in debt bondage and confiscated their meager earnings (RCP 1922).

LITERACY AND CASTE

Brothel keepers maintained women in bondage through spurious techniques such as taking thumbprints. As we see from the testimony of Akootai's coworkers, brothel inmates assumed that these thumbprints were enormously significant; their low literacy levels compounded the tyranny of brothel keepers. About nine out of ten Indian prostitutes were unschooled, a far higher percentage than in the general female population: 160 per 1,000 females were literate, while 95 per 1,000 prostitutes were literate.[17] These literacy levels are the closest reflection of prostitutes' disadvantaged background, since the census tables do not provide details on family income or occupation. Table 6 highlights distinctions between European and other prostitutes: the few prostitutes from Europe were found to be literate, while those from all other areas were recorded as largely illiterate.

The other major indicator of women's social status is caste, which colonial officials recorded in minute terms, in keeping with the colonial obsession with classification (Cohn 1996). The majority of Hindu prostitutes belonged to lowest orders in the caste hierarchy, such as Kunbis, Mahars,

TABLE 6. Literacy among prostitutes according to country of birth, Bombay city, 1921

Country of birth	Total	Literate	Illiterate
British India	2,398	255	2143
Goa	510	20	490
Arabia, Turkey, Egypt	30	0	30
China and Japan	50	3	47
Europe	7	7	0
Total	2,995	285	2,710

Source: Census of India 1921, vol. 9, section 20, table 6.

and Dheds.[18] They also belonged to groups that dedicated girls to temples and were professional dancers and singers such as Kalavantins, Bhavins, and Naikins; castes of roving entertainers such as Kolhatis; and descendants of slaves captured in war, Bandis.[19]

HEALTH

Venereal sores, the immediate provocation for Akootai's revolt, were a very common problem. The Report of the Prostitution Committee found a widespread and growing incidence of syphilis and gonorrhea. Table 7 presents statistics for the incidence of venereal disease in the E ward of the city, which included areas tolerating brothels, such as Kamathipura, and its neighboring areas Nagpada, Byculla, and Mazagaon.

In municipal dispensaries and hospitals in this part of the city, a considerable percentage of those who came to be treated for other diseases showed signs of venereal disease. An astounding 30 percent of the total outpatients at the J.J. Hospital were infected with venereal disease. Yet the stigma attached to the disease was so widespread that there was no hospital in Bombay at which a VD sufferer could "count upon reception as an in-patient" (RCP 1922, M10). Racial distinctions were drawn in particularly acute terms in this respect: while upper-rung European prostitutes could count on private doctors' visits to their brothel houses, Indian prostitutes had to rely on the spurious methods used by brothel keepers to treat

TABLE 7. Incidence of venereal disease in selected hospitals of the E ward of Bombay

Hospital	Number of patients	Percentage of total patients with VD	Percentage admitted to treat VD	Percentage of other patients discovered with VD
J.J. Hospital	3146	29.8	13.1	16.7
Bellasis Rd.	293	30.7	3.8	26.9
Foras Rd.	56	26.7	7.1	19.6
Motlibai Women's	197	28.1	23	5.1
Motlibai Children's	98	0	0	18.3

Source: Appendix D, *Report of the Committee on Prostitution in Bombay,* 1922, M19. The figures were collected by the League for Combating Venereal Disease.

Note: The Bellasis Road and Foras Road hospitals are municipal dispensaries. Patients at Motlibai Children's Hospital were afflicted with congenital syphilis.

them, such as the application of "caustic" to their genitalia reported in Akootai's murder trial.

The Report of the Committee on Prostitution recommended that adequate free medical care be provided to prostitutes. Although the Women's Venereal Disease Clinic financed by the Bombay Municipality could be found on Lamington Road, it did not run smoothly. In 1927, observers found that brothel keepers prevented infected workers from continuing medical treatment at this clinic because of the loss of earning time. Brothel keepers usually "refused the offers of hospital accommodation" extended to their inmates, and opposed efforts to secure regular attendance of women for examination and treatment (GD 1927–28b, M156).

LIVING ARRANGEMENTS

Indian brothels were domestic spaces where women lived with dependent children and their elderly. The Report of the Prostitution Committee characterized Indian prostitutes as leading "semi-family lives . . . with . . . young dependent children" (GD 1922, M3). According to the 1921 census, in areas of the city dominated by working-class Indian residents, such as Girgaon, Fanaswadi, and Khetwadi, prostitutes each had about one dependent. However, in segregated areas such as Kamathipura and Tardeo, the ratio of dependents to prostitutes was 1 in 34 or 1 in 33. The Report of the Prostitution Committee analyzed this difference as evidence that the character of the sex trade in Bombay had undergone recent changes. The 1921 census section on "Prostitution in Bombay" also noted a qualitatively new type of prostitution, where women had far fewer dependents. The steady inflow of single women from other regions into the trade could have contributed to this ratio in the segregated areas. Still, many prostitutes were literally at home in brothels, having been born there.

Children of brothel workers tended to join the profession owing to the paucity of alternatives. In 1922, the report of a committee of social reformers noted that "young dependent children . . . if girls, are inevitably turned to the trade" (GD 1922, M3). As police and social workers' records very rarely report on the welfare of sons of prostitutes, it is difficult to get a clear sense of what happened to boys. Only four cases of reported trafficking in police records from 1924 to 1934 involved boys (HD 1927a, 55, 56; HD 1928a, 70, 71). The offenses involving male trafficking victims were described as imitating the patterns of enticement used in cases involving girls. A reasonable surmise is that male children also entered the sex trade as pimps or in businesses directly supporting brothels such as music, tailoring, or laundering. Although music was a prominent option for male children of courtesans, it may not have been available for children of all brothel workers. Male petty traders certainly had a noticeable physical presence on the principal streets in Kamathipura, as "barbers . . . tea shop owners . . . ice-cream hawkers . . . picture sellers . . . and magicians" (Krishnan 1923, 38–59). Such options possibly allowed sons to remain in the proximity of their families. Official accounts stress the pervasive presence of nonclient men in brothels, casting them all as auxiliaries: "Males living on the earnings of [prostitutes] were about as numerous as the women themselves, according to the Police. The men acted as pimps and servants in some cases, in other cases they victimized the girls" (HD 1932, 16).

Social workers viewed it as a challenge that daughters of brothel workers entered prostitution automatically.[20] The Bombay Vigilance Association and the League of Mercy extensively intervened in brothel-based families and regularly competed with prostitute mothers' authority as parents. In one case, the Bombay Vigilance Association tried to send a girl whose mother "was leading a bad life" to a "training Home," but the mother took her out "on the pretence of getting her married" (HD 1927a, 101). The League of Mercy similarly trained its vision on mothers who were prostitutes. In 1926, it reported on one mother who "[drank] and led a bad life" and who was purportedly "planning her eldest girl's ruin." The organization tried to remove the girl from her mother's custody and place her in a boarding school but could only put her in the custody of relatives. We then are told that the mother broke a promise and took the girl away (HD 1927a, 71). In another case, the League of Mercy managed to send off the children of a nurse to boarding school, because the mother was declared to be "a well-known procuress . . . with many girl victims" (HD 1927a, 71). Occasionally, however, such efforts were counterproductive: a 1932 report of a Prostitution Commission mentions that

> Sometimes the only result of detaining a girl in a home was that she returned to the brothel as a more accompl[i]shed and educated girl and thus more attractive to customers. A case was related to the Commission of a prostitute woman suggesting to her young daughter to resort to a rescue institution to be able to earn more in prostitution. (HD 1932, 22)

That social workers were so unsuccessful in detaching children from prostitute mothers speaks to the strength of the emotional bonds, or at least the maternal prerogative, in brothels.

Physically, brothels were not independent buildings as much as groups of rooms rented by brothel keepers. The rooms themselves were usually a part of a two- or three-story structure known as a chawl. In the first two decades of the twentieth century, the cityscape of Bombay was transformed by chawls. Chawls were a product of Bombay's urban planning, in that they were expressly built to house working-class families—those of mill workers, dockers, and construction workers (Edwardes 1910; Hazareesingh 2001). The typical unit of living space in a chawl was a one-room tenement, which contained a sleeping space, a hearth, and a washing area. The City Improvement Trust constructed 9,311 such tenements between 1909 and 1918 (Hazareesingh 2001). The average size of a room was 12 x 8 x 8 feet, and it was typically divided by a partition within. The average living space for brothel inmates, according to the Prostitution Committee Report, was a room slightly larger than this average chawl room. It was about 150 square feet with an attached smaller room in which the women cooked and ate. At times, twelve women were confined within such a room (RCP 1922, M10). A photograph taken inside an Indian brothel on Cursetji Sukhlaji Street by Dr. K. S. Patel (mentioned in chapter 1) depicts an even larger room of about twenty by fifteen feet, with four single beds and less than a foot's width between beds. At one end of the room there is a tap used for cooking and washing purposes. The notes accompanying the photograph also note that the *dhoti* (wrap) of the male was slung across the top of bedposts as a curtain (HD1921c). This kind of shared brothel space made for a form of sexual commerce that lay at one end of the scale of discreetness, in the terminology mentioned in note 1 of the Introduction.

Chawl living was inherently communal and crowded. The one-room tenements each opened out on to a common verandah in which were located taps and latrines.[21] Even with its minimal amenities and space, the average monthly rent for a room ranged from three-and-a half to five rupees, which often surpassed the means of mill workers. Hence chawls did not solve the problem of inadequate housing for working classes. Bombay's population growth between 1901 and 1921 led to what Hazareesingh (2001, 247) terms a "housing famine" in the years following World War I. In such conditions, brothels served not simply as spaces where sexual services were

rendered but also spaces of potential rest for working-class clients—a phenomenon also observed by White (1990) in the context of colonial Nairobi.

A peculiar feature of some buildings such as Akootai's were the barred
doors on their ground floor rooms, which gave them the appearance of
cages. Police introduced these bars in the 1890s in order to prevent disturbances, because men milled around the front of brothels. As the rooms
opened onto the streets, the bars forced men to form lines outside rather
than overwhelm the women (Edwardes 1923, 93–94). The Report of the
Prostitution Committee found that by the 1920s, however, that the bars
also "screened women from unwelcome attention of the police" (RCP 1922,
M9). However, the cages themselves functioned to incite voyeurism. A
passage from O. U. Krishnan's *Night Side of Bombay*, in its walking tour
of major streets of Kamathipura, described the cages thus:

> In these cages . . . half a dozen women of various ages and in a bewildering
> variety of diseases . . . sit ravenously peering out through the iron bars of the
> doors extending unsolicited and solicited invitations to the passers-by . . .
> In front of every door [you find] a crowd of hooligans of the worst type . . .
> peering in, as if they are viewing a menagerie of curious animals from some
> unknown land yet undiscovered. (Krishnan 1923, 45–46)

The simultaneous function of brothels as domestic and work spaces meant
that family life and prostitution were not experienced as mutually incom-
patible domains. Brothel inmates developed quasi-sibling relationships because of their forced intimacy and common struggles, as in Akootai's brothel.
Relatives of prostitutes moved in and out of brothels with ease. Some relatives of brothel workers (such as Naikoo) retained long-standing relations
with brothel keepers and visited brothels on repeated occasions, sometimes
even to retrieve family members. Thus, ties of actual and fictive kinship ran
across and within the walls of brothels, facilitating the entry of new brothel
workers and disciplining existing workers. Marriage did not provide a bul-
wark against, or even preclude, prostitution.

THE RESONANCE OF AKOOTAI'S DEATH

While Akootai's life speaks to us through multiple, highly mediated sources,
her death doubtlessly produced unexpected effects. The very cruelty of her

murder served as a focal point for abolitionist energies, and the Duncan Road case became a standard referent in calls for legal reform. Her collectively spoken subaltern voice—for it was Akootai's brothel inmates who represented her—became an indirect means for living brothel workers to protest their own treatment. At the same time, her story circulated widely because the key perpetrator, Syed Mirza, conformed to prevailing narratives of Pathan criminality. All in all, this story confirmed for the police the general abjectness of Indian underclasses and spurred bourgeois Indian residents to launch the legislative "rescue" of similarly placed women.

The grisly details of Akootai's murder were linked to the unchecked power of brothel keepers and the prevailing common conditions of indebtedness, illiteracy, and illness. As shown in the survey data, many prostitutes such as Akootai were from other parts of the country, lived in tenements very much like hers, were untrained in reading, and suffered poor health. When the police used Akootai's story to publicize the enormity of abuse by brothel keepers, they disingenuously ignored how colonial policies were responsible for the power of brothel keepers. As explained in chapters 2 and 3, during periods of regulation and antitrafficking, the police tacitly supported brothel keepers' power as a means to preserve order in brothels.

Akootai's death served as a fillip for those seeking to outlaw prostitution. Newspapers such as the *Times of India, Bombay Chronicle,* and the *Indian Social Reformer* called for setting up an inquiry into conditions in brothels in Bombay. The committee in turn proposed new legislation, which emerged as the Bombay Prevention of Prostitution Act. The next chapter elaborates this history.

c h a p t e r 5

Abolition and Nationalism

Episodes such as the Duncan Road murder trial are rarely the sole cause of new phases in legislation. More typically, they play the role of crystallizing public sentiments that already point in an aligned direction. In Bombay, for instance, there were already currents of public opinion and lawmaking that favored abolishing prostitution. Demographic shifts and urban crowding had engendered anxieties about the moral regulation of public spaces. The trial also coincided with the gathering strength of nationalism, whose ideological construction of Indian womanhood presented a ground on which to contest existing colonial policies on prostitution. The details of Akootai's death ignited public antipathy toward the world of brothels and propelled efforts to write a comprehensive stand-alone law, the Bombay Prevention of Prostitution Act. This chapter explores the wider moral, political, and demographic context that produced the abolitionist phase in Bombay's laws on prostitution. Tracing the checkered story of the enforcement of this law, it also shows how abolition, like regulation, could not solve the problem of violence against prostitutes. A closer look at police and prison records, at the end of the chapter, underscores the broad pattern of criminalizing prostitutes that characterized Bombay's sex trade.

REGULATING PUBLIC SPACES

The moral panic about prostitution that produced abolitionist laws arose in the context of demographic shifts in Bombay. In the first two decades of the twentieth century, immigrants flocked to Bombay in search of jobs in its mills, factories, and docks. Between 1901 and 1921, the city's population in census records crossed the one million mark, increasing by 65 percent from 776,006 in 1901 to 1,175,914 in 1921. Yet the number of residential buildings "only increased by 11 percent" in the period 1901–21 (Hazareesingh 2001, 244). With its limited space as an island, Bombay in this period could be rightfully be described as "the most densely populated city in the world" (Klein 1986, 732). And of its various areas, Bombay's Kamathipura was one of the most crowded. There were more than 500 people to an acre living in Kamathipura in 1911, a number matched only by two of its neighboring wards, Nagpada and Kumbharwada (Edwardes 1910). Apart from sex workers, large numbers of mill and factory workers resided in this part of the city. In Nagpada, "model chawls" (apartment buildings for factory workers) had been built at the turn of the century (Edwardes 1910, 41). In nearby Tardeo, there were eighteen mills and eighteen factories (Edwardes 1910, 43) and Tarwadi, not far to the northwest of Kamathipura, was the site of thirteen spinning and weaving mills (Edwardes 1910, 43). Thus, although its streets were termed a red-light zone in the official imagination, Kamathipura was increasingly claimed as a residential area by new tides of workers in the early twentieth century.

The anxiety that prostitution was no longer confined to identifiable spaces heightened during this period of high congestion. As areas of Bombay grew in population, there were successive calls for the removal of prostitutes from thoroughfares. For instance, in 1904, the preeminent Parsi daily *Jam-e-Jamshed* noted that Falkland Road, an "open haunt of vice," was also a street that led "the mass of the working community from the northern parts of the town to their place of business . . . schools, markets, and theatres" (December 26, 1904). In August 1903, the *Punch Dand* newspaper complained about the prevalence of prostitutes in Bhuleshwar, to the north of Kamathipura. Abolition can thus be seen as an effort to remove prostitution from public view: as the population of the city grew, there were fewer and fewer parts of the city that middle-class residents were willing to cede to prostitution. The demand for removing brothels altogether from the city was a logical outcome; as the *Sanj Vartman* newspaper put it, "If such places are at all to exist, they should be removed to some quarter out of the city" (September 22, 1909).

The movement to abolish brothels also drew on a long record of anti-prostitution activism by missionaries. The earliest attempt to curtail brothels, for instance, was Reverend R. H. Madden's and Wallace Gladwin's proposal to import statutes from the British 1885 Criminal Law Amendment Act suppressing brothels. Madden was the superintendent of Seamen's Rest in Bombay, and Gladwin was the publisher of *India Watchman,* a missionary magazine published in Bombay aimed at "exposing sin of every grade" (*Missionary Monthly* 1897, 4). They had long complained that "houses of ill fame" were a "local nuisance to passers by" because of their indecent behavior (HD 1893, 117). The governor-in-council, however, doubted that enacting laws along the lines of the British Criminal Law Amendment Act would be effective. His view was that "the total suppression of prostitution [seemed] out of the question" given "the varying customs and even the religious observations of a heterogeneous population" (HD 1893, 117). Other missionaries of the Vigilance Committee signed a memorial complaining about the annoyances caused to pastors and mission workers by the residents of Cursetji Sukhlaji Street. In response, however, the Judicial Department of the Government of Bombay explained that "it [was] a lesser evil to segregate brothels as far as possible in one quarter" (HD 1892). Colonial administrators proved resistant to disturbing the efficient system of sexual recreation that serviced the mercantile navy and the military.

The popularity of abolition in the aftermath of the Duncan Road murder trial was also related to a host of other prohibitionist stances popular among social reformists. Demands to ban the sale of liquor and censor indecent films and dance performances, for instance, accompanied the call to abolish brothels. According to the newspaper *Akhbar-e-Islam,* "The chief cause of the spread of prostitutes is liquor and the Council should therefore try to put an end to liquor traffic" (August 12, 1921). When the Bombay Government did not respond to petitions asking for prohibition, the newspaper *Shri Shivaji* accused it of endangering mill workers through a "trap in the shape of liquor shops" (December 13, 1921). Newspapers expressed nervousness about the rapid rise of cinema halls: *Dnyan Prakash* commented on the "bad effect produced in the mind of young boys and students" by "indecent pictures" (January 27, 1923); the *Muslim Herald* declared that films were made to "excite lower passions" (May 28, 1921).

In 1926, when "singing and dancing girls" were introduced into the theaters of Bombay, there was a general outcry: *Sanj Vartaman* asked the government to put a stop to "dances of women presenting themselves half-naked," which were "calculated to produce a bad impression on the minds of the people and to create an atmosphere of immorality" (October 13, 1926). *Jam-e-Jamshed*, the leading daily of the Parsi community, received several letters against the practice and called on the police commissioner and Censor Board for a ban (October 23, 1926).

Dancing girls were classified alongside prostitutes, with both forming the obverse of the chaste woman idealized by missionaries, social reformists, and nationalists alike (Chatterjee 1989, Kumar 1994, Whitehead 1995). When the government proposed to send groups of dancing girls from India to the Empire Exhibition in England, the *Sindhi* newspaper carried the angry response: "It is a pity that India, land of women of high types, should take pride in exhibiting her dancing girls" (October 13, 1923). Another paper, *Al Wahid*, also noted in a similar nationalist vein that "the famous British dancer Miss Maud Allen on her visit to India was forbidden to dance in public with her naked body in the interest of British prestige in India. It is a pity that we cannot impose our wishes on the Government in a matter of this kind. We are a subject people and must put up with such humiliations until we break our shackles" (October 14, 1923). Yet another asked if the exhibit was "a device to show the world that Indians are a very backward and semi-barbarous people? Though India has sold its wealth, its morality, and its handicrafts, still we must not allow its honor to be sold" (*Raja Hansa*, September 30, 1923).

In this coalescing nationalist worldview, the nation's honor was predicated upon the desexualized representation of its women. Public figures such as dancing girls, whose chastity was placed in question, emblematized the notion of compromised national honor. Such nationalist constructs relied on a proprietal view of women's bodies; women's bodies were meaningful only in relation to the nation to which they belonged. The analogy between national honor and female sexual chastity presumed that all non-marital sex was necessarily a form of violation. The prostitute or dancing girl was a meaningful symbol only within an ideological field that denied alternative understandings of sex, such as one where sexual activity was de-linked from notions of honor. This a priori framing of prostitutes/dancing girls as compromised figures produced the many unidirectional efforts to recuperate them in the name of the nation. The early women's movement in India also contributed to this nationalist fixing of the prostitute as an object of rescue, as I will show.

WOMEN'S ACTIVISM, NATIONALISM, AND MORAL HYGIENE

Women's organizations in this period took positions that in many ways echoed the nationalist approach to prostitution. Congress, the largest Indian nationalist party, had taken an early abolitionist position on the issue when it resolved to supports efforts to repeal the CDA in 1888 and 1892 (Kumar 1994). Eradicating prostitution, and particularly the institution of temple dancing or *devadasis,* was also one of the earliest galvanizing issues in the Indian women's movement. For both middle-class feminists and nationalists, the ideal female citizen was an educated mother who served as a guardian of the moral polity.[1] Prostitutes and dancing girls were the necessary antithesis of such a construct. Both nationalists and feminists largely framed the women in question—sex workers, dancers, and singers—as uniformly pitiable figures who could be recuperated through monogamous marriage. Women's organizations framed their position in a language that was shared by missionaries and nationalists alike, one of "moral hygiene" (Whitehead 1998). Eradicating prostitution and other "social evils" such as drinking and child marriage would, they believed, purify the nation's body.

An increasingly vocal middle-class women's movement led the way in banning temple dancing, or the *devadasi* system, which they termed prostitution because temple dancers did not marry and sometimes sexually serviced male patrons. In taking on this issue, women's organizations aimed to undercut the patriarchal entitlements of upper-caste men who patronized temple dancers (Kumar 1994). Three national women's associations, the Women's Indian Association (WIA), founded in 1917, the All India Women's Conference, AIWC, founded in 1926, and the National Council of Women in India (NCWI), founded in 1925, all promoted legislation on this issue. The WIA journal *Stri Dharma* carried editorials against prostitution regularly, most often referring to the *devadasi* system (Whitehead 1998). A prominent WIA member, Dr. Muthulaksmi Reddy, led a well-known agitation against the *devadasi* system and authored legislations "preventing the dedication of innocent girls to temple service, and [encouraging] their marriages" (*Stri Dharma* 1932, 609–10; Basu and Ray 1990). Such laws that were intended to prevent temple dancers from becoming prostitutes implicitly enforced middle-class values of patriarchal marriage (Jordan 1993, Srinivasan 1988, Whitehead 1996). The WIA's efforts proved particularly successful in Madras presidency: in 1929 the local legislative council passed a law that reduced a *devadasi*'s claim on temple property. This measure was intended to strike at the heart of the institution, since the wealth (and matrilineal inheritance patterns) of many *devadasis* allowed them to resist marriage. It followed on the heels of judicial activism curtailing dancing girls' property rights and adoption rights (Parker 1998). Other women's organizations also took strong stands against prostitution: the AIWC issued a resolution supporting legislative efforts at banning brothels and preventing the dedication of *devadasis* (Basu and Ray 1990). The NCWI and the Bengal Women's Union also agitated against the sale of women into prostitution (Kaur 1933).

The stances of women's organizations on prostitution are consistent with the terms on which women in general entered the political arena. Unprecedented numbers of women were drawn into nationalist politics in the 1920s, but women's public participation was predicated on their adherence to strict standards of sexual purity. Although women's organizations carried out charitable works in rehabilitating prostitutes and although they spoke the language of common womanhood, they did not feature prostitutes as partners in struggle. Prostitutes themselves were not viewed as legitimate nationalist actors.

Two episodes related in Mohandas Gandhi's journals dramatize this point. In 1921, 350 prostitutes volunteered to become members of the Congress party, on the heels of Gandhi's attempt to broaden membership of the party to anyone who could pay a fee of fourteen annas. The women also contributed to the Tilak Swaraj Fund, set up by Gandhi as a means to support Congress's activities for social amelioration. When they expressed a wish to seek office in Congress committees, Gandhi refused and met with them to explain his objections. At the meeting, Gandhi tried to bar them from Congress committees by declaring that no one "could officiate at the altar of *Swaraj* [self-rule] who did not approach it with pure hands and a pure heart" (Gandhi 1942, 183). He advised the women to give up their profession and take up spinning instead.

The women's nationalist fervor was not so easily redirected. Only "eleven of them promised to give up" their way of life "and take up spinning the next day." But "the others said they would take time to think, for they did not wish to deceive [him]" (Gandhi 1942, 183). Over the next few years, these other women remained Congress members, were elected as delegates, and even founded an association whose manifesto promoted helping the poor and nursing the sick, spinning and weaving, skills training among prostitutes, and adopting nonviolence. In 1925, when Gandhi encountered this group again, he reacted with intense anger that their association provided musical training, which he viewed as a continuation of their profession, and declared their organization's manifesto "obscene." He angrily advised the women "to do humanitarian work before reforming themselves." He regretted that "public opinion" and their own "modesty" had not made them "refrain from seeking Congress membership." He called the women "more dangerous than thieves, because they steal virtue" and described them as akin to "unrepentant professional murderers." Their "tremendously dangerous powers of mischief" disqualified them from becoming members of the *satyagraha* (civil disobedience) movement (Gandhi 1942, 186–88). Gandhi displayed a similarly deep suspicion of the motives of another group of Congress volunteers in Madaripur. When they formed "an association of fallen sisters," he declared it "dangerous, especially for young men" and urged the women to "concentrate all their energies on . . . [opening] men's eyes to the bestial diabolical character of their offense" rather than performing Congress work (CWMG 31, 295). Gandhi reserved some of his strongest language for prostitutes, terming them "wrecks of society," and akin to "thieves" (CWMG 23, 112; CWMG 40, 42).

Gandhi's reaction is not surprising to feminist scholars who have studied the modes of women's nationalist participation (Forbes 1996; Kishwar 1985; Kumar 1994; Patel 1988). While they credit Gandhi with mobilizing large numbers of women, they also point out that he also heavily circumscribed women's political expression. Gandhi constituted the ideal nationalist woman as selfless, plain-dressed, and high-minded, with none of the threatening allure for heterosexual men that prostitutes supposedly held. Indeed, he even presented all women as being potential temptresses: a 1917 issue of the *Indian Social Reformer* reported that he declared "money, land and woman" to be "the source of all evil"—a comment that drew the ire of women's activists (*Indian Social Reformer* 1917b).

For Gandhi, the only acceptable fallen sister was a repentant one; in other words, one who entirely supported herself by spinning, with no trace of her former profession. She had to lose all markers of sexual appeal if she wished to join the freedom struggle. He saw prostitutes principally as symbols of men's lust; he confessed that their presence reminded him of his own identity as a man and that he "hung his head in shame" before them (Gandhi 1942, 181–82). Although Gandhi's intense aversion to prostitutes was to some extent idiosyncratic, his opinions exemplify a paradox in the nationalist approach to prostitution. On the one hand, nationalists called for pity toward prostitutes, whose "honor" and "chastity" had been stolen by "unscrupulous" men. Gandhi even rhetorically declared that stealing the honor of a woman was far more "hurtful to society" than "stealing property" (1942, 198–99). On the other hand, he saw prostitutes themselves as "thieves of virtue" and "unhealthily forward" if they did not display any shame (1942, 179).

This contradictory approach to prostitutes—seeing them as blameworthy and as victims—marked nationalist positions in discussions about abolition. For instance, the newspaper *Kaiser-I-Hind* stated with no sense of irony that "this evil [of brothels] ought to be checked by removing some of the inmates of houses to some distant locality and keeping a proper supervision over them. There is also a growing feeling that some special law ought to be passed in order to give the police and legal authorities the power to save the unfortunate women who fall into the clutches of brutal brothel keepers from ill treatment and a life of compulsory slavery" (August 14, 1921). The impulse to save women from falling into evil rested uneasily alongside the preconception that such women were themselves evil.

ABOLITIONISM IN LAW

The 1902 City of Bombay Police Act (Act IV) was the first to rule brothel keeping and soliciting as illegal.[2] It made Bombay the first city in the subcontinent to outlaw brothel keeping. However, these measures were buried within a series of other sections about the reorganization of the police force and were not publicized: although several newspapers carried stories about the 1902 Police Act, none of them mentioned the sections relating to prostitution.[3] When one considers the novelty of these measures against brothel keeping, their minimal publicity indicates a weak intent to implement them. Such a conclusion is borne out by the uneven enforcement of this law: police did not apply the section against brothel keeping, and sporadically applied only the section against soliciting. The commissioner of police authorized officers to arrest without warrant any person found soliciting, and "114 prostitutes were dealt with" for this offense within the first year of its being in effect (HD 1903). Table 11 shows that a large number of women were imprisoned for a few years following the act, perhaps as a result of the focus on soliciting. However, there were no arrests of brothel keepers reported. When brothels did figure in police reports, it was as the scene of non-prostitution-related crimes that the police pursued. For instance, in one case, police constables arrested two soldiers who committed a theft in a brothel (ARPTIB 1915, 26). In another case, a wealthy Arab prostitute on Falkland Road complained about a robbery, and the CID (Central Investigation Division) and the divisional police coordinated in arresting the thief (ARPTIB 1914, 6). On the whole, the 1902 act did not make much of a dent in the scale of organized prostitution.

The political climate in India became more conducive to abolitionism after the 1919 Government of India Act set up a Central Legislative Assembly premised on the principle of greater self-governance by Indians. Such a climate extended into presidency-level politics as well, spurring abolitionist measures. On the heels of the Duncan Road murder trial, a bill was introduced in 1918 to amend the 1902 Police Act, drawing on details of how Akootai and her inmates were maintained in bondage. A new section now prohibited brothel keepers from withholding and lending apparel, ornaments, and property to women; it also declared as illegal all civil suits by brothel keepers for the recovery of debts, apparel, and ornaments, aiming to curtail the kind of power Syed Mirza wielded.[4] The bill also repeated section 370 of the Indian Penal Code banning slavery when it penalized the detention of women against their will—an understandable form of repetition given the public outrage over Akootai's bondage. The bill was passed into law in 1920 as the City of Bombay Police Amendment Act. Despite the changes in the police law to protect brothel inmates, the police reports for the years following the 1920 amendment show no reference to prosecutions under the new section.[5] As a result, reformists began to call for a separate law dealing comprehensively with prostitution (HD 1917b).

In 1921, a citizens' group led by Kanji Dwarkadas—a key social reformer in Bombay politics—petitioned the government to set up a committee "to thrash out the [prostitution] question in all its aspects" (*Bombay Chronicle*, August 24, 1921). In response, the Government of Bombay instituted the Committee on Prostitution, composed of prominent reformist citizens, social workers, and officials described in chapter 4 (RCP 1922, M7).[6] This committee suggested many legal changes, the most far-reaching of which was the elimination of the brothel system: brothel keepers, procurers, pimps, and bullies. The committee held that this measure would reduce the flow of girls from the rural areas into Bombay, as there would be no regular source of demand. Without the open advertisement, public display, and easy access provided by brothels, the scale of prostitution would decrease, they argued. They also argued that brothels specifically caused inertia and laziness among inmates, as women waited for customers; in the absence of brothels, they felt, prostitutes might be forced out of the profession alto- gether.[7] Significantly, the three dissenters to these recommendations were the key British administrators on the committee: the municipal commis- sioner, the commissioner of police, and a military official. At the end of the 1922 report, they inserted a signed statement of dissent that "the abolition of prostitution in India is ill-advised because India has tolerated hereditary prostitution" (RCP 1922, v/26/803/4).

The Committee on Prostitution nonetheless put forward a bill in 1923 to curtail brothels, and it was met with frenzied enthusiasm by newspapers (*Bombay Samachar,* June 14, 1921; *Sanj Vartaman,* June 11, 1921). Members on the Legislative Council who supported the bill used the nationalist argu- ment that the British legislators were being hypocritical by condoning pros- titution in India. G. B. Trivedi, council member from Bombay, asked, "If the brothel can be prohibited in England, then, why should it not be pro- hibited in Bombay?" (Bombay Legislative Council Debates 1923, 515.) Oth- ers gave voice to the moral panic in the city, for instance remarking that the degree of commercialized prostitution in Bombay was "second only to cities of the United States" (Bombay Legislative Council Debates 1923, 54). A distinctly middle-class self-righteousness also marked legislators' stances. In deriding prostitutes and prostitution, middle-class abolitionists could set themselves apart from what they viewed as the depraved wealthy as well as the ignorant poor. The principal clients of prostitutes were, after all, migrant and floating workers, or wealthy merchant classes who patronized entertainers, or foreign sailors and soldiers. Mr. S. K. Bole, representing Bombay City North in the legislative council, raised an accusing finger at "mercantile communities" and called for the bill to target "kept mistresses" (Bombay Legislative Council Debates 1923, 508–9). R. R. Kale, member

from Satara district, made a similar attempt to increase the reach of the law
by suggesting that all immoral sexual intercourse—of a woman with any
man other than her husband—be banned. Legislators tried to outdo each
other in the stringency of their proposals, playing a game of moral one-
upmanship. The pressure of the organized abolitionist groups such as the
Bombay Vigilance Association and the Social Purity Committee also shaped
debates on the 1923 bill. Some legislative council members read out letters
of approval from important members of the Social Purity Committee, indicating that the opinion of organized abolitionists was critical in legitimiz-
ing the actions of the council (Bombay Legislative Council Debates 1923,
516). The Bombay Vigilance Association placed a member on subsequent
committees considering changes to the law.[8]

When the 1923 bill was passed as the Bombay Prevention of Prostitution
Act (henceforth BPPA), however, its final form steered away from introducing any vastly new measures. The 1923 act targeted pimping, soliciting,
procuring, and detaining women against their will in a brothel, but not
brothel keepers and owners. Some members, such as Ibrahim S. Haji, had
convincingly argued that landlords of houses used as brothels were not necessarily engaged in any criminal activity, and that unless they themselves
were found on the brothel premises, they ought not to be punished (Bombay Legislative Council Debates, 511). In other words, the BPPA largely
repeated sections contained in the 1902 Police Act and Indian Penal Code.[9]
It thus serves as a good example of a law that represented a condensing of
public opinion rather than an innovation against forced prostitution. The
1923 act went through repeated amendments in the 1920s and 1930s, in
flailing efforts to eradicate brothel keeping, as described in the next section.

THE COURSE OF THE BPPA, 1926–48

Despite the alarm with which abolitionist lawmakers viewed prostitution,
the police force largely viewed it as an entertaining sidebar to the drier
offenses they otherwise worked on. The language of the 1917 annual report,
the same year as the Duncan Road murder trial, provides a case in point:
three cases of procuring minor girls and women are prefaced thus: "Among
the more interesting cases investigated: Slave Traffic" (ARPCB 1917, 19). The
police reports fixated on cases reflecting odd customs or extreme brutality.
Police described the murders of prostitutes, for instance, with greater detail

than the arrest and conviction of brothel keepers, traffickers, or procurers. From 1860 to 1922, six cases of murders of prostitutes are described at length in annual police reports, with only three cases of Indian traffickers described with the same level of detail.[10] These reports also regularly mentioned the religion and caste of perpetrators and victims, seeking to attribute crime to local traditions, sects, and culture (Chandavarkar 1998).

Thus, although the Bombay Prevention of Prostitution Act was passed with great fanfare in 1922, the police did not set about implementing it with the same fervor of lawmakers. For three years following the passage of the BPPA, police reports showed no prosecutions under the new law. In 1925, the newspaper *Vilas* reported that procurers carried on their trade, and prostitutes on Foras Road continued to solicit passersby. It blamed the corrupt police force thus: "Our yellow-turbaned policemen care a fig for the law so long as they get some bribe" (June 27, 1925). Indeed the police force seemed ignorant of new laws: in 1925, the police investigated a brothel keeper's complaint against an inmate about a theft of ornaments, oblivious to the ban on such civil suits by brothel keepers in section 8 of the BPPA (ARPCB 1926, 13). The surgeon-general of Bombay continued to feel in 1926 that "the closing of brothels of a better class would not be a measure of hygienic utility if it resulted in the women so dishoused becoming clandestine prostitutes" (GD 1927–28b, M35).

After a few years, some Bombay Legislative Council members began to express alarm over the lack of impact of the 1923 law. In 1926, the council debated an amendment to make punishments more stringent. S. A. Sardesai of Bijapur district declared that Indians were "left far behind America, Germany and Europe . . . in [preventing] prostitution" (HD 1926a, 4). S. K. Bole (after whom a major road in central Bombay is now named) described a visit to a friend's place whose neighborhood was "formerly a family locality where married people lived" and where "now [his] friend alone [lived] surrounded by prostitutes." He declared that "where there [were] decent localities these prostitutes should not be allowed to live" (HD 1926a, 7–8). R. G. Pradhan of Nasik district affirmed that "in this city of Bombay you find prostitutes living as neighbors with respectable families" and that "in some cases one floor is occupied by a respectable family and another floor by prostitutes." He asked the council to consider "what a pernicious influence it [could] have on the morals and general life of the city, particularly upon young minds" (HD 1926a, 9).

In such a climate, the amendments to the BPPA in Act XI of 1926 made soliciting harder: it became possible for any police officer to arrest without warrant someone suspected of soliciting, and the punishment increased from eight days to three months in prison, and the fine increased from fifty to one hundred rupees.[11] As these changes had little effect on brothels, abolitionist groups began to step up pressure. The Bombay Vigilance Association made pamphlets calling for punishing brothel keepers and providing equal punishment for male and female procurers. It held public protest meetings in "about thirty social institutions" and "passed resolutions in the City Corporation" to that effect (HD 1929, 7). Visiting delegates of the British Social Hygiene Association also made recommendations to the government to ban brothels. Prostitution was such a popular issue in the public sphere that newspaper editors assumed the mantle of reformists, such as the editor of the prominent Gujarati daily *Jam-e-Jamshed,* Phirozsha Marzban, who proposed a bill in 1929 to control prostitution.

The resulting Act XII of 1930 made the law harsher on brothels: landlords who allowed their premises to be utilized as brothels were guilty of abetting prostitution. The act expanded the definition of a brothel to cover any place used for "immoral purposes." Most significantly, female procurers and brothel keepers became as equally liable as male ones, and the punishment increased from two to three years' imprisonment without bail.[12] Bombay became the only place in the subcontinent apart from Burma where brothel keeping was clearly outlawed. Although the Suppression of Immoral Traffic Act had been passed in Calcutta in 1923, it did not target brothels unless they "annoyed neighbours" or were located in specified places. The Madras Immoral Traffic Act of 1930, which was similar, was delayed in enforcement.[13]

The 1930 act struck a serious legal blow to organized prostitution in Bombay. Police targeted a number of European brothels, and several European women then left for Calcutta (HD 1932, 10). Yet many brothel owners adapted to the law by replacing tolerated brothels with a system of room tenancy: about 5,000 women in prostitution rented separate rooms in their own names in order to circumvent laws (ARPCB 1931, 10; ARPCB 1932, 11). The new wider definition of the brothel in 1930 meant that police could now serve such individual prostitutes with notices if they received complaints from neighbors. However, no such complaints were forthcoming in areas such as Kamathipura, where prostitutes were a majority of the inhabitants.

Thus, although brothels were illegal, segregated prostitution continued in effect (HD 1932, 15). And in the words of the police, although the brothel keeper had "disappeared into obscurity," there was "no doubt that she still plie(d) her trade" (HD 1932, 16).

Another form of a cover for brothels was the Turkish bath house and massage parlor. Police reports for 1930, 1931, and 1932 refer with frustration to an increasing number of such establishments.[14] The law did not address this issue until after the country's independence in 1947. Act XXVI of 1948 extended the definition of brothels to cover "Turkish baths, massage establishments, beauty parlors, manicure rooms, pedicure rooms, knitting rooms, embroidery rooms, or any other similar place by whatever name or description knowingly permits prostitutes."[15] In addition, "the partitioning of rooms or places into cubicles, by any means including cloth or canvass curtains, wood, cement, corrugated iron, asbestos or brick partitions . . . for the purposes of prostitution" was also not allowed.[16] This post-Independence formulation was far more comprehensive than previous ones; savvy legislators tried to account for every possible loophole.

The large number of amendments to the BPPA—in 1926, 1927, 1930, 1931, 1945, and 1948—is indicative of the political weight that the issue of prostitution carried. The debates over these amendments featured a number of very exercised legislators laying blame at the government's door. Yet despite the vocal debates, most of the amendments were cosmetic changes, with the only major change occurring in 1930. Prostitution in turn assumed new forms, in response to new provisions of the law.

ENFORCEMENT OF THE BPPA

Tables 8–11 indicate the number of arrests and convictions under the BPPA and its amendments throughout the 1920s and 1930s. They detail the enforcement of individual sections of the BPPA dealing with brothel keeping, soliciting, pimping, and procuring. Each of the tables collates annual arrest and conviction figures under separate sections of the BPPA, from 1927 to 1949. Taken together, they indicate that preventing murders such as Akootai's was in no way the priority of the enforcement practices: police largely targeted those found soliciting customers, while brothel keepers remained beyond the reach of the law.

Brothel Keeping

Table 8 collates arrest and conviction figures under the BPPA's section 8, which penalized illegal detention of women in brothels, and section 9, which targeted the occupying and managing of brothels. As the table demonstrates, police took no significant action against brothel keepers for the first few years of the law's enforcement. Even when cases were brought to court, convictions were few. Meanwhile, the number of brothels did not recede: in their 1930 annual report, police acknowledged that there were at least "600 brothels" in the city (ARPCB 1930, 11).

TABLE 8. Number of cases and convictions for brothel keeping under BPPA, 1924–49

Year	Section 9			Section 8		
	Cases	Convicted	Acquitted	Cases	Convicted	Acquitted
1924	0	0	0	0	0	0
1925	0	0	0	0	0	0
1926	0	0	0	0	0	0
1927	0	0	0	0	0	0
1928	0	0	0	0	0	0
1929	0	0	0	0	0	0
1930	0	0	0	2	1	1
1931	0	0	0	19	9	10
1932	0	0	0	5	4	1
1933	0	0	0	0	0	0
1934	0	0	0	1	0	1
1935	0	0	0	0	0	0
1936	9	3	0	1	0	1
1937	101	0	0	1	1	0
1938	89	15	0	0	0	0
1939	86	11	0	1	0	0
1940	149	7	0	18	11	5
1941	85	9	0	8	6	2
1942–45	—	—	—	—	—	—
1946	10	0	0	0	0	0
1947	140	1	0	0	0	0
1948	185	61	0	1	0	0
1949	396	0	0	2	0	0

Source: Annual Report of the Police in the City of Bombay for 1927–49. Figures for 1942–45 are not available since wartime police reports were incomplete.

Starting in 1937, the number of brothel keeper arrests suddenly increased, as a result of the amendment to the BPPA that widened the pool of offenders to include individual prostitutes in single rooms, which were also now legally defined as brothels. Yet throughout the period when multiple arrests were made (1937–49), there were few convictions of brothel keepers. The familiar difficulty, that "girls were reluctant to give evidence against wrongdoers in court and in some cases deliberately turn round and side with the defense," persisted (ARPCB 1927, 13). Brothel keepers also benefited from loopholes in the law, posing as servants of brothel inmates who received wages or as boardinghouse owners who received rent from each inmate (ARPCB 1930, 11). There was also a genuine difficulty in distinguishing brothel keepers from brothel workers, because many women shifted between these roles. As noted in Akootai's story (chapter 4) as well as the Favel investigation records (chapter 3), brothel mistresses and supervisors were typically former prostitutes who continued to transact sexual services on an intermittent basis.

SOLICITING

Table 9 displays the stringent enforcement of the BPPA section 3, which targeted soliciting. There were far more arrests and convictions than for sections 8 and 9. Police interpreted the 1923 act as a license to prosecute large numbers of female prostitutes—the easiest target when battling prostitution. The table demonstrates how severely the new law affected prostitutes. Arrests of prostitutes for soliciting were far higher than those of brothel keepers, pimps, and procurers. The number of females arrested under this section was consistently higher than that of males—who were often pimps for women, according to police reports. The arrests for soliciting were also higher after 1926, because warrants were not needed.

Tables 8 and 9 together show that a disproportionate number of prostitutes were arrested and convicted compared to brothel keepers under the BPPA. The police saw the public nuisance of prostitutes as a greater problem than forced prostitution. The numbers of arrests and convictions for soliciting were higher than for any other offense, whether brothel keeping, pimping, or procuring (ARPCB 1927–50). Despite the fact that the BPPA was initiated to target the growing number of brothels and repeated amendments were made to it over the years to enable this goal, the police merely stepped up arrests of prostitutes for soliciting. The next section provides

TABLE 9. Number of cases of soliciting in Bombay city under BPPA, 1927–1950

Year	Section 3 arrests	Male	Female	Convicted	Acquitted	Pending
1927	0	0	0	0	0	0
1928	35	15	20	34	1	0
1929	26	5	21	23	3	0
1930	28	3	25	27	1	0
1931	41	3	34	39	1	1
1932	196	—	—	192	4	0
1933	196	—	—	195	1	0
1934	208	—	—	204	2	2
1935	215	—	—	208	3	4
1936	152	—	—	150	2	0
1937	163	20	143	163	5	0
1938	161	23	138	157	3	1
1939	178	14	164	168	8	2
1940	200	23	177	195	3	2
1941	143	15	128	134	8	1
1942–45	—	—	—	—	—	—
1946	254	58	196	239	12	0
1947	201	68	133	177	9	0
1948	474	68	406	287	6	182
1949	—	—	—	—	—	—
1950	378	38	340	262	33	41

Source: Annual Report of the Police in the City of Bombay, 1927–50. Figures were occasionally not available because of gaps in primary sources or wartime suspension of data collection.

Note: Figures for 1931 also included 5 *hijras* (transsexuals or eunuchs), which have not been included in the male or female categories in the table.

evidence of prostitutes' criminalization in sources such as census figures and prison reports. It shows that this pattern in the enforcement of the BPPA was repeated across the years between 1860 and 1947.

PROSTITUTES IN THE CENSUS

Given the dubious social status of prostitutes, census numbers for prostitutes are not reliable indices of the actual number of women who engaged in sexual commerce. Nonetheless, the census classifications provide a window onto tracking the formation of colonial categories and the social valence they carry. The classification "prostitute" was present in the tables of censuses of India taken between 1864 and 1931. Its location within the layout of the census indicates the changing social status of prostitutes. In 1864, "prostitution" was listed as one of the occupations under the section "Luxuries and Dissipation," among others such as "bracelet dealer," "musician," "photographer," "toymaker," "watchmaker" and "liquor seller." There was a section for "unproductive occupations" but "prostitution" was not classified under it. With the 1871 census, "prostitution" shifted to the "Miscellaneous" section near the end of census tables, where the categories of "Disreputable Professions" were named. In an indication of the stigma now attached to the profession, this location held steady over subsequent censuses; prostitutes remained a category under either the "Miscellaneous Persons" or "Unproductive Occupations" section.

Although census figures, like most official records, do not provide comprehensive listings for the number of women in prostitution, at the very least they indicate the number of women who were identifiably prostitutes, such as workers in brothels whose supervisors cooperated with census officials, or those who were in the profession by heredity. On the whole, we can assume that census figures undercounted prostitutes. For instance, the 1921 census counted 2,955 prostitutes in the city, but the police report for that year counted 5,169 (HD 1932, 15).

The number of prostitutes listed in each census from 1864 to 1931, collated in Table 10, speaks meaningfully about the effects of laws in various periods. It is striking that the largest-ever census returns were in 1864, of 9,536 prostitutes, at a time when prostitution had not yet been cast as a criminal activity. During the CDA era (1870–71; 1880–88), when state control of prostitution increased, far fewer women identified themselves as prostitutes. Thus, the 1871 and 1881 censuses show much smaller returns than 1864, of 1,651 and 1,524 prostitutes respectively.

The CDA (which targeted unregistered prostitutes for escaping medical examinations) reduced the willingness of women to identify themselves as prostitutes. As chapter 2 described, many women who identified as prostitutes in the 1864 census went into hiding. After the repeal of the CDA, the numbers rose in 1891, also due to the wider classification, "females in disreputable professions." The figures for 1901 are closer to those for 1881; the 1911 census did not make a clear count of prostitutes. The 1921 census reveals a rise in the numbers of prostitutes. The passing of the 1923 BPPA law on its heels meant that women again became reluctant to identify themselves as prostitutes, because of police targeting soliciting. Accordingly, there is a drop in the 1931 figures.

On the whole, Table 10 indicates the shifting social approbation of prostitutes, as well as women's responses to being criminalized. During periods when laws on prostitution were being enforced, fewer prostitutes came forward to contribute to census numbers. Within the census reports, the changing classification of prostitution[17] from a legitimate occupation to an unproductive and disreputable miscellaneous category displays its growing stigmatization.

PROSTITUTES IN PRISON, 1875–1931

Like census figures, prison reports attest to the growing criminalization of prostitutes. The earliest administrative reports of Bombay jails counted the "prostitutes" among female prisoners. From 1855 to 1870, a column for "prostitutes" was found in the "occupations" table, along with other items such as "dancing girls" and "maidservants." From 1871 onward, the "occupations" table for women was dropped, but the classification "prostitutes" was retained as part of the marital status columns. Women were now either

TABLE 10. Number of women classified as "prostitutes" in Bombay city, 1871–1931

Year	Number of returns under classification "Prostitute"
1864	9,536
1871	1,651
1881	1,524
1891	3,676
1901	1,942
1911	—
1921	2,849
1931	1,136
1941	—
1951	—

Sources: Census of Island of Bombay 1864, table 60, 84; Census of Bombay 1872, table 71, 134; Census of India: Bombay City & Island 1881, 71; Census of India 1891, Bombay, table 17-B, 371; Census of India: Bombay 1901, vol. 9, part 2, table 15, 106; Census of Bombay Town and Island 1912, vol. 8, part 2, 88 89; Census of India: Bombay 1922, vol. 9, part 2, city table 7; Census of India: Cities of the Bombay Presidency 1931, vol. 9, part 2, city table 7, 199; Census of India: Bombay, Saurashtra, and Kutch 1951, vol. 4, part 1: Bombay, 95.

"married," "unmarried," or "prostitutes." Apart from the addition of a column for "widows" in 1879, these terms remained the only ways of classifying female prisoners until Independence. After Independence, the word "unattached" replaced "prostitutes" in jail documents. The change in the connotation of "prostitute" in the 1871 prison report mirrors that found in the 1871 census, as discussed in the previous section. The change shows the general decline in the status of prostitutes at the onset of the CDA.

In Table 11, I present collated figures from annual prison reports across the late colonial period and compare the number of imprisoned prostitutes with the total number of female prisoners. Figures before 1875 and after 1931 for only Bombay city were not available in the annual reports of the prisons, and so the first phase of the CDA (1870–71) and the latter years of the BPPA are not covered in this table. Even though all imprisoned women who were termed "prostitutes" were not necessarily in prison for practicing prostitution,[18] the trends in their imprisonment are consistent with the

TABLE 11. Number of prostitutes in prisons relative to female prisoners in Bombay city, 1875–1931

Year	Number of prostitutes	Number of female prisoners
1875	12	105
1876	12	74
1877	8	128
1878	13	206
1879	1	17
1880	2	20
1881	4	23
1882	6	17
1883	39	162
1884	22	108
1885	18	93
1886	33	94
1887	31	105
1888	25	89
1889	20	97
1890	6	69
1891	16	87
1892	5	116
1893	13	72

TABLE II. (*continued*)

Year	Number of prostitutes	Number of female prisoners
1894	33	90
1895	16	120
1896	22	170
1897	13	156
1898	13	146
1899	26	302
1900	36	303
1901	13	335
1902	24	513
1903	87	463
1904	123	472
1905	344	645
1906	243	725
1907	367	609
1908	298	570
1909	201	467
1910	234	485
1911	91	364
1912	140	522
1913	94	361
1914	65	294
1915	39	226
1916	17	228
1917	7	213
1918	2	234
1919	7	290
1920	24	194
1921	19	156
1922	39	160
1923	125	255
1924	12	174
1925	40	178
1926	27	126
1927	38	126
1928	31	106
1929	12	86
1930	22	139
1931	25	137

Source: *Annual Report of the Bombay Jails* 1875–1922, statement 2; *Administrative Report of the Bombay Jail Department* 1923–31, statement 2.

general pattern of prostitutes' criminalization from 1875 to 1931. In periods when laws such as the CDA and the 1923 BPPA were in effect, greater numbers of women classified as prostitutes were found in prisons. In the second phase of the CDA, from 1880 to 1888, there was an increase in the number of prostitutes in prison. The number dropped slightly in 1890 and stayed steady for a few years. The next major increase occurred in 1904, which followed the passing of the 1902 Police Act. The sharp drop in numbers between 1914 and 1919 may be attributed to changed priorities of the police force during World War I. After the passing of the 1923 BPPA, the number of prostitutes in prison steadily rose again.

Taken as a whole, these prison figures indicate that during every period when any significant policy initiative dealing with prostitutes was taken, there was a rise in the number of prostitutes imprisoned. Even when these policies were aimed at curtailing forced prostitution, such as the 1902 act and the 1923 BPPA, prostitutes were punished. The mere existence of laws on prostitution, whatever the content, contributed to the *perception* of prostitutes as criminals. The laws increased pressure on police to appear effective, and in turn, this pressure made those who solicited even more vulnerable. Thus for those in the sex trade, the content of laws was less important than the publicity that the lawmaking process garnered for their profession. Despite the success of abolitionist movement, motivated by cases such as Akootai's murder, conditions giving rise to brothel keepers' coercion were not altered.

c o n c l u s i o n

The Failed Promise of Laws:
Contemporary Reflections

The British colonial period is typically characterized as a time when Victorian standards of restraint reconstituted sexual relations in India. The laws that changed sexual relations in that era, such as those permitting widow remarriage and banning child marriage and homosexuality, all upheld an ideal of desexualized femininity. This book demonstrates that in the case of laws on prostitution, contrary to the presumably Victorian tendencies toward restricting or abolishing prostitution, British colonial administrators not only tolerated but also institutionalized sexual commerce. In the course of ostensibly seeking to curb venereal disease and coercive prostitution, the colonial state instituted an orderly and racially stratified sex industry. Relying on the support of orthodox Indian legislators to preserve an appearance of unobtrusive rule, and seeking to avoid the costs of ill health among its functionaries, the colonial government acted in ways that refuted both its purported civilizing mission and the metropolitan British state's internationalist commitments to antitrafficking. Middle-class Indian nationalists and reformists utilized colonial measures and legal currents to advance an agenda that positioned the state differently but in ways that did not significantly reduce the problem of violence against prostitutes.

Colonial administrators frequently relied on what Partha Chatterjee (1993) has termed the "rule of colonial difference"—the viewing of colonies as exceptions to liberal political universals. For instance, they propagated the notion that prostitution was a long-standing Indian tradition in formulating CDA-era policies, and justified public intervention into the lives of prostitutes with the claim that such women felt no shame about their profession. When brothels were banned in Britain as a consequence of an abolitionist movement in the 1880s, colonial legislators ignored calls to follow suit in India. In the antitrafficking era, the problem of prostitutes trafficked into Bombay from other parts of India was discounted as less serious than that of women trafficked from Europe.

Although colonial officials aimed to rigidify differences between rulers and the ruled, the universalism inherent in the language of law emboldened nationalist and reformist Indian legislators to compel administrators to apply standards more evenly. Middle-class residents of Bombay placed pressure on the government to confine prostitutes to segregated neighborhoods. Legislators urged that the standards applied to prostitutes in Britain and trafficked foreign women in India be similarly applied to Indian women. By the 1920s, the colonial government had to bow to pressures from abolitionists and introduce measures to curb organized prostitution, in order to provide the illusion of action. Laws, then, functioned as expressions of intent, as postures in the process of communication between the ruling British authorities and a formative Indian public sphere.

The use of law as rhetoric—communication aimed at persuading a defined audience—explains its redundance. Laws themselves were not formulated with a consideration of the practicalities of enforcement. Ambitious measures such as the CDA rules and the 1902 Police Act exceeded the enforcement capabilities of the state. One can conclude that the laws engendered their own evasion by their stringency and hence incited further legislation. The same crimes—soliciting, brothel keeping, procuring—drew repeated legislation over the late colonial period. In some cases, such as the 1920 Police Act and 1923 BPPA, laws appeared to repeat themselves within a margin of only two or three years.

A divergence between the law and its enforcement was a necessary feature of the colonial state's actions, given the ambitious and universalist language of the laws. Many of the archived files cited in this book demonstrate that Bombay's police readily acknowledged both their inability to enforce prostitution laws and their reluctance to do so. In the CDA era, the social experiment of disease control was restricted principally to European women in order to conserve resources; in the antitrafficking era, police attended exclusively to narrowed definitions of the problem; and in the abolitionist phase, only those women who visibly solicited in public spaces were targeted, leaving brothel owners and supervisors largely unaffected.

One consequence of such ambivalent and selective law enforcement was the development of a venal link between the police force and brothel keepers. Given the minimal resources available for implementing prostitution laws, police relied on brothels and brothel keepers to maintain order and facilitate medical checks. Women who individually solicited clients were arrested, as were those who did not subject themselves to registration and medical checkups. Prostitutes were thus driven into brothels by the threat of violence outside them. Brothel keepers in turn terrorized inmates by claiming to protect them from the police. Soliciting was forced into hiding to allow its reconstitution as the primary crime of prostitution.

The history of laws on prostitution in Bombay is therefore aptly characterized by Foucault's insight that mechanisms of prohibition expand the circuits of power. Laws constituted new kinds of crimes; they created the conditions of their own violation and set up an iterative dynamic of exercising and evading power. As laws on prostitution grew in number through the late colonial period, they simultaneously institutionalized the phenomenon that they addressed. Laws such as the CDA were productive of new meanings, potentially targeting a range of women not previously classified as prostitutes, such as temple dancers and courtesans. The "common prostitute" and the brothel became staple features of the new understanding of prostitution. Although appearing to be barriers, prohibitions extended the reach of power: newly defined offenses such as soliciting and evasion of medical examination drew many subaltern women into the ambit of state control. Whether they were aimed at curbing or regulating prostitution, and whether or not they were regularly enforced, the laws constituted women as objects of surveillance.

The laws also constituted sexual relations as worthy of medical attention and native women as objects of prohibited desire. In the process, laws incited the pornographic imagination of state actors. In the case of both the CDA and antitrafficking conventions, the law provided occasions for the police to watch women in the sex trade and engage closely with them. The dramatic and intimate encounters narrated in this book between policemen and prostitutes were not accidents as much as opportunities that were occasioned by regular law enforcement practices.[1] The CDA also facilitated the access of medical professionals to the bodies of Indian women in ways that were unthinkable in the broader civilian context.

Yet another effect of prostitution laws was the geographic transformation of Bombay's sex trade. Prostitution was progressively confined to fewer and fewer areas through police enforcement of segregation laws. Whereas in 1860, eight sections of the city had more than 500 prostitutes, by 1921, there were only two sections with over 500 prostitutes, as shown in chapter 3. It was the area where European prostitutes resided that came to be seen as the red-light zone, largely because of the official attention paid to this neighborhood. Today, that area, Kamathipura, remains the identifiable center of prostitution in Bombay. Even the physical layout of the streets in Kamathipura has not changed—during my fieldwork, I was able to use a map composed in 1901 to navigate my way walking around the area; although some of the major streets have been renamed under the Shiv Sena government in the past decade, most passersby refer to Sukhlaji Street, Duncan Road, Foras Road, Falkland Road, and Grant Road by these older names. The layout and numbering of lanes in the heart of Kamathipura remains the same.

These physical continuities provide an occasion to speculate on other similarities between the context I have studied and Mumbai in the present. The colonial Indian state, of course, differed in its imperatives from the post-Independence developmentalist Indian state. As Rajeswari Sunder Rajan (2003) notes, while the colonial state was committed to the discourse of "civilizational otherness and the pragmatics of rule," which led to its placating orthodox forces, "the postcolonial state claims a more absolute mandate" (199–200). The current state is expected to uphold both the rights and welfare of all its citizens in nondiscriminatory ways. And yet, it is simultaneously required to placate a new set of orthodoxies, such as global discourses of public health, trafficking, and neoliberalism that reinscribe colonial patterns of state-civilian relations. In the next section, I draw some parallels between the present context and the colonial past and comment on the contemporary relevance of my study.

THE STATE, FUNDERS, AND
PROSTITUTION LAWS TODAY

In July 2007, a curious news announcement made headlines around the world: the numerical estimate of people living with AIDS in India had been sharply revised to half of what it was previously thought to be. Whereas the National AIDS Control Organization (NACO) in India had earlier estimated that in the past decade there had been a steady increase of HIV-infected people to about 5.2 million, a 2006 survey drawing on the help of UNAIDS and WHO placed the estimate at around 2 to 3 million people (BBC 2007; UNAIDS 2007). The UNAIDS website (UNAIDS 2007) attributed this revision to more accurate measurement techniques, but such a stark difference in numbers compels the question of why the earlier estimates were so high. What rhetorical purpose did such estimates serve? An indication may be found in the immediate response to the story from voluntary organizations and NACO. Warning against complacency, the head of NACO declared that "there is no question of reducing even a dollar towards the fight against AIDS" (BBC 2007, 7 July). As the use of the word "dollar" here demonstrates, NACO and other voluntary organizations rely heavily on presenting India as a site of an AIDS problem that its government cannot surmount without foreign donors. In their newly dominant discourse, the state is represented as being inadequate on many fronts: not only does it lack resources but it also is in denial about its outdated laws. Its political representatives are seen as having outmoded perceptions about Indian sexuality. Indian society, in this view, needs to shake off its repressive shackles (a refrain ripe for Foucauldian critique). In such a climate, the high estimates of HIV prevalence are intended to shock the state and society into taking greater action; they contest a misplaced complacency about Indian sexual conservatism.

NACO, a body funded largely through a $200 million World Bank loan, is the key proponent of such a position. Established in 1992 as a central coordinating agency for AIDS-control efforts in the country, it is an interesting example of a public-private partnership: although a government organization, it positions itself as an administrative, rather than political, body, coordinating the various NGOs and medical organizations rather than representing the voice of the political leadership. It has led a long campaign to raise awareness about AIDS and, in particular, has instituted HIV-surveillance programs around the country (Verma et al. 2004). NACO has also been the chief advocate of a policy at odds with existing laws on prostitution: to decriminalize sex workers.

NACO has identified sex workers as one of its principal target populations. Its annual HIV Prevention Sentinel Surveillance, for example, uses the help of city municipal corporations to make AIDS testing more widely available among sex workers (Verma et al. 2004). Its proposed change in law is, however, less motivated by sex workers' interests than by an instrumentalist view of such workers as vectors of disease who need to be accessed and treated in the interests of the general public. The recent proposals for overhauling Bombay's sex trade through licensing must be seen in this context of ascendant public health discourses. NACO is not alone in proposing licensing. City corporations have proposed even more stringent measures to control AIDS—the Calcutta mayor proposed licensing of brothel workers based on mandatory AIDS testing.[2] While sex workers' organizations generally cooperate with the goals of AIDS prevention agencies, many of them are opposed to the system of licensing proposed by local governments and NACO.[3] Well-known groups such as Darbar Mahila Samanwaya Committee in Calcutta and VAMP (Veshya Anyay Mukti Parishad—sex workers' forum against injustice) in Sangli call for decriminalization but not licensing of sex workers. (A national network of sex workers, Bharatiya Patita Uddhar Sabha—Indian sex workers union—has, however, endorsed licensing.)

The merits of licensing can clearly be refuted by my historical narration of the CDA. Not only did regulating prostitution not show any clear effect on venereal disease incidence figures; it rendered women in the sex trade more vulnerable to state coercion. But apart from this specific historical lesson, my study also engenders a suspicion of the majoritarian tendencies in discourses of public health. Public health interventions circulate as measures intended to benefit the population as a whole. However, they often do so at the expense of some, and they often become vehicles for the developmentalist state to trumpet its badly needed successes and satisfy external funding agencies. The needs of those targeted, then, become secondary to the imperative of successful "public" outcomes.

The call for licensing also draws on a globalizing discourse of sex workers' rights. This discourse has an almost unidirectional focus on renaming prostitution as sex work. The criminalization of prostitutes is a central problem in the sex trade, as this book amply demonstrates, but I find the discourse of sex workers' rights, particularly as advanced by sex radicals, to be quite inadequate on multiple counts. First, it elides the possibility that prostitution may not always be experienced as formal work, even if it can be analytically understood as such. Brothels can, for instance, be experienced less as workplaces and more as extensions of family life, filled with forms of domination and obligation characteristic of the family (Tambe 2006). For many in the sex trade, the sex radical goal of performing undomesticated sexualities is illusory.[4] Second, the analytical distinction in labor studies between workers and supervisors may not hold water in contexts where sex workers adopt the role of brothel keepers on a fluid basis and even earn enough to become brothel owners at some point in their lives. Laws and policies that seek to isolate and criminalize brothel keeping and pimping may end up finding resistance on both these counts from sex workers themselves. Third, the celebration of prostitution as a form of work potentially misidentifies the affective core of pro–sex worker activism. For many of those in the sex trade, the argument for decriminalization is rooted in the principle of respect for them as citizens, bearers of rights, or simply as human beings. The work that they do, or their activities as prostitutes, may well be construed as the very locus of their hardships, and not their source of self-valorization, dignity, or joy. The increasingly popular adoption of sex work as an all-encompassing category collapses variations in the experience of sexual commerce.

Across the globe, the discourse of antitrafficking has also gained a new legitimacy. The ambitious U.S. Victims of Trafficking and Violence Protection Act of 2000 has increased border patrols and withheld foreign aid to countries that do not fight trafficking (Halley et al. 2006). USAID funding for antitrafficking projects in South Asia, as well as with other regions, has multiplied (Shah 2006). The historical record of such measures is, however, weak: the coordinated action between police in different countries under the League of Nations did not prevent trafficking; the laws merely introduced new avenues for police corruption. Although traffickers were sporadically deported, a lucrative nexus developed between police and brothel keepers to monitor the citizenship of prostitutes. The foreignness of trafficked victims was insidiously constructed as a part of the social problem of trafficking. In contemporary times, increased police attention does not bode well for immigrants everywhere who already bear the heavy weight of state surveillance.

Many feminist and human rights groups broadly agree that decriminalizing sex workers is a worthy goal.[5] Decriminalization would help those in the sex trade organize for better working conditions and reduce the hold of brothel keepers. However, the means to accomplish decriminalization are not as obvious. In the present Indian context, decriminalization would ultimately be more of a matter of changes in enforcement practices rather than changes in the text of laws. Since Indian independence, both the two major laws on prostitution, the Suppression of Immoral Trafficking Act (1956) and the Immoral Trafficking and Prostitution Prevention Act (1986), have not declared engaging in commercial sex itself to be illegal.[6] Yet, like their counterparts across the previous century, they have been enforced in ways that have largely criminalized women in the sex trade. The figures that sex workers fear the most are neither customers, brothel keepers, nor procurers but the police (Human Rights Watch 2002). Newspapers regularly report raids on brothels, and yet brothel workers continue to complain about the regular *hafta* (bribe) that they have to provide to police when hauled into police stations after these raids. Surely it is time to shift our political imagination away from the promise of laws and law enforcement.

While the state's role in controlling prostitution has typically been conceptualized either in terms of its abolitionist or its regulationist potential, state power itself, as well as the unintended effects of legislation, has been less well understood. Many activists and even police officials in Mumbai agree that additional legislation is unnecessary—Pravin Patkar of the anti-trafficking group Prerna, and Pradnya Sarvade, a deputy commissioner of police (Preventive Section) both declare that there are enough laws on paper to address prostitution-related problems and that what is needed is more effective enforcement. But there are few voices willing to doubt the very wisdom of turning to the police as instruments of redressal. My book shows how the criminalization of trafficking drove women fearful about their legal status further into the clutches of brothel keepers. At a time when calls are rife for crackdowns on trafficking in Bombay, it is worth pondering the constitutive power of the law, its role as rhetoric, and the unintended consequences of its ineffectual enforcement.

While deceit and egregious abuse certainly play a role in leading women, and particularly children, to enter the sex trade, these are not the sole, or primary, reasons for the proliferation of commercial sex. The number of migrant women in the global sex trade has risen in the past decade, especially of those hailing from countries where neoliberal restructuring has reduced livelihood options for women.[7] When trafficking is cast as a law-and-order problem, the conditions that drive family members to sell daughters or that make brothel life appealing to women are left ignored. Increasing levels of poverty and the promise of a better life in cities drives countless children and women to eagerly trust those termed traffickers. Sexual commerce can potentially offer money, escape, and forms of relative agency absent in other kinds of work. The law does not, and cannot, address such dimensions of the sex trade. Projects that expand alternative occupations for women are one useful solution encouraged by states and NGOs, but a more long-term approach would reverse urban-centered development priorities and challenge the orthodoxy of market fundamentalism.

The role of legal reform is currently undergoing serious feminist questioning in India. Whereas feminists have made remarkable advances in pushing through progressive laws on a host of issues such as dowry, female feticide, and girls' education, there is now a generation of scholars calling for greater understanding of the disciplinary dimensions of state power (Kapur 2005, Sunder Rajan 2003). Vigilance seems especially necessary when the state is an emissary of universalizing discourses of public health and sex workers' rights. My study provides a cautionary view of the gaps in, and scope for abuse of, universalist discourses associated with prostitution. By focusing on the unintended consequences of an earlier generation of anti-trafficking and public health–inspired laws, *Codes of Misconduct* ultimately urges caution about approaching the law as an unproblematic instrument of reform.

ACKNOWLEDGMENTS

In its earliest incarnation this book was a dissertation project, and so I start by acknowledging the generous support and insightful critiques of my committee members at American University. Thanks especially to my chair Vidya Samarasinghe for her infectious confidence and sharp academic instincts, to Deborah Rosenfelt for her astute suggestions and encouragement across many years, and to Geoffrey Burkhart for his many helpful questions. I also appreciate Mustapha Kamal Pasha's help in the formative stages. Suzanna Walters at Georgetown University shared in the project's transformation into a book.

Grants I received from American University and Georgetown University enabled me to travel for fieldwork in 1999–2000, 2002, and 2004. The following institutions and individuals facilitated my research: Maharashtra State Archives, Mumbai (in particular the ever-helpful A. K. Karadhe); the National Archives of India; the British Library, particularly Jill Geber at the Oriental and India Office Collections; the Library of Congress, especially Mohan Gadre and Alan Thrasher; the Bombay University library; the Nehru Memorial Museum and Library; Mr. Navalgund at the library of the National Law School of India; David Nelson at the South Asia collection of the library of the University of Pennsylvania; the Cambridge University South Asian studies collection; the School of Oriental and African Studies library; the Indian Law Institute library; the Georgetown University library; and Robarts Library at the University of Toronto. Marcel Fortin and Amanda Wagner at Robarts Library helped me navigate GIS software and graphics programs in fashioning a reproducible map. Thanks also to Samantha Laforêt, Rachel Levee, and Shannon Black for invaluable research assistance funded by a Connaught Foundation New Faculty Grant.

My stays with friends have added warm memories to this project. Thanks to Keshwar and Homi Ghadiali in London and Anuradha and Ashok Gokhale in Bombay. The Indian Social Institute in New Delhi and YWCA in Bombay also provided calm refuge. For stimulating conversations in the project's early stages, I thank Uma Chakravarti, Janaki Nair, Kumkum Sangari, Shruti Tambe, Sujata Patel, Sharada Dwivedi, Frank Conlon, Salman Akhtar, Asiya Siddiqui, Chaya Datar, Sharadchandra Gokhale, Anil Awachat, Sharmila Rege, Shefali Chandra, Preeti Pai Patkar, and Pravin Patkar.

My greatest debts are to colleagues, anonymous reviewers, and friends who have read all or parts of this work. Thanks to Janaki Nair, Pratiksha Bakshi, Urvashi Butalia, Srimati Basu, and anonymous reviewers at the University of Minnesota Press and Zubaan for reading the entire manuscript and for their many excellent suggestions. Thanks to Dana Collins and Megan Sweeney for sharing generously of their minds while at Georgetown; also Pensri Ho, Tim Pilbrow, Pamela Fox, You-Me Park, and Leona Fisher in faculty reading groups. Thanks to Rajeswari Sunder Rajan, Chandra Mohanty, Richa Nagar, Aparna Devare, Harald Fisher-Tiné, Kamala Kempadoo, Diane Blair, Rachel Sturman, and Sonali Sathaye for commenting on my work and presenting venues to share it. At the University of Toronto, thanks to Marianna Valverde for her sage advice on the opening chapters, and also for the exciting intellectual community of my colleagues Alissa Trotz, Michelle Murphy, Lynne Viola, Kanishka Goonewardena, Melanie Newton, Ato Quayson, Joshua Barker, Kerry Rittich, Bonnie McElhinny, Jacqui Alexander, Judy Taylor, and many others.

At the University of Minnesota Press, thanks to Jason Weidemann for shepherding the manuscript and Lynn Walterick for her careful eye. At Zubaan, thanks to Urvashi Butalia. The refereeing process for my related publications has been very helpful.

I enjoyed the happy haven of my friendship with Aparna Devare and Salil Joshi as I first formulated this work, and they continue to nourish me. Gayatri Vedantam and V. K. Viswanath's unfailing kindness, technological wizardry, and good humor saved my day on many occasions—much love. Thanks also to Vatsala Vedantam and V. L. Sastry for their quiet support. Shruti Tambe, Ganesh Vispute, and Richa Nagar are model public intellectuals whose work inspires me. For their help in my transition to a new academic home, warm thanks to Kiran Mirchandani, Ashwin Joshi, Maya Bhullar, Karan Singh, Kathryn Morgan, Angela Fleury, Shubhra Gururani, Pat and David Sculthorpe, Shahrzad Mojab, and Jane Abray.

Finally, thanks to those whose love centers me: Baba has been a model of fortitude, and his good humor and passionate pursuits have taught me how to live well. Abhi's wit and music brighten many lives, and especially mine. To Shankar, my gratitude runs deep: your friendship, love, and intelligence have sustained and sharpened my work through the years. And to Anya: thank you for the boundless joy.

CHRONOLOGY OF LAWS RELEVANT TO PROSTITUTION IN BOMBAY

Year	Law	Items of Law Relevant to Prostitution
1812	Police Regulation	Title 6: Police require lists of all brothels and names and dwellings of all prostitutes; brothel keepers responsible for order on premises.
1827	Police Regulation	Title 14: Enticing away of women made an offense.
1860	Indian Penal Code	Sections 366–369: Kidnapping and abduction for illicit intercourse made an offense.
		Sections 372–373: Selling and buying of persons under eighteen for prostitution an offense.
1860	Bombay Police Reform (Act ILVIII)	Section 14: Upon receiving complaints from neighbors, police commissioner can order any brothel keeper to discontinue such use of premises.
1864	Foreigners' Act	Non-British subjects may be deported from British India if suspected of criminal activity.

Year	Law	Items of Law Relevant to Prostitution

REGULATIONIST ERA

1867	Bombay Cantonment Act (Act III)	Inspection of brothels for preventing spread of venereal disease; registration of public prostitutes; prohibition of prostitution by unregistered women; extension of rules beyond cantonment limits authorized, but not the penalties for breach of rules.
1870	Contagious Diseases Act (applied to Bombay) (India Act XIV)	Compulsory registration and medical examination of prostitutes; brothel keepers to furnish to police information about particulars of each prostitute and dates of medical examination undergone by them; segregation of prostitutes by neighborhood.
1872	Suspension of CDA due to inadequate financing	
1880	Reintroduction of CDA	
1888	Repeal of CDA	

ANTITRAFFICKING ERA

1894	International Society for the Suppression of White Slave Traffic	Member countries sign agreement to keep a watch at ports against traffickers
1897	Repeal of Cantonment Act (XV)	Cantonment Authority prohibits brothel keeping and the residence of public prostitutes within the limits of regimental bazaars.
1902	Bombay City Police Act (IV)	Section 28: Police can order persons to stop use of a premise as a brothel.

Year	Law	Items of Law Relevant to Prostitution
1902 (*continued*)		Section 120: Soliciting will be punished with imprisonment of eight days and/or a fine of Rs 50.
		Section 20: Police commissioner can direct a prostitute to vacate her place of residence.
1910	International Society for the Suppression of White Slave Traffic	Member countries agree that anyone who procured, enticed, or led away, even with her consent, a woman or girl under age for immoral purposes, [would] be punished, notwithstanding that the various acts constituting the offense may have been committed in different countries.
1921–22	International Convention on Trafficking	Indian laws on trafficking of women and children harmonized with international law.

ABOLITIONIST ERA

Year	Law	Items of Law Relevant to Prostitution
1920	Bombay City Police (Amendment) Act	Section 126 A: Penalizes detention of women against their will; bans brothel keepers from withholding and lending of apparel, ornaments, and property; and allows civil suits to recover inmate debts.
1923–24	Indian Penal Code Amendments to Sections 361–373	Age of consent in cases of kidnapping, abduction, sale, and purchase of girls for prostitution raised to 18 years.
1923	Bombay Prevention of Prostitution Act (XI)	Section 9: Brothel keepers could be ordered by magistrates or police to stop use of a specified house, room, or place as a brothel.

Year	*Law*	*Items of Law Relevant to Prostitution*
1923 (*continued*)		Section 3: Soliciting punishable by eight days' imprisonment and/or a fine of Rs 50.
		Section 6: Procuring of girl or woman punishable by three years in prison or fine of Rs 2000 or whipping.
1924	Cantonment Act (II)	Commanding officer may remove brothels, prostitutes from cantonments.
1926	Amendment of 1923 Prostitution Act (IX)	Soliciting punishable by three months in prison and/or fine of Rs 100; arrest without warrant possible.
1930	Amendment of 1923 Prostitution Act (XII)	Brothel owning: brothel owners, in addition to brothel keepers, could be imprisoned.
		Procuring: female as well as male procurers liable.
1934	Bombay Devadasi Protection Act (X)	The dedication of women or girls to temples or deities punishable by imprisonment for one year and/or fine; all dedication ceremonies declared unlawful; no marriage contracted by a devadasi deemed invalid.
1948	Amendment of 1923 (XXVI)	Definition of brothel expanded; Prostitution Act covers Turkish baths, partitioned cubicles, etc., used for prostitution. Definition of soliciting expanded to include "any act of gross indecency."

NOTES

INTRODUCTION

1. A few observations on the terms in this book. I use the city's new name, Mumbai, when referring to the present, and I retain the older name, Bombay, in historical contexts. Also, I refer to Bombay city rather than Bombay presidency at all times. In this book, I use the terms "sex trade" and "sexual commerce" interchangeably to refer to the exchange of sexual services for money or goods. I intentionally use the terms "prostitute" and "prostitution" in order to stay faithful to the context of nineteenth and early-twentieth-century discourses. I use the term "sex worker" in the contemporary context because of its positive political valence, although it has some pitfalls, as I discuss in chapter 7. I sometimes use "brothel worker" or "brothel inmate" as specific descriptors. The term "sex industry" refers to a gamut of forms of sexual commerce, particularly organized forms such as brothels, and also related activities such as pornography and escort services. The sex industry can be typologized along the following axes: (a) ownership: from self-employed (streetwalkers, call girls) to supervised activities (brothels); (b) spatial organization: from identifiable regular spaces of sexual commerce (brothels) to contingent spaces (parks, motel/hotel rooms); (c) forms of services offered: from nonphysical contact (phone sex, bar dancing) to physical contact (penetrative sex); (d) discreetness, which often corresponds strongly with social class: from exclusive services that retain the client's anonymity to street prostitution where the number and types of observers are unpredictable.

2. Dr. K. S. Patel's extensive responses to a survey on prostitution are found in HD 1921c.

3. See ARPCB 1930, 11; and ARPCB 1931, 10; ARPCB 1932, 11. Suspicions about massage parlors also came up repeatedly in my private conversations with anonymous interlocutors during a 2004 trip to Bombay.

4. See newspaper reports such as *Times of India*, August 9, 2004, "Police Increase Vigil at Five-Star Hotels, Pubs," 3 (Times News Network). Antitrafficking advocate

Pravin Patkar also suggested a significant Uzbek presence in Mumbai's sex trade (private conversation, 2002).

5. See the film *Chandni Bar* (Bhandarkar 2001), recipient of the 2002 IIFA Best Picture award and Suketu Mehta's Pulitzer-nominated *Maximum City* (2004) as examples of recent works focused on the issue of dance bars.

6. For example, at a screening of the documentary *Born into Brothels* in Washington, D.C., in February 2005, I witnessed a representative of an antitrafficking group approach one of the filmmakers with a proposal to use the film to expand support for antitrafficking campaigns. The film is not strictly about trafficking, but the images of Indian brothel life served the group's purposes.

7. See sections 372 and 373 of the Indian Penal Code dealing with selling or buying someone for the purpose of prostitution, as well as section 366 dealing with kidnapping for illicit purposes.

8. In June 2004, the state governor had suggested licensing sex workers on the heels of a proposal by the national human resources development minister to regulate prostitution across the country.

9. While a number of recent books map the history of regulating prostitution in urban centers such as Buenos Aires (Guy 1991, 2000), Calcutta (Banerjee 2000), Mexico City (Bliss 2001), Nairobi (White 1994), Singapore, Hong Kong, Calcutta, and Bombay (Levine 2003), Shanghai (Hershatter 1997), and Stockholm (Svanstrom 2001), this book emphasizes to a far greater extent the disjuncture between lawmaking and law enforcement.

10. In 1999 Sweden became the first country in the world to prohibit buying sexual services, defining prostitution as a form of violence against women, following the formulations of Swedish feminist groups. In the United States, radical feminists have been instrumental in influencing the government's position in instituting Trafficking in Persons Reports, as Halley et al. (2006) explain.

11. Some of the best reviews of feminist debates on sexual commerce include Bell 1994, Chapkis 1997, Kempadoo and Doezema 1998, McClintock 1993, Millett 1973, Overall 1992, 1994, Pateman 1988, Queen 1997, Sunder Rajan 2003, Shrage 1994, Sullivan 2003 and Zatz 1997.

12. A typical representative of the liberal approach is the U.S. group COYOTE (Call Off Your Old Tired Ethics). See Chapkis 1997 for details.

13. "Sex radical" is the self-identified term used by feminists who emphasize the potential of commercial sex to express agency. For examples of sex radical writing, see Bell 1994, Chapkis 1997, Queen 1997, and Vance 1984.

14. In order to probe the effectiveness of the laws in these phases, I analyze police files, annual law enforcement reports, annual prison records, judicial memoranda, court cases, social workers' records, and newspaper articles. Some of these sources such as prison records include quantitative data, which I collate from various years into tables, in order to facilitate comparison and analysis across years. Other sources such as newspaper articles, petitions by civilians, and social workers' records provide a sense of how laws were received.

15. See Chapkis 1997, Kempadoo and Doezema 1998, McClintock 1993, Shrage 1994, and Zatz 1997 on these legal and conceptual benefits of treating prostitution as sex work.

16. These quotes are taken from the July 15, 2003 BBC news story "India Fights to Promote Condoms," which noted that India had the second highest number of HIV infections in the world (http://news.bbc.co.uk/2/low/south_asia/3067325.stm); and Jordan's (2002) story in the *Sunday Times*. The problem of "trafficking" from Nepal and Bangladesh to Bombay has been mapped for a decade now (see, for instance, Friedman 1995).

17. Examples include documentaries and feature films such as *Sex Workers in India* (Aronson 2004), *The Selling of Innocents* (Gupta 1997), *The Day My God Died* (Levine 2003), *Chameli* (Mishra 2004).

18. It is hard to know how accurate these numbers are. The figures I cite are based on estimates given to me by public health organizations such as Population Services International and People's Health Organization (interviews, August 2004). Sanghera's (1996, 103–4) review shows that the numbers "surpass[ed] those of Amsterdam, Hamburg, and Bangkok."

19. Travelers' accounts enthusiastically note the diversity of Bombay's population. See, for instance, J. H. Stocqueler's (1844) description, quoted in Karkaria's (1915) anthology: "The crowded ways, peopled with professors of almost every known creed, and natives of almost every land; the open shops, filled with goods to suit all tastes," 323–25. See also Hall (1832) quoted in Karkaria (1915, 268–69): "As I gazed around me in wonder and delight, I could fix my eye on nothing I had ever seen before. The dresses, in endless variety of flowing robes and twisted turbans, flitted like a vision before me. The Hindoos, of innumerable castes, were there each distinguished from the other by marks drawn with brilliant colours on his brow. There stood Persian merchants with shawls and other goods from cashmere [Kashmir], mingled with numerous Arab horse-dealers careering about; Malays from the straits of Malacca, chatting familiarly with those good-natured merry fellows, the long-tailed Chinese, whose most ungraceful Tartar dress and tuft contrast curiously in such a crowd with the tastefully arranged drapery and gorgeous turbans of the Mahomedans and Hindoos."

20. Bombay was reported to have the largest number of European prostitutes in the country in 1912: 126, in comparison with the reported 50 in Calcutta, 2 in Madras, and 6 in Karachi (HD 1913, 221).

21. The secretary to the Government of Bombay was the central authority implementing the International Conventions on Trafficking of 1904 and 1921 in India (HD 1932, 2).

22. Meyer (1953, 268, 275) notes five well-known types of harlots: the harlot of the rulers, city harlot, secret harlot of good family, harlot of the gods, and harlot of the bathing places.

23. The types of courtesans were: bawds, female attendants, unchaste women, dancers and actresses, artisan's wives, runaway wives, women living on their beauty, and courtesans skilled in dancing and music (Vatsyayana 1962, 237).

24. Edwardes (1910, 202) reports that the proportion of females to 1,000 males in Bombay city was 649 in 1872, 664 in 1881, 586 in 1891, and 595 in 1906.

25. See Spivak 1988 on the dilemma of representing the voice of the subaltern. By definition, subaltern entities are beyond the reach of official discourse, for subalterns are, paraphrasing Marx, the group that cannot represent themselves but must be represented.

1. THE COLONIAL STATE, LAW, AND SEXUALITY

1. Washbrook (1981, 686) finds that "paranoia" arose among colonial rulers after the 1857 revolt underlined the vulnerability of the British Raj. According to Hutchins (1967) as well, the mutiny led to an abandonment of efforts to reform Indians and an inclination to conciliate them. Particularly, he notes that colonial policy in the late nineteenth century was increasingly disposed to preserve those Indian traditions useful to colonial rule.

2. The "colonial mode of production" has been the subject of considerable study and debate in South Asian studies. Perhaps the most widely cited elaboration of this concept is by Alavi (1975, 1251–57), who sees it as a "composite unity," distinct from both a feudal and capitalist mode of production, but possessing attributes of both. Its overarching feature is the mediation of the economy by an imperial center. Different segments of the economy, such as industry and agriculture, were increasingly delinked from one another and connected primarily to the center. Generalized commodity production existed but mostly served the metropolitan center. Surplus was appropriated by the colonial state in order to extend capital formation in the metropolitan center. Landlessness also increased the supply of labor to urban centers, maintaining low wage levels, which in turn secured higher profits in metropolitan centers. Banaji (1972) also notes that in this mode of production, local accumulation of capital was blocked. It was only in times of world economic crisis that expansion of local manufacturing occurred, as in the interwar period.

3. The early volumes by the Subaltern Studies Collective have made a striking contribution to recounting Indian colonial history "from below." The central aim of this group, whose stalwarts include Ranajit Guha, Shahid Amin, Gyanendra Pandey, and David Arnold, has been to counter bourgeois nationalist and colonial history by recovering the consciousness of nonelite social groups. The authors reach beyond the army connotation of the term "subaltern" (meaning someone of inferior rank) to a Gramscian sense of a nonhegemonic social group (Gramsci 1971, 53). See *Subaltern Studies* volumes I–X, especially Volume I, vii–viii.

4. This label is applied to a set of historians focusing primarily on eighteenth-century Indian states who stress continuities between the precolonial and colonial states and adopt an analytical, generalization-seeking approach to Indian history. The title emerged soon after the publication of a set of essays in *Modern Asian Studies* 7, no. 3 (1973). Some works commonly identified with this school are Bayly 1983, Bose and Jalal 1998, and Chandavarkar 1994, 1998.

5. The clearest expression of this position is found in Robert Lingat's *The Classical Law of India* (1998, 257–60). Baxi (1986) offers a useful critique of such approaches.

6. In his critique of two important Subaltern Studies pieces in which the law figures prominently, Guha's "Chandra's Death" and Amin's "Approver's Testimony," Baxi (1992, 251–52) calls for treating community adjudication as "non-state legal systems."

7. Baxi (1992) argues that when looking microscopically at case law, one finds that courts did not adhere strictly to previous decisions, and there was no rigid uniformity, certainty, or consistency in the system.

8. Cohn (1987, 479) sees the introduction of contract relations in India as characterized by "failure to understand the nature of Indian society, assumptions based on British practice" and "mistakes and short term practical considerations."

9. Queen Victoria guaranteed nonintervention in religion in the following proclamation: "We declare it to be our royal will and pleasure that . . . all shall alike enjoy the equal and impartial protection of the law; and we do strictly charge and enjoin all those who may be in authority under us that they abstain from all interference with the religious belief or worship of any of our subjects on pain of our highest displeasure" (quoted from Kosambi 1996, 269).

10. In two well-publicized cases involving child brides in Bengal and Bombay, the colonial state ruled in favor of husbands, aligning with religious orthodox elements.

11. The relationship between the capitalist state, the family-household system, and the wage-labor system has been addressed by Marxist and socialist feminists such as Barrett (1980) and Eisenstein (1977). The role of twentieth-century welfarist legislation in assigning homemaking and childcare to women has been particularly well established (Abramovitz 1988, Nair 1996a). A central issue of debate is whether the capitalist state can be classified as a necessarily, or only historically, male-dominant entity. Barrett (1980), Brown (1995), and Connell (1990) argue against an essentialist notion of a "male" state, nonetheless exploring how states reproduce male dominance through their various imperatives. Brown (1995), in particular, identifies how male dominance is perpetuated through the juridical, bureaucratic, capitalist, and prerogative dimensions of the state.

12. *Devadasis* were women dedicated from childhood to serve temple deities, and who were barred from marriage. They were often accomplished dancers, performing at public arenas on religious occasions. Nair (1996a) details the erosion of matriliny among Nayars and *devadasis* through successive legislations in the second half of the nineteenth century, 150–69.

13. As examples, Chakravarti (1998) points to tracts produced by practitioners of medicine on immorality within high-caste Hindu homes, which listed abortions, liaisons between widows and other householders, and murder of females in the name of family honor.

14. Pheterson (1996) has best elaborated this point in her work on the whore stigma. This critique is shared across a range of feminist writing; see, for instance, McClintock (1993), MacKinnon (1989), and Walkowitz (1980).

15. Such economic usefulness of prostitution is of course not restricted to the colonial context. The economic role of prostitutes has been framed within a contemporary global perspective by Enloe (1989) and Peterson and Runyan (1993). These feminist

international relations theorists highlight the important role sexual servicing has played in sustaining cross-national tourism and foreign military presences.

16. Foucault 1991 (99) probes the rise of the concept of "population" in governance. See also Foucault 1990, 25.

17. For a good introduction along these lines to Foucault's life and works, see Paul Rabinow's introduction in Foucault 1984, especially 7–11.

18. The strategies outlined here were first tried out by the bourgeoisie on themselves, Foucault claims. It was only in the late nineteenth century that the juridical and medical control of perversions utilized by the privileged classes came to be applied to working classes as well (121).

19. Freud's work represents this standard account (Foucault 1990, 150).

20. The implications of this proposition for subject formation are dramatically clarified by Judith Butler (1997), who delves into the contradictions in the formation of sexual identity.

21. See especially Foucault 1990, 82–102. In these sections, Foucault relates his theory of power to the subject of sexuality. He insists that we should move beyond the juridical notion of power, with its antecedents in unitary regimes of monarchies.

22. The notion that the law did not express the will of the state in an absolute sense is actually closer to Foucault's conceptualization of penological reform in *Discipline and Punish* (1979) than his work on sexuality.

23. In sections of *History of Sexuality*, Foucault uses the term "law"as shorthand for the order of juridical monarchy. He stresses that a feature common to all Western monarchies was that they were constructed as systems of law and expressed themselves through theories of law. He therefore makes "law" synonymous with the power of the king.

24. Foucault's stated aim is to "define the regime of power-knowledge-pleasure that sustains discourse on sexuality in our part of the world" (11). Spivak (1988) takes him to task for this geographically limited perspective, terming it a sanctioned ignorance.

25. British men who came to India were often of a middle-class extraction, seeking to expand their personal fortunes and rise in social status. There was, therefore, a pretense of aristocratic status, which Hutchins (1967) wryly notes.

26. Whitehead (1996, 193–95) notes that a key turning point was the acceptance of the germ theory of disease transmission, which was accepted by the British Medical Association in the 1890s and a decade later by the Indian Medical Association. The germ theory drew great attention to hygiene in child-rearing practices.

2. A FAILED EXPERIMENT?

1. One of the earliest books on the CDA in the Indian context was Ballhatchet 1980. Walkowitz (1980) in the same year described the CDA's history in the British context. On South Africa, see Van Heiningen's (1984) article. Others who have written about it in the context of Calcutta are Banerjee (1998) and Pauline Rule (1987). On Bombay, see Ramanna (2000). On northern India, see Whitehead (1995). On its implications for British feminists, see Burton (1994). For a superb comparative treatment, see Levine (2003).

2. See, again, Ballhatchet (1980), Banerjee (1998), Burton (1994), Levine (2003), McClintock (1993), Van Heiningen (1984), and Whitehead (1995).

3. I have in mind here Levine (2003), McClintock (1993), and Van Heiningen (1984). Even though Levine's work comparing CDAs across Asia scrupulously attends to distinctions between the regions, she still presents them largely as a success.

4. Levine (1994, 1996) and Whitehead (1995) use examples mostly from north and east India and only occasionally from west and south India.

5. The institutions of governance in Bombay were shaped by the requirements of the East India Company. The Charter of 1661 granted the East India Company the command over garrisons and power to set up courts of civil and criminal justice. A succession of governors ruled Bombay from 1664 onward, both under the East India Company and under the British Crown after 1862. In the early nineteenth century, a number of rudimentary institutions of governance were systematized: the administrative organization of the police force in 1812, the settlement of revenues in the 1820s, and an independent municipal administration in 1845, consisting of both European and Indian Justices of Peace.

6. The Police Rule, Ordinance, and Regulation of 1812 specified that a small fee had to be taken from each registered house of prostitution in order to defray the expense of watching these "dangerous trades, houses or modes of life" (Kapse 1987, 203).

7. Regulation of 1827, title 14, article 3 reads: "The Court of Petty Sessions shall have power of summary convictions in all cases of persons enticing or conveying away married females or unmarried females under the age of thirteen, out of the protection, and against the will of the Husband or Father . . . for the purpose of prostitution in any way . . . such offenders to be punishable by fine not exceeding five hundred rupees . . . or imprisonment . . . for a time not exceeding six months." Quoted in Kapse 1987, 216.

8. At the time, men and parents often attempted to survive famine and high revenue payments through selling women and children as domestic servants, wives, concubines and prostitutes (Singha 1998).

9. This quote is found in a letter from the secretary of Government of India to Government of Bombay, Judicial Department 1838, vol. 68/512, 44, cited in Kapse 1987, 2.

10. Officially, only 12 percent of British soldiers abroad were allowed to have wives, but the actual number was even smaller (Arnold 1993, 84).

11. E. F. Chapman, Quartermaster General in India, wrote in a circular memorandum that "the employment of Dhais, and insistence upon the performance of the acknowledged duties, is of great importance" (June 17, 1886), printed in Andrews and Bushnell 1898, 3–4.

12. These various justifications are discussed by Ballhatchet (1980). The widespread belief that masturbation was harmful to the body was backed by official medicine, as seen in the surgeon general's statement that "(masturbation) as is well-known, leads to disorders of both body and mind" (Government of Bombay 1886).

13. Upper-class army officials cast soldiers as mechanical objects in need of maintenance and worthy of state spending. One report on the health of troops warned that

"the British soldier, as he lands in India, is a very costly article, and I think it is only wise economy to leave no means untried for the preservation of his health and efficiency" (RHBBC 1877, 39).

14. P. D. Gaitonde (1983) writes in a history of medicine under Portuguese colonialism that Indian physicians in the sixteenth century were unfamiliar with syphilis and termed it *phiranga roga* (or foreign disease) as it was believed to have been brought in by the Portuguese. See also Arnold 1993, 84.

15. Arnold (1993, 23, 28–43) terms this the "environmentalist" paradigm of medicine. See for instance, the words of the surgeon general: "There is an additional gravity attaching to disorders when they occur in the Eastern Tropics." Moore, 6.

16. The Cantonment Act was applied in 1867 in Bombay with some alterations. The rules were less harsh than those followed elsewhere: the Bombay government published a notification that although the act would be operated beyond cantonment limits, penalties could not be imposed for breaches of rules in these areas (HD 1887). Right from the inception of the regulation, it appears that the Bombay government followed a lenient course in applying the central government's measures.

17. See Levine 2003 on the sequence of its application in other colonies such as Hong Kong, Singapore, and Queensland.

18. I thank Janaki Nair for this insight.

19. In the English CDA of 1864, a woman could be detained by medical examiners for only twenty-four hours; she could be imprisoned for refusing to submit for an exam for only one month. No such limits were specified in the Indian CDA of 1868 or the Bombay rules of 1870.

20. Ironically, the largest numbers of syphilis cases were contracted during a stay in England. The entry on Bombay reads "240 men stationed for three and a half months, each man with 39 days leave, incurred only 2 cases of venereal ulcer." After the stay in England, "5 cases of syphilis were found following 33 days in port" (RWCDA 1883, 7).

21. In the medical officer's words, "Of the 12 cases occurring in HMS Bacchante, 6 presented during the month of March pointed to a common origin, and it appears that 4 contracted syphilis from one defaulter, who also contaminated 3 soldiers," (GD 1887, vol. 37, 276).

22. See Arnold 1993 on the history of the Indian Medical Service and the intimate connection between the military and state medicine.

23. The importance of medical authorities in the operation of the Bombay CDA is evident in the enforcement responsibility given to the surgeon general and the chief medical officer of lock hospitals. They hired personnel, set up medical examination centers, ran the lock hospitals, and provided reports on the working of the CDA to the government (RACDAB 1870, section XII, regulations 1, 2, 3). In the interval between the first phase of the application of the CDA (1870–71) and the second phase (1880–88), it was the sanitary commissioner's office that stepped up pressure on the government to reintroduce the Acts.

24. 1,651 people were classified as "prostitutes" in the 1871 census, and 1,524 in 1881. See chapter 5 for details.

25. Parliamentary Papers 1883, vol. 50, 540–42. Enclosure: Letter from the Sanitary Commissioner for the Government of Bombay, GD, A-535, June 28, 1876.

26. As the surgeon general noted in 1887, "Nothing would render the Act more unpopular with natives than any semblance of intereference with 'kept women'" (GD 1887c, 156).

27. See RWCDA 1887, July, describing the case of Coolsum. See also newspaper reports confirming that women had left for Bandra: *Bombay Samachar*, May 26, 1871; *Satya Watta,* June 9, 1870.

28. When visiting brothels by night, Inspector Foard found a number of women who frequented them "no doubt for the purpose of prostitution," but who are alleged to be friends or relations of registered prostitutes (GD 1887c, 149–51).

29. In the case of Purbuttee's prosecution, the magistrate declined to proceed with the case because the only available witness was another prostitute, Tuckoo, whom the magistrate found "a woman of bad character" (GD 1887a, 173).

30. When the Act was introduced, the municipality and the government had reached an agreement for sharing the costs.

31. The chief Indian trading communities were the Gujarati and Jain *Banias* (traders), Parsis, Konkani Muslims, Bohra Muslims, and Marathas.

32. This was a citizens' organization that aimed to represent the needs of the people before the British government. See Dobbin 1972, 80–86.

33. The editors of *Jam-e-Jamshed* on May 9, 1871 congratulated the "people of Bombay" and repeated that "it is not just to tax the honest and moral for the convenience of the vicious."

34. *Rast Goftar,* December 26, 1881; *Indu Prakash,* December 27, 1881; *Gujarati,* January 2, 1882.

35. Military Collection 315, L/MIL/7/13826.

36. The quartermaster general in India advised, in a circular to all commanding officers, that "in the regimental bazaars it is necessary to have a sufficient number of women, to take care that they are sufficiently attractive, to provide them with proper houses, and above all to insist upon means of ablution being always available." Quoted in Andrews and Bushnell 1898, 3–4.

3. RACIAL STRATIFICATION
AND THE DISCOURSE OF TRAFFICKING

1. Pamela Haag (1999), for instance, mentions that "white slavery" was referenced in one billion pages between 1900 and 1924 in the United States.

2. The League of Nations, commonly termed the precursor of the United Nations, was an international organization founded in 1919 aspiring to preserve territorial integrity and cooperation between nations of the world. It oversaw international conventions against trafficking.

3. As I explain in the final section of the chapter, third-party procurers were those responsible for transporting and selling women or girls from one locale to brothels in another locale.

4. One antitrafficking report supports the claim that Bombay had a high number of Europeans with the following figures: there were about 9,000 Europeans (5,000 of whom were male) in Bombay, but around 4,000 in Calcutta and 3,000 in Madras in 1932 (HD 1932, 25).

5. The following excerpt from a 1937 antitrafficking report illustrates in detail how Bombay was the point of entry to other cities for one pair of women: "Miss Erma Edith Contin, Swiss subject, [and] Marie Josephine Bottai, a French subject, came to India by SS Comorin on the 27th March 1936. Miss Conti registered herself as a prostitute and went to reside in Calcutta. Miss Bottai went to Madras and then to Singapore by the SS Rajulla on 16 June 1936. She was reported to have lived on prostitution during her stay in India" (Political Department 1937, 1).

6. For instance, a 1922 Prostitution Committee's report found "34 Japanese houses with 80 inmates" (GD 1922, appendix B, 11).

7. These specific countries were also part of a circuit of traffickers mapped by Hyam (1990, 144), with movement occurring from Russia, Poland, Austria, France, and Germany to Asia and South America. Apart from the economic constraints that drove women into this profession, state policies also facilitated trafficking circuits in some of these "sending" countries: France had in place a system of regulated brothels, which made it an easier recruiting ground, while the Russian czarist state issued prostitutes a "yellow card" in place of a passport, which allowed for their easy identification by recruiters (Carter 1945).

8. These observations are based on the reasoning used by police commissioner Frank Souter to move prostitutes out of Duncan Road in 1888: that it was a thoroughfare for those traveling south from Byculla. By the 1920s, Byculla was a well-established white suburb: the Anglo-Indian and Domiciled European Association was housed on Sankli Street in Byculla, for instance.

9. Bohras were a subsect of Muslims hailing from Western India and were influential traders. See manuscripts of petitions from Bohra community (GD 1888b, 109–15; 199–221). For petitions from self-styled "respectable poor" residents, see GD 1888c, 29, and also 267–69. These residents held that the arrival of European prostitutes disturbed their peace.

10. See also the residents' letter in the *Bombay Gazette*, titled "The Bombay Social Pest," May 18, 1888, 5: "It is hoped police will send the late residents of Cursetji Suklaji Street back to their old abode as soon as possible, and relieve us poor sufferers from the nuisance we have had to put up with for nearly a year."

11. This petition has a row of thumbprints next to Indian women's names, led by one man's name, suggesting that it could have been a brothel landlord trying to present the letter as an Indian prostitutes' petition.

12. Indian constables, who were primarily Marathi-speaking immigrant recruits from Ratnagiri, rarely interacted with European brothel workers. For more on the hierarchical structure of Bombay's police force, see Chandavarkar 1998.

13. The number of European prostitutes did increase considerably just before World

War I but went down during the war as German and Austrian women were deported (HD 1913a, 221; ARPTIB 1915, 17).

14. Favel "dropped the hint that he was the only Jew in the Police who had won a King's medal and something ought to be done to celebrate it," and Meyer obliged with the picnic (Judicial Department Proceedings 1917, 100).

15. Buenos Aires was a "principal target" for anti–white slavery campaigns because of the large number of European prostitutes (Guy 2000, 79). Hyam (1990) also notes that "Buenos Aires was something of an international Mecca or Golconda magnet" in the "geography of white slavery" (145).

16. Oxford English Dictionary, 2nd ed. In a rare sixteenth-century usage, "traffic" also meant "a prostitute."

17. I thank Janaki Nair for a reminder of this important point. See also Sinha (2006).

18. For instance, see Alfred Dyer's (1892) widely circulated article "Slave Trade in European Girls to British India," which compiles cases of trafficked girls in Bombay from different missionary newspapers.

19. In this sense, brothels were business ventures in which ownership and management were to some extent synonymous, and the brothel had a corporate existence potentially independent of the building in which it was housed.

20. See the testimonies of Phooli, Moti, and Paru for examples of amounts earned per customer in an Indian brothel (HD 1917a).

4. AKOOTAI'S DEATH

1. In Spivak's (1988) definition (which paraphrases Marx), the subaltern is the group that cannot represent itself but must be represented. The Subaltern Studies Collective specifically draws on Gramsci's (1971) usage of the term "subaltern."

2. The details narrated here are principally gathered from the testimonies in the Duncan Road murder case (HD 1917a). Most important are the statements of Phooli, Moti, and Paru, who were brothel workers alongside Akootai. In addition, I have used the statements of Tarabai, who cooked for them; Jijabai, who also worked in the brothel; Gajrajsingh Akbarsingh, who collected rents from the brothel keepers; Vithoo Jagoji, the police constable; Lingabai, an assistant of Gangabai; Naikoo, Akootai's cousin; Ganpat Keshav, who registered the death; and Laxman Bala, who carried the corpse.

3. Jijabai had a different relationship with the brothel keepers than the other inmates; she was "brought" to the brothel by a man named Abdul, and although she stated that she did not know the arrangement between Mirza and Abdul, she was not kept under lock and key.

4. A curry stone is a heavy pestle used with stone mortars to grind curry pastes. It is usually about one foot long and four inches wide at the base.

5. There were some differences in earning among the inmates. Moti's claim of nearly fifty customers per day was intended to upstage her companions, revealing how the prevailing measure of a prostitute's worth was based on the needs of brothel keepers. See testimony of Moti, HD 1917a.

6. See testimony of Gajrajsingh Akbarsingh, rent farmer (HD 1917a).

7. Naikoo testified: "My cousin Akootai used to earn in accused no. 1's brothel and I used to go to see her. I also used to borrow money from accused no. 1 who is a Pathan. I have paid him off. I do not owe him anything now" (HD 1917a).

8. Akootai hailed from the southern Kolhapur district, where it is possible that Kannada words were a part of the dialect.

9. See testimony of Tarabai (HD 1917a).

10. See testimony of Phooli (HD 1917a).

11. Interestingly, he asked his neighbor, Sulleman Oomer, whose mistress also ran a brothel, to stay behind and "sit near" Gangabai because "she [was] alone and would get frightened." This line indicates on the one hand that Gangabai was feeling fearful but also that Mirza felt he needed to have an associate keep a watch on Gangabai (see testimony of Tarabai).

12. See testimony of Ganpat Keshav (HD 1917a).

13. See ARSCB for 1871 (trial of Morad Husain Ali); 1873 (trial of Nusserwanjee Nowrojee); and 1874 (trial of Purushram Ganesh); ARPTIB 1892 (trial of Abdullah Gopichand); ARPCB 1918 (trial of Syed Mirza); and ARPCB 1921 (trial of Umrao Singh and Beldev Mullu).

14. Several newspaper reports prefaced their initial mention of Mirza with an identification of his ethnicity, including the *Bombay Chronicle*, February 22, 1917, and the *Times of India*, April 6, 1917. The *Advocate of India* editorialized: "The Pathans are a great nuisance in Bombay and other parts of India. They are great bullies and are a terror particularly in country districts;" it endorsed "early legislative measures to stop such terrorism and blackguardism" (July 4, 1916).

15. As Dirks (2002) and Cohn (1996) have analyzed, the late colonial state in India became increasingly ethnographic in its aim to predict and control recalcitrance and unruliness. It identified castes and tribes that were likely to be disorderly and marked them as criminals. The Pathans were one such classification.

16. Wacha surmised that "possibly the police were accomplices and cases of the nature were never heard. If heard now, it is suspected that the police has not had its '*bakshis*' [bribe] from these inhuman monsters" (HD 1917c).

17. *Census of India* 1921, paragraph 168.

18. See Edwardes (1910) on the caste makeup of Kamathipura's brothel workers. Edwardes and his assistants who helped compile the Gazetteer of Bombay concluded that prostitutes in Kamathipura were "largely Mhars from Deccan and Dheds from Gujarat" (Edwardes 1910, 190).

19. See Table II of Section 20, Prostitution in Bombay, Census of India 1921. For an account of castes involved in prostitution, see the entries in Enthoven 1920 on "*bhavins*" (145–47), "*kalavantins*" (130–32), and "*bandis*" (58).

20. The ascendant role of public health in the 1920s and the notion of scientific mothering allowed social reformist institutions to pronounce expertise on childrearing. See Whitehead (1996) for more on the rise of scientific mothering in the 1920s.

21. See Edwardes's (1910) chapter on population, written with the help of H. A. Talchekar, for a description of chawls.

5. ABOLITION AND NATIONALISM

1. For an excellent articulation of this ideal construct of the female citizen from the 1930s, see Kaur's (1933) description of the women's movement in India. It confirms aspects of Chatterjee's (1989) well-known argument that Indian womanhood was configured as a site of spirituality. See also Sinha's (1997, 2006) influential analyses of how the woman question was framed in Indian nationalist discourse in the 1920s.

2. Section 28 of the Act IV of 1902 defined the brothel keeper as someone "who occupies or manages or acts or assists in the management of, or upon any woman who resides in, uses, or frequents, any house, room or place in which the business of a common prostitute is carried on." It is significant that this act did not make all brothels illegal, as it left the serving of notices up to the discretion of the commissioner of police. Section 120 specified soliciting thus: "Whoever in any street or public place or place of public resort, or within sight of, and in such manner as to be seen or heard from, any street or public place, whether from within any house or building or not, a) by words, gestures or otherwise, attracts or endeavors to attract attention for the purposes of prostitution; b) solicits or molests any person for the purposes of prostitution; c) willfully and indecently exposes his person." The punishment was imprisonment for up to eight days or a fine up to fifty rupees.

3. For stories on the 1902 Police Bill and Act, see *Indu Prakash*, February 20 and 27, and March 10; *Voice of India*, April 26; *Jam-e-Jamshed*, March 17 and 24; *Gurakhi*, February 23 ; *Rast Goftar*, March 2, 16, and 27. All of these discuss the 1902 Act without referring to sections 28 or 120 dealing with brothel keepers and soliciting.

4. See Section 126 A of "A Bill to Further Amend the City of Bombay Police Act 1902" (HD 1918).

5. There were no prosecutions under the new section 126 A of the Police Act in the annual police reports (ARPCB), 1920–23. In 1923, the Bombay Prevention of Prostitution Act was passed, consolidating section 126 A with other measures.

6. Such a committee had been proposed in the immediate aftermath of the Akootai murder. See letter from Labhshankar Laxmidas of the Bombay Humanitarian Fund to the police, April 7, 1917, calling for a special commission to be appointed to study prostitution (HD 1917b).

7. There is a strain of contempt for brothel prostitutes in the committee's report. It held that the women had an "inborn or acquired laziness" and if forced to leave brothels, they would be unlikely to "adapt themselves to the changed conditions and join the clandestine class" (RCP 1922, M12, M15).

8. Mr. Hoosenally Rahimtoola, member of the Bombay Vigilance Association, was included on the select committee to consider amending the BPPA in 1926 (HD 1926a, 12).

9. Section 5 targeted pimping: "Any male person who knowingly lives, wholly or in part, on the earnings of prostitution"; sections 6 and 7 targeted procuring and importing of women into Bombay for prostitution; and section 8 banned the detention of a woman against her will in a house or room for the purpose of prostitution.

10. For descriptions of murders of prostitutes, see ARPCB 1871, 1873, 1874, 1892, 1918, 1921. For examples of similarly lengthy descriptions of trafficking cases, see ARPCB 1917. The few descriptions of trafficking cases mention peripheral information that is peculiar but irrelevant, such as one man's bankruptcy after a pilgrimage to Mecca, which led him to force his wife to work in a brothel (ARPCB 1917, 9).

11. See changes to section 3 by Act XI of 1923.

12. See changes in sections 8 and 9 introduced by Act XII of 1930.

13. For a comparison of policies on prostitution in different regions of India in 1932, see Responses to the League of Nations Questionnaire (HD 1932, 5–6).

14. See ARPCB 1930, 11; ARPCB 1931, 10; ARPCB 1932, 11.

15. See changes to section 4 introduced by Act XXVI of 1948.

16. See changes to section 2 introduced by Act XI of 1948.

17. The classification "prostitutes" varied in its specificity from census to census. Although the 1864, 1871, and 1881 censuses counted "prostitutes," the 1891 census had a vague category ("females in disreputable professions"), of which prostitutes formed the bulk, according to census notes (the figure in Table 10 reflects all "females in disreputable professions"). In 1901, "prostitutes and pimps" were counted but in 1911, "prostitutes" were included with "beggars, vagrants, receivers of stolen goods, and cattle poisoners." Since this classification was very broad, the figure for that year is left blank. In 1921 and 1931, numbers for "prostitutes and pimps" were listed clearly among "Unproductive Occupations." The 1941 census was abbreviated because of war and showed no occupations. Censuses after Independence did not include prostitution.

18. Data on the cause of imprisonment were not available.

CONCLUSION

1. I have in mind examples such as Inspector Foard catching Jumna and her partner having sex; Inspector Nolan's encounters with Murriam in six different brothels; Inspector Favel receiving services in, and sharing profits from, brothels; Dhunji Deoji searching for his mistress in a Kamathipura brothel; and Vithoo Jagoji discovering Akootai's body. See chapters 2, 3, and 4 for details.

2. The mayor of Kolkata (Calcutta) announced in April 2004 that the Kolkata Municipal Corporation (KMC) would issue licenses to sex workers who were brothel-based and willing to take a mandatory HIV test (Dar 2004).

3. The Kolkata mayor's proposal was opposed by the city's largest sex worker's rights organization, DMSC (Durbar Mahila Samanwaya Committee) and was soon retracted.

4. See Bell 1994, Chapkis 1997, Queen 1997, and Vance 1984. See also, as an Indian example, VAMP's newsletter http://www.vampnews.org/about_us.html.

5. The Human Rights Watch (2002) report *Epidemic of Abuse* explains at great length the problem of police harassment of sex workers and NGOs that interact with them, such as VAMP in Sangli and Samraksha in Bangalore.

6. See D'Cunha 1991, Kotiswaran 2001, and Sunder Rajan 2003 for reviews of post-Independence laws on prostitution.

7. Eastern Europe, where countries have been shell-shocked by market reforms, and Mexico, where farming has suffered under multilateral trade agreements, are primary "sending" countries to the United States, for example. See Thorbeck and Pattanaik 2002 on migration and the sex trade on a global scale.

BIBLIOGRAPHY

BOOKS AND JOURNAL ARTICLES

Abbe Dubois, J. A. 1906. *Hindu Manners, Customs, and Ceremonies.* Translated by H. K. Beauchamp. Oxford: Clarendon.

Abramovitz, Mimi. 1981. *Regulating the Lives of Women: Social Welfare Policy from Colonial Times to Present.* Boston: South End.

Agarwal, Bina. 1994. *A Field of One's Own: Gender and Land Rights in South Asia.* Cambridge: Cambridge University Press.

Agnes, Flavia. 1999. *Law and Gender Inequality: The Politics of Women's Rights in India.* Delhi: Oxford University Press.

Alavi, Hamza. 1975. "India and the Colonial Mode of Production." *Economic and Political Weekly* 10, special no. (August): 1235–62.

Anagol-McGinn, Padma. 1992. "The Age of Consent Act (1891) Reconsidered: Women's Perspectives and Participation in the Child-Marriage Controversy in India." *South Asia Research* 12, no. 2 (November 1992): 100–118.

Anderson, Michael, and Sumit Guha, eds. 1998. *Changing Concepts of Rights and Justice in South Asia.* Delhi: Oxford University Press.

Andrews, Kate, and Elizabeth Bushnell. 1898. *The Queen's Daughters in India.* London: Mogar and Scott.

Appadurai, Arjun. 1996. "Sovereignty without Territoriality: Notes for a Post-National Geography." In *The Geography of Identity,* edited by P. Yaeger, 40–58. Ann Arbor: University of Michigan Press.

Arnold, David. 1993. *Colonizing the Body: State Medicine and Epidemic Disease in Nineteenth-Century India.* Berkeley: University of California Press.

———. 1997. "The Colonial Prison: Power, Knowledge and Penology in Nineteenth-Century India." In *A Subaltern Studies Reader,* edited by R. Guha, 140–78. Minneapolis: University of Minnesota Press, 1997. Originally published in *Subaltern*

Studies 8 (1994), edited by D. Arnold and D. Hardiman, 148–87. Delhi: Oxford University Press.

Asad, Talal. 2002. "Ethnographic Representations, Statistics, and Modern Power." In *From the Margins: Historical Anthropology and its Futures,* edited by Brian Axel, 66–91. Durham, N.C.: Duke University Press.

Ballantyne, Tony. 2003. "Rereading the Archive and Opening up the Nation-State: Colonial Knowledge in South Asia." In *After the Imperial Turn: Thinking with and Through the Nation,* edited by Antoinette Burton, 102–24. Durham, N.C.: Duke University Press.

Ballhatchet, Kenneth. 1980. *Race, Sex, and Class under the Raj: Imperial Attitudes and Policies and Their Critics, 1793–1905.* New York: St. Martin's Press.

Banaji, Jairus. 1972. "For a Theory of Colonial Modes of Production." *Economic and Political Weekly* 2, no. 52: 2498–502.

Banerjee, Sumanta. 1993. "The 'Beshya' and the 'Babu': Prostitute and her Clientele in Nineteenth-Century Bengal." *Economic and Political Weekly* 28, no. 45: 2461–72.

———. 1998. *Dangerous Outcast: The Prostitute in Nineteenth-Century Bengal.* Calcutta: Seagull Books.

———. 2000. *Under the Raj: Prostitution in Colonial Bengal.* New York: Monthly Review Press.

Barrett, Michele. 1980. *Women's Oppression Today: Problems in Marxist Feminist Analysis.* London: Verso.

Barry, Kathleen. 1984. *Female Sexual Slavery.* New York: New York University Press.

———. 1995. *The Prostitution of Sexuality: The Global Exploitation of Women.* New York: New York University Press.

Basu, Aparna, and Bharati Ray. 1990. *Women's Struggle: A History of the All India Women's Conference, 1927–1990.* New Delhi: Manohar.

Baxi, Upendra. 1986. *Towards a Sociology of Indian Law.* New Delhi: Satrahan Publications.

———. 1992. "'The State's Emissary': The Place of Law in Subaltern Studies." In *Subaltern Studies 7: Writings on South Asian History and Society,* edited by Partha Chatterjee and Gyanendra Pandey, 247–64. New Delhi: Oxford.

———. 1993. *Marx, Law, and Justice.* Bombay: N. M. Tripathi.

Bayly, Christopher. 1983. *Rulers, Townsmen, and Bazaars: North Indian Society in the Age of British Imperialism, 1770–1870.* Cambridge: Cambridge University Press.

BBC. 2007. "Sharp Drops in India Aids Levels. 6 July. http://news.bbc.co.uk/2/hi/south_ asia/6276398.stm. (accessed July 30, 2007).

Bell, Shannon. 1994. *Reading, Writing, and Rewriting the Prostitute Body.* Bloomington: Indiana University Press.

Berman, Jacqueline. 2003. "(Un) popular Strangers and Crises (Un) bounded: Discourses of Sex-trafficking, the European Political Community, and the Panicked State of the Modern State." *European Journal of International Relations* 9, no. 1 (March): 37–86.

Bindel, Julie, and Liz Kelly. 2004. *A Critical Examination of Responses to Prostitution in Four Countries: Victoria, Australia; Ireland; the Netherlands; and Sweden.* Evidence Received for Prostitution Tolerance Zones (Scotland) Bill Stage 1. http://www.scottish .parliament.uk/business/committees/lg/inquiries-04/ptz/lg04-ptz-res-03.htm (accessed February 4, 2004).

Bliss, Katherine. 2001. *Compromised Positions: Prostitution, Public Health, and Gender Politics in Revolutionary Mexico City.* University Park: Pennsylvania State University Press.

Block, Fred. 1977. "The Ruling Class Does Not Rule: Notes on the Marxist Theory of the State." *Socialist Revolution* 7, no. 3: 6–28.

Bolitho, Hector. 1954. *Jinnah: Creator of Pakistan.* London: John Murray.

Bose, Sugata, and Ayesha Jalal. 1998. *Modern South Asia: History, Culture, Political Economy.* London: Routledge.

Bristow, Edward. 1983. *Prostitution and Prejudice: The Jewish Fight against White Slavery.* London: Oxford University Press.

Brown, Wendy. 1992. "Finding the Man in the State." *Feminist Studies* 18, no. 1 (Spring): 7–34.

———. 1995. *States of Injury: Power and Freedom in Late Modernity.* Princeton, N.J.: Princeton University Press.

Bullough, Vern, and Bonnie Bullough. 1993. *Women and Prostitution: A Social History.* Buffalo, N.Y.: Prometheus.

Burton, Antoinette. 1994. *Burdens of History: British Feminists, Indian Women, and Imperial Culture, 1865–1915.* Chapel Hill: University of North Carolina.

———. 2003. *Dwelling in the Archive: Women Writing House, Home, and History in Late Colonial India.* New York: Oxford University Press.

———. 2003a. "Introduction: On the Inadequacy and the Indispensability of the Nation." In *After the Imperial Turn: Thinking with and through the Nation,* edited by A. Burton, 1–23. Durham, N.C.: Duke University Press.

Butler, Judith. 1990. *Gender Trouble: Feminism and the Subversion of Identity.* New York: Routledge.

———. 1997. *The Psychic Life of Power: Theories in Subjection.* Stanford, Calif.: Stanford University Press.

Califia, Pat. 1988. *Male Sluts.* Boston: Alyson.

Carroll, Lucy. 1989. "Law, Custom, and Statutory Social Reform: The Hindu Widows' Remarriage Act of 1856." In *Women in Colonial India: Essays on Survival, Work, and the State,* edited by J. Krishnamurthy, 1–26. Delhi: Oxford University Press.

Carter, Dyson. 1945. *Sin and Science.* Toronto: Progress Books.

Chadha, Monica. 2003. "India Fights to Promote Condoms." *BBC online,* http://news .bbc.co.uk/2/low/south_asia/3067325.stm (accessed July 16 2003).

Chakraborty, Usha. 1963. *Condition of Bengali Women around the Second Half of the Nineteenth Century.* Calcutta: Bardhan Press.

Chakravarti, Uma. 1989. "Whatever Happened to the Vedic Dasi? Orientalism, Nationalism, and a Script for the Past." In *Recasting Women: Essays in Colonial History,* edited by K. Sangari and S. Vaid, 27–87. New Delhi: Kali for Women.

————. 1993. "Conceptualizing Brahminical Patriarchy in Early India: Gender, Caste, Class, and State." *Economic and Political Weekly* 28, no. 14 (April 3): 579–85.

————. 1996. "Wifehood, Widowhood, and Adultery: Female Sexuality, Surveillance, and the State in Eighteenth-Century Maharashtra." In *Social Reform, Sexuality, and the State,* edited by Patricia Uberoi, 3–22. New Delhi: Sage.

————. 1998. *Rewriting History: The Life and Times of Pandita Ramabai.* New Delhi: Kali for Women.

Chandavarkar, Rajnarayan. 1994. *The Origins of Industrial Capitalism in India: Business Strategies and the Working Classes in Bombay, 1900–1940.* Cambridge: Cambridge University Press.

————. 1998. *Imperial Power and Popular Politics: Class, Resistance, and the State in India, c.1850–1950.* Cambridge: Cambridge University Press.

Chapkis, Wendy. 1997. *Live Sex Acts: Women Performing Erotic Labor.* New York: Routledge.

Chatterjee, Indrani. 1999. *Gender, Slavery, and Law in Colonial India.* New York: Oxford University Press.

Chatterjee, Partha. 1989. "The Nationalist Resolution of the Women's Question." In *Recasting Women: Essays in Colonial History,* edited by Kumkum Sangari and Sudesh Vaid, 233–53. New Delhi: Kali for Women.

————. 1993. *The Nation and its Fragments: Colonial and Postcolonial Histories.* Princeton, N.J.: Princeton University Press.

Chatterjee, Ratnabali. 1993. "Prostitution in Nineteenth-Century Bengal: Construction of Class and Gender." *Social Scientist* 21, nos. 9–11: 159–72.

Chowdhury, Prem. 1996. "Contesting Claims and Counter-Claims: Questions of the Inheritance and Sexuality of Widows in a Colonial State." In *Social Reform, Sexuality and the State,* edited by Patricia Uberoi, 65–82. California: Sage Publications.

Cohn, Bernard. 1987. *An Anthropologist among Historians.* Delhi: Oxford University Press.

————. 1996. *Colonialism and its Forms of Knowledge: The British in India.* Princeton, N.J.: Princeton University Press.

Connell, R. W. 1990. "The State, Gender, and Sexual Politics." *Theory and Society* 19, no. 4: 507–44.

Cooper, Frederick, and Ann Laura Stoler, eds. 1997. *Tensions of Empire: Colonial Cultures in a Bourgeois World.* Berkeley: University of California Press.

Crago, Anna-Louise. 2003. "Unholy Alliance." *Rabble,* May 21. http://www.alternet.org/story.html?StoryID=15947 (accessed June 1 2004).

Dang, Kokila. 1993. "Prostitutes, Patrons, and the State: Nineteenth-Century Awadh." *Social Scientist* 21, nos. 9–11: 173–96.

Dar, Sujoy. 2004. "In India, Kolkata Mayor's Plans to Legalize Sex Work Trigger Debate." Inter Press Service, April 14, 2004. http://www.cyberdyaryo.com/features/ f2004_0414_02.htm (accessed June 1, 2004.)

Das, Veena. 1996. "Sexual Violence, Discursive Formations, and the State." Special issue of *Economic and Political Weekly* (September): 2411–23.

D'Cunha, Jean. 1991. *The Legalization of Prostitution: A Sociological Inquiry into the Laws relating to Prostitution in India and the West.* Bangalore: Wordwatch.

Dirks, Nicholas B. 2002. "Annals of the Archive: Ethnographic Notes on the Sources of History." In *From the Margins: Historical Anthropology and Its Futures,* edited by Brian K. Axel, 47–65. Durham, N.C.: Duke University Press.

Dobbin, Christine. 1972. *Urban Leadership in Western India: Politics and Communities in Bombay City, 1840–1885.* London: Oxford University Press.

Dossal, Mariam. 1989. "Limits of Colonial Urban Planning: A Study of Mid-Nineteenth-Century Bombay." *International Journal of Urban and Regional Research* 13, no. 1 (March): 19–31.

Dyer, Alfred. 1892. "Slave Trade in European Girls to British India." *Bombay Guardian* (July): 1–4.

Edwardes, S. M. 1910. *Gazetteer of Bombay City and Island.* Vol. 1. Bombay: Times Press.

———. 1923. *Bombay City Police: A Historical Sketch.* London: Oxford University Press.

———. 1983 [1924]. *Crime in British India.* New Delhi: ABC Publishing.

Eisenstein, Zillah. 1977. "Constructing a Theory of Capitalist Patriarchy and Socialist Feminism." *Insurgent Sociologist* 7, no. 3 (Spring): 3–17.

El Saadawi, Nawal. 1983. *Woman at Point Zero.* London: Zed Books.

Engels, Dagmar. 1983. "The Age of Consent Act of 1891: Colonial Ideology in Bengal." *South Asia Research* 3, no. 2 (November): 107–31.

Enloe, Cynthia. 1989. *Bananas, Beaches, and Bases: Making Feminist Sense of International Politics.* Berkeley: University of California Press.

———. 2000. *Maneuvers: The International Politics of Militarizing Women's Lives.* Berkeley: University of California Press.

Enthoven, R. F. 1920. *The Tribes and Castes of Bombay.* Vol.1. Bombay: Government Central Press.

Forbes, Geraldine. 1996. *Women in Modern India.* Cambridge: Cambridge University Press.

Foucault, Michel. 1979 [1977]. *Discipline and Punish: The Birth of the Prison.* Translated by A. Sheridan. New York: Vintage, 1977; reprint, New York: Vintage 1979.

———. 1984. *The Foucault Reader.* Edited by P. Rabinow. New York: Pantheon.

———. 1990. *The History of Sexuality.* Vol. 1, *An Introduction.* New York: Vintage. Originally published in 1978.

———. 1991. "Governmentality." In *The Foucault Effect: Studies in Governmentality,* edited by G. Burchell et al., 87–104. Chicago: University of Chicago Press.

Gaitonde, P. D. 1983. *Portuguese Pioneers in India: Spotlight on Medicine.* Bombay: Popular Prakashan.

Gandhi, Mohandas. 1921. "Notes." *Young India,* June 8, 1921. *Collected Works of Mahatma Gandhi,* vol. 23, no 112.

———. 1925. "Speech at Public Meeting, Madaripur," June 13, *Collected Works of Mahatma Gandhi,* vol. 31, no 295.

———. 1927. "Speech at Public Meeting, Chidambaram," September 11, published in *The Hindu,* Spetember 13, 1927, *Collected Works of Mahatma Gandi,* vol. 40, no. 42.

————. 1942. *Women and Social Injustice.* Ahmedabad: Navjivan Publishers.

Ghosh, Durba. 2004. "Household Crimes and Domestic Order: Keeping the Peace in Colonial Calcutta, c.1770– c.1840." *Modern Asian Studies* 38, no. 3: 599–623.

————. 2006. *Sex and the Family in Colonial India: The Making of Empire.* Cambridge: Cambridge University Press.

Glickman, Nora. 2000. *The Jewish White Slave Trade and the Untold Story of Raquel Liberman.* New York: Garland Publishing.

Gramsci, Antonio. 1971. *Selections from the Prison Notebooks of Antonio Gramsci.* Edited and translated by Q. Hoare and G. N. Smith. New York: International Publishers.

Guha, Ranajit. 1997 [1987]. "Chandra's Death." In *A Subaltern Studies Reader, 1986–1995,* edited by R. Guha, 34–62. Minneapolis: University of Minnesota Press, 1997. Originally published in *Subaltern Studies 5,* edited by R. Guha, 135–65. Delhi: Oxford University Press, 1987.

Guthrie, Jeannine. 1995. *Rape for Profit: The Trafficking of Nepali Girls and Women into India's Brothels.* Washington, D.C.: Human Rights Watch.

Guy, Donna. 1991. *Sex and Danger in Buenos Aires: Prostitution, Family, and Nation in Argentina.* Lincoln: University of Nebraska Press.

————. 2000. *White Slavery and Mothers Alive and Dead: The Troubled Meeting of Sex, Gender, Public Health, and Progress in Latin America.* Lincoln: University of Nebraska Press.

Haag, Pamela. 1999. *Consent: Sexual Rights and the Transformation of American Liberalism.* Ithaca, N.Y.: Cornell University Press.

Halley, Janet, et al. 2006. "From the International to the Local in Feminist Legal Responses to Rape, Prostitution/Sex Work, and Sex Trafficking: Four Studies in Contemporary Governance." *Harvard Journal of Law and Gender* 29, no. 1: 335–425.

Hartsock, Nancy. 1990. "Foucault on Power: A Theory for Women?" In *Feminism/Postmodernism,* edited by L. Nicholson, 157–75. New York: Routledge.

Hastings, D. J. 1986. *Bombay Buccaneers: Memories and Reminiscences of the Royal Indian Navy.* London: BACSA.

Hazareesingh, Sandip. 2001. "Colonial Modernism and the Flawed Paradigms of Urban Renewal: Uneven Development in Bombay, 1900–1925." *Urban History* 28, no. 2: 235–55.

Heimsath, Charles. 1964. *Indian Nationalism and Hindu Social Reform.* Princeton, N.J.: Princeton University Press.

Hershatter, Gail. 1997. *Dangerous Pleasures: Prostitution and Modernity in Twentieth-Century Shanghai.* Berkeley: University of California Press.

Hubbard, Phil. 1998. "Sexuality and Immorality in the City." *Gender, Place, and Culture* 5, no. 1: 55–76.

Human Rights Watch. 1993. *A Modern Form of Slavery: Trafficking of Burmese Women and Girls into Brothels in Thailand.* Washington, D.C.: Human Rights Watch.

————. 2002. *Epidemic of Abuse: Police Harassment of HIV/AID Outreach Workers in India* 14, no. 5 (C). New York. http://64.233.161.104/ search?q=cache:DroGmAs

VCGsJ:www.hrw.org/reports/2002/inda2/indiao602-o1.htm+NACO+and+prosti tution&hl=en (accessed June 1, 2004.)

Hutchins, Francis G. 1967. *The Illusion of Permanence: British Imperialism in India*. Princeton, N.J.: Princeton University Press.

Hyam, Ronald. 1990. *Empire and Sexuality: The British Experience*. Manchester: Manchester University.

Jacobson, Matthew F. 1998. *Whiteness of a Different Color: European Immigrants and the Alchemy of Race*. Cambridge, Mass.: Harvard University Press.

Jaggar, Allison. 1985. "Prostitution." In *The Philosophy of Sex: Contemporary Readings*, edited by Alan Soble, 348–68. Totowa, N.J.: Rowman and Allanheld.

Joardar, Biswanath. 1984. *Prostitution in Historical and Modern Perspectives*. New Delhi: Inter-India Publications.

John, Mary, and Janaki Nair. 1998. *A Question of Silence: The Sexual Economies of Modern India*. New Delhi: Kali for Women.

Jordan, Bobby. 2002. "The HIV Counsellors Who Sell Their Bodies At Night." *Sunday Times of South Africa*. April 7, 2002. http://www.aegis.org/news/suntimes/2002/ ST020402.html. (accessed February 11, 2008).

Jordan, Kay. 1993. "Devadasi Reform: Driving the Priestesses or the Prostitutes Out of Hindu Temples?" In *Religion and Law in Independent India*, edited by R. D. Baird, 257–77. Delhi: Manohar Publications.

Kadam, V.S. 1996. "Dancing Girls of Maharashtra." In *Images of Women in Maharashtrian Literature and Religion*, edited by Anne Feldhaus, 61–89. Albany: State University of New York Press.

Kaplan, C., and I. Grewal. 2002. "Transnational Practices and Interdisciplinary Feminist Scholarship: Refiguring Women's and Gender Studies." In *Women's Studies on Its Own*, edited by R. Wiegman, 66–81. Durham, N.C.: Duke University Press.

Kapse, S. R. 1987. *Police Administration in Bombay, 1600–1865*. Bombay: Himalaya.

Kapur, Ratna. 2005. *Erotic Justice: Law and the New Politics of Postcolonialism*. London: GlassHouse Press.

Karkaria, R. P. 1915. *The Charm of Bombay: An Anthology of Writings in Praise of the First City in India*. Bombay: Taraporewala, Sons and Co.

Kaur, Amrit. 1933. "Women's Movement in India." *Stri Dharma* 16, no. 4 (February): 177–238.

Kautilya. 1992. *The Arthashastra*. Edited and translated by L. N. Rangarajan. New Delhi: Penguin Books.

Kempadoo, Kamala. 2001. "Women of Color and the Global Sex Trade: Transnational Feminist Perspectives." *Meridians: Feminism, Race, Transnationalism* 1, no. 2 (Spring): 28–51.

Kempadoo, Kamala, and Jo Doezema, eds. 1998. *Global Sex Workers: Rights, Resistance, and Redefinition*. New York: Routledge.

Kincaid, Dennis. 1973. [1939]. *British Social Life in India (1608–1937)*. London: Routledge and Keegan Paul.

Kishwar, Madhu. 1985. "Gandhi on Women." *Economic and Political Weekly* 20: 1691–1702, 1753–58.

Klein, Ira. 1986. "Urban Development and Death: Bombay City, 1870–1914." *Modern Asian Studies* 20, no. 4: 725–54.

Kosambi, Meera. 1985. "Commerce, Conquest, and the Colonial City: Role of Locational Factors in the Rise of Bombay." *Economic and Political Weekly* 20, no. 1 (January 5): 32–37.

——. 1986. *Bombay in Transition: The Growth and Social Ecology of a Colonial City, 1880–1980.* Stockholm: Almqvist and Wiksell International.

——. 1996. "Gender Reforms and Competing State Controls over Women: The Rakhmabai Case (1884–1887)." In *Social Reform, Sexuality, and the State,* edited by P. Uberoi, 265–90. New Delhi: Sage.

Kosambi, Meera, and John Brush. 1988. "Three Colonial Port Cities in India." *Geographical Review* 78, no. 1 (January): 32–47.

Kotiswaran, Prabha. 2001. "Preparing for Civil Disobedience: Indian Sex Workers and the Law." *Boston College Third World Journal* 21, no. 2 (Spring): 161–242.

Krishnan, O. U. 1923. *The Night Side of Bombay.* Bombay: Krishnan/ Tatvavivechaka Press.

Kristof, Nicholas. 2004. "Loss of Innocence." *New York Times,* January 28, A25.

Kumar, Radha. 1994a. *The History of Doing: An Illustrated Account of Movements for Women's Rights and Feminism in India, 1800–1990.* New Delhi: Kali for Women.

——. 1994b. "Women in the Bombay Cotton Textile Industry, 1919–1940." In *Dignity and Daily Bread: New Forms of Economic Organizing among Women in the Third World and the First,* edited by S. Rowbotham and S. Mitter, 53–72. London: Routledge.

——. 1998. "Sex and Punishment among Mill Workers in Early-Twentieth-Century Bombay." In *Changing Concepts of Rights and Justice in South Asia,* edited by M. Anderson and S. Guha, 179–97. Delhi: Oxford University Press.

League of Nations. 1943. *Prevention of Prostitution: A Study of Measures Adopted or under Consideration Particularly with Respect to Minors.* Geneva: League of Nations.

Lerner, Gerda. 1986. *The Creation of Patriarchy.* Oxford: Oxford University Press.

Levine, Philippa. 1994. "Venereal Disease, Prostitution, and the Politics of Empire: The Case of British India." *Journal of the History of Sexuality* 4, no. 4: 579–602.

——. 1996. "Rereading the 1890s: Venereal Disease as 'Constitutional Crisis' in Britain and India." *Journal of Asian Studies* 55, no. 3 (August): 585–612.

——. 2003. *Prostitution, Race, and Politics: Policing Venereal Disease in the British Empire.* New York: Routledge.

Lingat, Robert. 1998. *The Classical Law of India.* Translated by J. D. M. Derrett. Delhi: Oxford University Press. Originally published in 1973.

MacKinnon, Catharine. 1989. *Towards a Feminist Theory of the State.* Cambridge, Mass.: Harvard University Press.

——. 1993. "Prostitution and Civil Rights." *Michigan Journal of Gender and Law* 55: 13–31.

Malabari, Phiroze. 1910. *Bombay in the Making: Being Mainly a History of the Origin and Growth of the Judicial Institutions in the Western Presidency, 1661–1726*. London: T. Fisher Unwin.

Mani, Lata. 1989. "Contentious Traditions: The Debate on Sati in Colonial India." In *Recasting Women: Essays in Colonial History*, edited by K. Sangari and S. Vaid, 88–126. New Delhi: Kali for Women.

Manucci, Niccolao. 1966. *Storia do Mogor/ Mogul India, 1653–1708*. Vol. I. Translated by William Irvine. Calcutta: Editions Indian.

Marks, Lara. 1996. "Race, Class, and Gender: The Experience of Jewish Prostitutes and Other Jewish Women in the East End of London at the Turn of the Century." In *Women, Migration, and Empire*, edited by J. Grant, 31–50. London: Trentham Books.

McClintock, Anne. 1993. "Sex Workers and Sex Work: Introduction." *Social Text* 11, no. 4 (Winter): 1–10.

———. 1995. *Imperial Leather: Race, Gender, and Sexuality in the Colonial Conquest*. New York: Routledge.

Mehta, Suketu. 2004. *Maximum City: Bombay Lost and Found*. New York: Alfred A. Knopf.

Meyer, Johan Jacob. 1953. *Sexual Life in Ancient India: A Study in the Comparative History of Indian Culture*. New York: Barnes and Noble.

Miliband, Ralph. 1969. *The State in Capitalist Society*. New York: Basic Books.

Millett, Kate. 1973. *The Prostitution Papers: A Candid Dialogue*. New York: Avon.

Mirelman, Victor. 1990. *Jewish Buenos Aires, 1890–1930: In Search of an Identity*. Detroit: Wayne State University Press.

Mohanty, Chandra. 2003. *Feminism without Borders: Decolonizing Theory, Practicing Solidarity*. Durham, N.C.: Duke University Press.

Moir, Martin. 1988. *A General Guide to the India Office Records*. London: British Library.

Moon, Katherine. 1997. *Sex between Allies: Military Prostitution in U.S.–Korea Relations*. New York: Columbia University Press.

Mukherjee, K. K., and Deepa Das. 1996. *Prostitution in Metropolitan Cities of India*. New Delhi: Central Social Welfare Board.

Mukherji, Santosh K. 1986. *Prostitution in India*. Reprint. New Delhi: Inter-India. Originally published in 1931.

Nair, Janaki. 1996a. *Women and Law in Colonial India: A Social History*. New Delhi: Kali for Women.

———. 1996b. "Prohibited Marriage: State Protection and the Child Wife." In *Social Reform, Sexuality, and the State*, edited by P. Uberoi, 157–86. New Delhi: Sage.

Natarajan, S. 1959. *A Century of Social Reform in India*. Bombay: Asia Publishing House.

Oldenburg, Veena Talwar. 1990. "Lifestyle as Resistance: The Case of the Courtesans of Lucknow, India." *Feminist Studies* 16, no. 2 (Summer): 259–88.

Overall, Christine. 1992. "What's Wrong with Prostitution? Evaluating Sex Work." *Signs: Journal of Women in Culture and Society* 17, no. 4 (Summer): 705–24.

————. 1994. "Reply to Shrage." *Signs: Journal of Women in Culture and Society* 19, no. 2 (Winter): 571–75.

Panigrahi, Lalita. 1972. *British Social Policy and Female Infanticide in India.* New Delhi: Munshiram Manoharlal.

Papanek, Hanna. 1994. "The Ideal Woman and the Ideal Society: Control and Autonomy in the Construction of Identity." In *Identity Politics and Women: Cultural Reassertions and Feminism in International Perspective,* edited by V. M. Moghadam, 42–75. Boulder, Colo.: Westview Press.

Parker, Kunal. 1998. "'A Corporation of Superior Prostitutes': Anglo-Indian Legal Conceptions of Temple Dancing Girls, 1800–1914." *Modern Asian Studies* 32, no. 3 (July): 559–633.

Patel, Sujata. 1988. "Construction and Reconstruction of Women in Gandhi." *Economic and Political Weekly* 33, no. 8 (February 20): 377–87.

Pateman, Carole. 1988. *The Sexual Contract.* Stanford, Calif.: Stanford University Press.

Peterson, Spike, and Ann Runyan. 1993. *Global Gender Issues.* Boulder, Colo.: Westview Press.

Pheterson, Gail. 1996. *The Prostitution Prism.* Amsterdam: Amsterdam University Press.

Philipson, Ilene, and Karen Hansen. 1990. "Women, Class, and the Feminist Imagination: An Introduction." In *Women, Class, and the Feminist Imagination: A Socialist-Feminist Reader,* edited by Karen Hansen and Ilene Philipson, 3–40. Philadelphia: Temple University Press.

Poulantzas, Nicos. 1969. "The Problem of the Capitalist State." *Left Review* 58, November–December: 67–78.

Pradhan, G. R. 1938. "Untouchable Workers of Bombay City." Ph.D. dissertation, University of Bombay.

Punekar, S. D., and K. Rao. 1962. *Prostitution in Bombay (with Reference to Family Background).* Bombay: Lalvani Press.

Queen, Carol. 1997. "Sex Radical Politics, Sex Positive Feminist Thought, and Whore Stigma." In *Whores and Other Feminists,* edited by Jill Nagle, 125–35. New York: Routledge.

Ramanna, Mridula. 2000. "Control and Resistance: The Working of the Contagious Diseases Acts in Bombay City." *Economic and Political Weekly* 35, no. 17 (April 22): 1470–76.

Rege, Sharmila. 1996. "The Hegemonic Appropriation of Sexuality: The Case of the *Lavani* Performers of Maharashtra." In *Social Reform, Sexuality, and the State,* edited by Patricia Uberoi, 23–38. New Delhi: Sage.

Rodriguez, Dulcinea Correa. 1994. *Bombay Fort in the Eighteenth Century.* Bombay: Himalaya Publishing.

Roe, Clifford G. 1911. *The Great War on White Slavery, or Fighting for the Protection of Our Girls.* Chicago: Clifford G. Roe.

Roy, Kumkum. 1995. "'Where Women Are Worshipped, There the Gods Rejoice': The Mirage of the Ancestress of the Hindu Woman." In *Women and the Hindu Right:*

A Collection of Essays, edited by T. Sarkar and U. Butalia, 10–28. New Delhi: Kali for Women.

Rozario, Rita M. 2000. *Broken Lives: Dalit Women and Girls in Prostitution in India.* Tumkur, India: Ambedkar Resource Center.

Rubin, Gayle. 1976. "The Traffic in Women: Notes on the 'Political Economy' of Sex." In *Toward an Anthology of Women*, edited by Rayna Rapp Reiter, 157–210. New York: Monthly Review Press.

Rudolph, Lloyd, and Susan Rudolph. 1967. *The Modernity of Tradition: Political Development in India.* Chicago: University of Chicago Press.

Rule, Pauline. 1987. "Prostitution in Calcutta, 1860–1940: The Pattern of Recruitment." In *Class, Ideology, and Woman in Asian Societies*, edited by Gail Pearson and Lenore Manderson, 65–79. Hong Kong: Asian Research Service.

Sanghera, Jyotsana. 1996. "The Necessity of Emotion: Writing Women's Lives in Blood and Tears." *Labour, Capital, and Society* 29, nos. 1 and 2: 100–124.

Sarkar, Tanika. 1993. "Rhetoric against Age of Consent: Resisting Colonial Reason and the Death of a Child-Wife. *Economic and Political Weekly* 28, no. 36 (September): 1869–79.

———. 2001. *Hindu Wife, Hindu Nation: Religion, Community, and Cultural Nationalism.* New Delhi: Permanent Black, and Indiana University Press.

Sarkar, Tanika, and Urvashi Butalia, eds. 1995. *Women and the Hindu Right: A Collection of Essays.* New Delhi: Kali for Women.

Sen, Samita. 1999. *Women and Labor in Late Colonial India: The Bengal Jute Industry.* Cambridge: Cambridge University Press.

Shah, Svati. 2006. "Producing the Spectacle of Kamathipura: The Politics of Red Light Visibility in Mumbai." *Cultural Dynamics* 18, no. 3: 269–92.

Sheppard, Samuel T. 1917. *Bombay Place-Names and Street-Names: An Excursion into the By-ways of the History of Bombay City.* Bombay: Times Press.

———. 1932. *Bombay.* Bombay: Times of India Press.

Shrage, Laurie. 1994. "Comment on Overall's 'What's Wrong with Prostitution? Evaluating Sex Work.'" *Signs: Journal of Women in Culture and Society* 19, no. 2 (Winter): 564–69.

Singha, Radhika. 1998. *A Despotism of Law: Crime and Justice in Early Colonial India.* Delhi: Oxford University Press.

Sinha, Mrinalini. 1997. *Colonial Masculinity: The Manly Englishman and the Effeminate Bengali in the Late Nineteenth Century.* New Delhi: Kali for Women.

———. 1999. "The Lineage of the 'Indian' Modern: Rhetoric, Agency, and the Sarda Act in Late Colonial India." In *Gender, Sexuality, and Colonial Modernities*, edited by A. Burton, 207–21. London: Routledge.

———. 2006. *Specters of Mother India: The Global Restructuring of an Empire.* Durham, N.C.: Duke University Press.

Sinha, S. N., and N. K. Basu. 1933. *History of Marriage and Prostitution: Vedas to Vatsyayana.* New Delhi: Khama Publishing.

Sleightholme, Caroline, and Indrani Sinha. 1997. *Guilty without Trial: Women in the Sex Trade in Calcutta.* New Brunswick, N.J.: Rutgers University Press.

Smith, George. 1879. *The Life of John Wilson.* London: John Murray.

Spivak, Gayatri Chakravorty. 1988. "Can the Subaltern Speak?" In *Marxism and the Interpretation of Culture,* edited by C. Nelson and L. Grossberg, 271–312. Urbana: University of Illinois Press.

Srinivasan, Amrit. 1988. "Reform or Conformity? Temple 'Prostitution' and the Community in the Madras Presidency." In *Structures of Patriarchy: State, Community, and Household,* edited by Bina Agarwal, 175–98. London: Zed.

Stokes, Eric. 1959. *The English Utilitarians and India.* Oxford: Clarendon Press.

Stoler, Ann Laura. 1995. *Race and the Education of Desire: Foucault's "History of Sexuality" and the Colonial Order of Things.* Durham, N.C.: Duke University Press.

———. 1997. "Making Empire Respectable: The Politics of Race and Sexual Morality in Twentieth-Century Colonial Cultures." In *Dangerous Liaisons: Gender, Nation, and Postcolonial Perspectives,* edited by A. McClintock, A. Mufti, and E. Shohat, 344–73. Minneapolis: University of Minnesota Press.

Sullivan, Barbara. 2003. "Trafficking in Women: Feminism and New International Law." *International Feminist Journal of Politics* 5, no. 1 (March): 67–91.

Sunder Rajan, Rajeswari. 2003. *The Scandal of the State: Women, Law, and Citizenship in Postcolonial India.* Durham, N.C.: Duke University Press.

Svanstrom, Yvonne. 2001. *Policing Public Women: The Regulation of Prostitution in Stockholm, 1812–1880.* Stockholm: Atlas Akademi.

Swarr, A., and R. Nagar. 2003. "Dismantling Assumptions: Interrogating 'Lesbian' Struggles for Identity and Survival in India and South Africa." *Signs: Journal of Women in Culture and Society* 29, no. 2 (Winter): 491–516.

Tambe, Ashwini. 2000. "Colluding Patriarchies: The Colonial Reform of Sexual Relations in India." *Feminist Studies* 26, no. 3: 587–602.

———. 2005. "The Elusive Ingénue: A Transnational Feminist Analysis of European Prostitution in Colonial Bombay." *Gender and Society,* 19, 2: 160–179.

———. 2006. "Brothels as Families: Transnational Feminist Reflections on 1920s Bombay *Kothas.*" *International Feminist Journal of Politics* 8, no. 2 (June): 219–42.

Thorbeck, S., and B. Pattanaik. 2002. Introduction. In *Transnational Prostitution: Changing Global Patterns,* edited by S. Thorbeck and B. Pattanaik, 1–9. London: Zed.

Uberoi, Patricia, ed. 1996. *Social Reform, Sexuality,, and the State.* New Delhi: Sage.

UNAIDS. 2007. "2.5 Million People Living with HIV in India. " July 6. http://www.unaids.org/en/MediaCentre/PressMaterials/FeatureStory/20070704_India_new_data.asp. (accessed July 30, 2007).

UN Office of Drugs and Crime (UNODC). 2004. *Protocol to Prevent, Suppress, and Punish Trafficking in Persons.* http://www.unodc.org/unodc/en/trafficking_protocol. html. (accessed May 4, 2004).

Valverde, Mariana. 1998. *Diseases of the Will: Alcohol and the Dilemmas of Freedom*. Cambridge: Cambridge University Press.

———. 2003. *Law's Dream of a Common Knowledge*. Princeton, N.J.: Princeton University Press.

Van Heiningen, Elizabeth. 1984. "The Social Evil in the Cape Colony, 1868–1902: Prostitution and the Contagious Diseases Acts." *Journal of Southern African Studies* 10, no. 2: 170–97.

Vance, Carole, ed. 1984. *Pleasure and Danger: Exploring Female Sexuality*. Boston: Routledge and Kegan Paul.

Vatsyayana. 1962. *The Kama Sutra: The Classic Hindu Treatise on Love and Social Conduct*. Translated by Richard F. Burton. New York: E. P. Dutton.

Verma, Ravi K., et al. 2004. *Sexuality in the Time of AIDS: Contemporary Perspectives from Communities in India*. New Delhi: Sage.

Visweswaran, Kamala. 1996. "Small Speeches, Subaltern Gender: Nationalist Ideology and its Historiography." In *Subaltern Studies 9*, edited by S. Amin and D. Chakrabarty, 83–126. Delhi: Oxford University Press.

Wagle, N. K. 1998. "Women in the Kotwal's Papers." In *Images of Women in Maharashtrian Society*, edited by Ann Feldhaus, 15–60. Albany: State University of New York Press.

Walkowitz, Judith. 1980a. "The Politics of Prostitution." *Signs: Journal of Women in Culture and Society* 6, no. 1 (Autumn): 123–35.

———. 1980b. *Prostitution and Victorian Society: Women, Class and the State*. Cambridge: Cambridge University Press.

———. 1992. *City of Dreadful Delight: Narratives of Sexual Danger in Late-Victorian London*. Chicago: University of Chicago Press.

Washbrook, David A. 1981. "Law, State, and Agrarian Society in Colonial India." *Modern Asian Studies* 15, no. 3: 649–721.

White, Luise. 1990. *The Comforts of Home: Prostitution in Colonial Nairobi*. Chicago: University of Chicago Press.

Whitehead, Judy. 1995. "Bodies Clean and Unclean: Prostitution, Sanitary Legislation, and Respectable Femininity in Colonial North India." *Gender and History* 7, no. 1 (April): 41–63.

———. 1996. "Modernizing the Motherhood Archetype: Public Health Models and the Child Marriage Restraint Act of 1929." In *Social Reform, Sexuality, and the State*, edited by P. Uberoi, 187–209. New Delhi: Sage.

Yang, Anand. 1985. "Introduction: Issues and Themes in the Study of Historical Crime and Criminality: Passages to the Social History of British India." In *Crime and Criminality in British India*, edited by Anand Yang, 1–25. Tucson: University of Arizona Press.

Zatz, Noah. 1997. "Sex Work/ Sex Act: Law, Labor, and Desire in Constructions of Prostitution." *Signs: Journal of Women in Culture and Society* 22, no. 21 (Winter): 277–308.

MANUSCRIPTS OF MEMORANDA, OFFICIAL CORRESPONDENCE, PETITIONS, AND PARLIAMENTARY HEARINGS

Bombay Legislative Council Debates. 1923. July 30–August 6. Vol. 10. Oriental and India Office Collections, British Library, London.

General Department. 1871a. Vol. 14. *Letter from Municipal Commissioner.* Maharashtra State Archives, Mumbai.

———. 1871b. Vol. 59. Maharashtra State Archives, Mumbai.

———. 1872a. Vol. 50. *Petition Submitted to the Governor and President in Council, Bombay, by Residents of Girgaum and its Vicinity, 29 January.* Maharashtra State Archives, Mumbai.

———. 1872b. Vol. 50. *Petitions to the Governor in Council from the Inhabitants of Belgaum.* Maharashtra State Archives, Mumbai.

———. 1873. Vol. 59. *Petition Submitted to the Governor and President in Council, Bombay, by Residents of Girgaum and its Vicinity.* 125–26. Maharashtra State Archives, Mumbai.

———. 1887a. File No. 2342. *Memo from Police Commissioner's Office, May 12.* Maharashtra State Archives, Mumbai.

———. 1887b. Vol. 37. *Petitions Submitted to the Governor and President in Council, by Residents of Cursetjee Sooklajee Street, 9 June.* Maharashtra State Archives, Mumbai.

———. 1887c. Vol. 37. *Memo from the Surgeon-General of Bombay, April 19.* Maharashtra State Archives, Mumbai.

———. 1888a. Vol. 42. Maharashtra State Archives, Mumbai.

———. 1888b. Vol. 42A. *Petition Submitted to the Governor and President in Council, Bombay, by Inhabitants of Fort, Chowpatti, Khetwadi, and Other Places in Bombay.* 407–8. Maharashtra State Archives, Mumbai.

———. 1888c. Vol. 42A. *Petition Submitted to the Governor and President in Council, Bombay, by Residents of Trimbuk Purushram Street.* 29–33. Maharashtra State Archives, Mumbai.

———. 1922. File no. 2792. *Prostitution in Bombay: Recommendations of the Committee Appointed to Consider the Means for Remedying the Evil of——*, M10. Maharashtra State Archives, Mumbai.

———. 1927–28a. File 548-B, vol. 3, M130. *Report of the British Social Hygiene Council.* Maharashtra State Archives, Mumbai.

———. 1927–28b. File 548-B, vol. 8. *Report of the British Social Hygiene Council.* Maharashtra State Archives, Mumbai.

Government of Bombay. 1886. *Memorandum on the Contagious Diseases Act* submitted by Surgeon-General W. J. Moore, October 1886, v/24/2289. Oriental and India Office Collections, British Library, London.

Home Department. 1884. Sanitary, *Home Department Sanitary Proceedings, December 1884, no. 38.* National Archives of India, New Delhi.

———. 1887. Sanitary, December, no. 47. *Penalties for breaches of rules under Cantonment Act XXII of 1864.* Maharashtra State Archives, Mumbai.

———. 1888a. Judicial. July, no. 83–89. *Abduction of European girls for immoral purposes.* National Archives of India, New Delhi.

———. 1888b. Judicial. Prog. No. 88. *Letter from A. P. McDonnell, Secretary Government of India, to W. J. Gladwin, Missionary, Bombay.* National Archives of India, New Delhi.

———. 1892. Judicial, July 25. *Resolution of Government of Bombay.* National Archives of India, New Delhi.

———. 1893. Police, July, Nos. 117–120. *Petition by Rev. R. H. Madden.* National Archives of India, New Delhi.

———. 1903. Police-A, July, vol. 20–23. *Memo from S. W. Edgerley to Government of India, 24 April, No. 2224.* National Archives of India, New Delhi.

———. 1912. Judicial A, November, Nos. 131–150. *Notes: Proposed Legislation to Check Immorality.* National Archives of India, New Delhi.

———. 1913a. Judicial, July No. 245. National Archives of India, New Delhi.

———. 1913b. Judicial A, *Letter to the Marquess of Crewe, 24 July 1913, File 289.* National Archives of India, New Delhi.

———. 1917a. Police-A, December 128–130. *High Court of Judicature, Bombay, 2nd sessions, 1917, case no. 13.* National Archives of India, New Delhi.

———. 1917b. Police-A, December 128–130. *Letter from Labshankar Laxmidas, Bombay Humanitarian Fund, to Hon. G.R. Lowndes, 7 April 1917.* National Archives of India, New Delhi.

———. 1917c. Police-A, December 128–130. *Letter from D. E. Wacha to Hon. Mr. G. R. Lowndes, Bombay, August 4, 1917.* National Archives of India, New Delhi.

———. 1917d. Police-A, December 128–130. *Vincent's Memorandum to the Judicial Department, August 11, 1917.* National Archives of India, New Delhi.

———. 1918. Police-A, November No. 19–20. *Bill to Amend Act IV of 1902.* National Archives of India, New Delhi.

———. 1920. *Police-A, Report by E. C. Shuttleworth, January, No. 24–29.* National Archives of India, New Delhi.

———. 1921a. File 469- IX. *The Evil of Prostitution in Bombay, Bombay Social Purity Committee. Report of the Prostitution Committee.* Maharashtra State Archives, Mumbai.

———. 1921b. File 469-III. *Prostitution in Bombay: Minutes of Evidence of Prostitution Committee.* Maharashtra State Archives, Mumbai.

———. 1921c. File 469- IX. *Questionnaire Reply from Dr. K. S. Patel of Venereal and Skin Hospital, Grant Road. Report of the Prostitution Committee.* Maharashtra State Archives, Mumbai.

———. 1922. Judicial 58/22. *Preface by S. M. Edwardes to Report on the International Conference on the Traffic in Women and Children,* July 1921, pp. 11–12. National Archives of India, New Delhi.

———. 1924. File P-35. *Annual Report on Traffic in Women and Children, for Submission to the League Secretariat.* Maharashtra State Archives, Mumbai.

———. 1925a. File P-133. *Annual Reports on Traffic in Women and Children, for Submission to the League Secretariat.* Maharashtra State Archives, Mumbai.

Home Department. 1925b. File 8514. *Prostitutes*. Maharashtra State Archives, Mumbai.
————. 1926a. Police 24/IV/26. *Bombay Legislative Council Debate on Bill VII of 1926, March 12, 1926*. National Archives of India, New Delhi.
————. 1926b. Police 36/1926. *Enquiry into Prostitution in India by a Committee Appointed under the Auspices of the League of Nations*. National Archives of India, New Delhi.
————. 1926c. File P-133. *Annual Reports on Traffic in Women and Children, for Submission to the League Secretariat*. Maharashtra State Archives, Mumbai.
————. 1927a. File P-133. *Annual Report on Traffic in Women and Children, for Submission to the League Secretariat*. Maharashtra State Archives, Mumbai.
————. 1927b. File 3338-IX a. Report of the Special Body of Experts on Traffic in Women and Children. *Proceedings Related to the Traffic in Women and Children, League of Nations*. Maharashtra State Archives, Mumbai.
————. 1928a. File P-133. *Annual Report on Traffic in Women and Children, for Submission to the League Secretariat*. Maharashtra State Archives, Mumbai.
————. 1928b. File 3338-IX. *Proceedings Relating to the Traffic in Women and Children, League of Nations*. Maharashtra State Archives, Mumbai.
————. 1929a. File P-133. *Annual Report on Traffic in Women and Children, for Submission to the League Secretariat*. Maharashtra State Archives, Mumbai.
————. 1929b. Police 24/IV/29. *Statement of Objects and Reasons for Amendment to Prostitution Act of 1923*. National Archives of India, New Delhi.
————. 1929–30. File 3338-XII. *Proceedings Relating to the Traffic in Women and Children, League of Nations*. Maharashtra State Archives, Mumbai.
————. 1930. File P-133. *Political Department Memo. Annual Report on Traffic in Women and Children, for Submission to the League Secretariat*. Maharashtra State Archives, Mumbai.
————. 1931. File P-133. *Political Department Memo. Annual Report on Traffic in Women and Children, for Submission to the League Secretariat*. Maharashtra State Archives, Mumbai.
————. 1932. Judicial, 914/32. *Responses to the League of Nations Questionnaire*. National Archives of India, New Delhi.
————. 1936. File 3015 VIIa. *Entertainment of Special Police Staff to Deal with Offenses. Amendment of the Prevention of Prostitution Act*. Maharashtra State Archives, Mumbai.
————. 1937. Judicial 56/8/37. *Notes from the Legislative Department for the Indian Delegate to the September Session of the League Assembly*. National Archives of India, New Delhi.
Kitchener. 1912. *Memorandum to All Army: "Our Army in India and the Regulation of Vice." Correspondence between India Office and the British Committee of the International Abolitionist Federation*. Oriental and India Office Collections, British Library, London.
Parliamentary Papers. 1883. 50/538–544. Enclosure: Letter from the Sanitary Commissioner for the Government of Bombay, General Department, A-535, June 28, 1876. University of Pennsylvania Library, Philadelphia.
————. 1888a. 77/234. University of Pennsylvania Library, Philadelphia.

————. 1888b. Vol. 50, *Letter from Commander of H.M.S. Beacon.* University of Pennsylvania Library, Philadelphia.

————. 1888c. Vol. 50, *Letter from Francis Carter.* University of Pennsylvania Library, Philadelphia.

————. 1893–94. 64/I/C.7148. University of Pennsylvania Library, Philadelphia.

Political Department. 1915. File 295-I-W. War Files. *List of German and Austrian Adult Males and Females Dealt with by the Civil Authorities in Bombay Presidency.* Maharashtra State Archives, Mumbai.

————. 1934. P-145. *Annual Report of White Slave Traffic.* Maharashtra State Archives, Mumbai.

————. 1935. P-145. *Annual Report of White Slave Traffic.* Maharashtra State Archives, Mumbai.

————. 1936. P-145. *Annual Report of White Slave Traffic.* Maharashtra State Archives, Mumbai.

————. 1937. P-145. *Annual Report of White Slave Traffic.* Maharashtra State Archives, Mumbai.

————. 1938. P-145. *Annual Report of White Slave Traffic.* Maharashtra State Archives, Mumbai.

Surgeon General's Report. 1887. No. 19 S. G. Oriental and India Office Collections, British Library, London.

ANNUAL REPORTS

POLICE

ARPCB *(Annual Report of the Police in the City of Bombay).* 1917–49. Oriental and India Office Collections, British Library, London.

ARPTIB *(Annual Report of the Police in the Town and Island of Bombay).* 1892–1916. Oriental and India Office Collections, British Library, London.

ARSCB *(Annual Report of the State of Crime in Bombay).* 1860–91. Oriental and India Office Collections, British Library, London.

ARWPTIB *(Annual Report on the Working of Police in the Town and Island of Bombay).* 1884–1917. University of Pennsylvania Library, Philadelphia.

JAILS

ARBJ *(Annual Report of the Bombay Jails).* 1875–1922. Oriental and India Office Collections, British Library, London.

ARBJD *(Administrative Report of the Bombay Jail Department).* 1923–1931. Oriental and India Office Collections, British Library, London.

ARMY

Military Collection. 315, L/MIL/7/13826. Oriental and India Office Collections, British Library, London.

Report of the Health of the Army. 1909. Oriental and India Office Collections, British Library, London.

RHBBC *(Report of the Health of British Troops in Bombay Command)*. 1877. v/24/307. Oriental and India Office Collections, British Library, London.

MEDICAL

Government of Bombay. 1885. *Report on the Working of the Contagious Diseases Act.* Surgeon General's Report, July 9. Oriental and India Office Collections, British Library, London.

RWCDA *(Reports of the Working of the Contagious Diseases Act)*. 1880–1888. Oriental and India Office Collections, British Library, London. Maharashtra State Archives, Mumbai; and National Archives of India, New Delhi.

CENSUS

Census of Bombay. 1872. University of Pennsylvania Library, Philadelphia.
Census of Bombay Town and Island. 1912. University of Pennsylvania Library, Philadelphia.
Census of India. 1921. Volume 9, part 1, section 20: Prostitution in Bombay. University of Pennsylvania Library, Philadelphia.
———. 1951. Bombay, Saurashtra, and Kutch. University of Pennsylvania Library, Philadelphia.
Census of India: Bombay. 1891. University of Pennsylvania Library, Philadelphia.
———. 1901. University of Pennsylvania Library, Philadelphia.
———. 1922. University of Pennsylvania Library, Philadelphia.
Census of India: Bombay City & Island. 1881. University of Pennsylvania Library, Philadelphia.
Census of India: Cities of the Bombay Presidency. 1931. University of Pennsylvania Library, Philadelphia.
Census of Island of Bombay. 1864. Oriental and India Office Collections, British Library, London.

SPECIAL COMMITTEE REPORTS

RCP. *Report of the Committee on Prostitution in Bombay.* 1922. Oriental and India Office Collections, British Library, London; Maharashtra State Archives, Mumbai.

COURT PROCEEDINGS

High Court of Judicature, Bombay, 2nd session. 1917. Home Department 1917, Police A, December 128–130. National Archives of India, New Delhi.
Judicial Department Proceedings. 1917. *Statement from F. A. M. Vincent, Police Commissioner to the Secretary to Government, Judicial Department, Bombay.* April 6, 1917, File no. 1456-M-3S. Oriental and India Office Collections, British Library, London.

NEWSPAPERS AND OTHER PERIODICALS

Summaries in *Report of Native Newspapers,* Maharashtra State Archives, Mumbai, or transcriptions in *Collected Works of Mahatma Gandhi.*

Advocate of India, Akhbar-e-Islam, Al Wahid, Bombay Chabuk, Bombay Chronicle, Bombay Gazette, Bombay Samachar, Dnyan Prakash, Gurakhi, Indian Social Reformer, Indian Spectator, Indu Prakash, Jam-e-Jamshed, Kaiser-I-Hind, Lokmanya, Native Opinion, Parsi Punch, Prabhat, Pratod, Punch Dand, Raja Hansa, Rajyabhakti, Rast Goftar, Sanj Vartaman, Satya Watta, Servant of India, Shri Shivaji, Sindhi, Sind Observer, Stri Dharma, Subhod Patrika, Times of India, Varatahar, Vritta Prakash, Young India.

ORIGINAL COPIES AND MICROFILMS

Obtained from Cambridge University Center of South Asian Studies, and University of Illinois, Urbana Library, Urbana-Champaign.

Bombay Chronicle. 1917a. "Slave Market of Bombay." April 6.
————. 1917b. "Woman's Death under Suspicious Circumstances." February 22, 4.
Indian Social Reformer. 1917a. "The Social Evil in Bombay." April 22, 401.
————. 1917b. "Gandhi and Women." May 16.
————. 1921a. "Prostitution in Bombay." August 14, vol. 31, 50.
————. 1921b. "Salvation Army Work in Bombay." October 1921, vol. 32, 9. University of Illinois, Urbana Library, Urbana-Champaign.
————. 1922. Report of the Prostitution Committee. August 27, vol. 32, 52; supplement pp. 1–6. University of Illinois, Urbana Library, Urbana-Champaign.
Missionary Monthly. 1897. January, vol. 1, 1. http://www.huntington.edu/ubhc/publi cations/missionary/1897/january/page4.htm (accessed July 24, 2007).

LAWS

Obtained from the National Law School library, Bangalore; Indian Law Institute library, New Delhi; National Archives of India, New Delhi; University of Pennsylvania Library, Philadelphia.

Bombay City Police Act. Act IV of 1902.
Bombay Prevention of Prostitution Act. Act XI of 1923; Amendment of BPPA by Act IX of 1927; Amendment of BPPA by Act XII of 1930; Amendment of BPPA by Act XXVI of 1948; Amendment of BPPA by Act XI of 1948.
City of Bombay Police Amendment Act of 1920.
Code of Civil Procedure. 1859.
Code of Criminal Procedure. 1861.
Indian Contagious Diseases Act. Act XIV of 1868.
International Convention for the Suppression of the White Slave Traffic. 1910 (HD 1913a).
IPC (Indian Penal Code). 1860.
RACDAB (Rules for the Administration of the CDA in Bombay.) 1870.
Regulation of 1827. Mumbai.
Rule, Ordinance and Regulation of 1812. Mumbai.

INDEX

abolitionism, xv, xvii, xxiii, xxvi, 2, 3, 10, 33, 81, 99–102, 104, 107–10, 121, 123, 124, 129, 165

age of consent, 1, 10, 11, 23, 137

AIDS, xi, xii, xiv, xvii, xviii, 126, 127

Akootai, xxvii, 79–100, 108, 113, 115, 121, 149–52

Arnold, David, 4, 14, 21, 29, 34, 35, 142, 145, 146, 155, 156

Baxi, Upendra, 5, 6, 142, 143, 156

Banerjee, Sumanta, xxv, 26, 28, 47, 140, 144, 145

Bellasis Road, 58, 59, 94

Bombay: history of, xi, xii, xv, xvii, xviii–xx, xxiv, xxv, xxvi, xxvii, 8, 11, 15, 27, 31, 45–50, 52, 53, 97–98, 100, 101, 109, 125, 141; map of, xxi, 125; ports in, xviii, xix, xx, 31, 33, 35, 53, 55, 69, 146; public sphere in, xxvi–xxvii, 45–50. *See also* housing

Bombay Prevention of Prostitution Act, 99, 100, 110, 111, 137, 138, 151

Bombay Vigilance Association, 72–74, 96, 110, 112, 151

Britain: political climate in, xii, xxiii, 4,

27, 28, 33, 50; prostitution laws of, xxiii, xxiv, 13, 15, 28, 33, 42, 63, 102, 109, 123, 124, 125

British. *See* European

British Social Hygiene Council, 112

brothel keeping, xiii, 27, 43, 64, 65–69, 77, 81, 82, 84, 85, 91–95, 97, 99, 107–15, 123, 128, 136

brothel mistress, 43, 64, 65, 67, 70, 74, 115

brothels: conditions in, 70, 82, 84, 85, 93, 95–98, 127–28; earnings in, 14, 70, 84, 85, 93, 96; as households, 86, 87, 95, 97, 98; law enforcement and police surveillance of, xviii, 13, 14, 27, 28, 38, 40, 41, 42, 51, 64–67, 76–77, 80, 100, 107–10, 113, 115, 129; rents and, 85, 97, 115; rise of, xi, xii, xix, xx, xxiv, xxvi, xxvii; spatial distribution of, 29, 35, 43, 52–63. *See also* European; prostitutes; sex work

Buenos Aires, 53, 68, 140, 149

Byculla, xxi, 58, 59, 62, 94, 148

Cairo, 53, 67

Calcutta, xxiv, xxv, 32, 38, 46, 47, 53, 54, 112, 127, 140, 141, 145, 148, 152

Ashwini Tambe is assistant professor of women's studies and history at the University of Toronto.